STICKY BOTTLE

STICKY BOTTLE

The Cycling Year According to Carlton Kirby

CARLTON KIRBY

BLOOMSBURY SPORT
LONDON • OXFORD • NEW YORK • NEW DELHI • SYDNEY

BLOOMSBURY SPORT
Bloomsbury Publishing Plc
50 Bedford Square, London, WC1B 3DP, UK
29 Earlsfort Terrace, Dublin 2, Ireland

BLOOMSBURY, BLOOMSBURY SPORT and the Diana logo are trademarks of Bloomsbury
Publishing Plc

First published in Great Britain 2023
Copyright © 2023, Carlton Kirby

Plate section images: author's personal collection, Getty Images, Alison Wragg and Thomas Larabi

Carlton Kirby has asserted his right under the Copyright, Designs and Patents Act, 1988, to be identified
as Author of this work

A catalogue record for this book is available from the British Library

Library of Congress Cataloguing-in-Publication data has been applied for

ISBN: HB: 978-1-4729-9459-2; eBook: 978-1-4729-9461-5; epdf: 978-1-4729-9456-1

2 4 6 8 10 9 7 5 3 1

Typeset by Deanta Global Publishing Services, Chennai, India
Printed and bound in Great Britain by CPI Group (UK) Ltd, Croydon CR0 4YY

Bloomsbury Publishing Plc makes every effort to ensure that the papers used in the manufacture of our
books are natural, recyclable products made from wood grown in well-managed forests. Our manufacturing
processes conform to the environmental regulations of the country of origin.

To find out more about our authors and books visit www.bloomsbury.com and sign up for our newsletters

CONTENTS

CONTENTS

FOREWORD
BY SEAN KELLY

He's only gone and written another book . . .

I've told you before that Carlton Kirby is a man few can shut up. I was wondering if his first book might be his last, but it clearly tickled many. He has quite the memory and a certain way about him when telling a story. Call it his Irish genes.

Now he's at it again, Lord help us. Of course I've got my own stories to tell: having spent my lifetime on the road, first as a professional rider and then as a commentator. And all those weeks, months and years that I've spent on the road in the good company of my many cycling friends live long in the memory.

They're a useful treasure chest when I'm commentating, helping to 'dress the day', especially on the longer, quieter stages when there's not much happening in the peloton. Plus, I hope it shows that I know my stuff when it comes to this fabulous sport. Cycling has given me a lifetime of enjoyment and a fair amount of success. I love it to its very bones.

As for Carlton, he can indeed tell a fine story – even if sometimes, on occasion, you might find yourself detecting just the faintest whiff about them.

This book is a window into a world we both share and love. Sure you may find yourself opening that very window to air the room a bit, but you'll be laughing all the same.

Enjoy!

Sean Kelly

INTRODUCTION

Over the past 35 years of calling races for the willing and the witless, I have passed through many borders. Beyond the bounds, some might say (but we will ignore them). This book is a journey through a cycling season of seasons. I've taken the calendar and given you a year of events and experiences, offering a few ideas you might like to try. Some of the races will certainly take a real effort to get yourself to; others no longer even exist. But as the months go by, I fondly remember them all – like they were yesterday, today and tomorrow once more.

I have been broadcasting on cycling since my days of running the sports desk at TV-am, the first breakfast station for ITV. It closed in 1992. I was left wondering what I'd do next when my colleague Jeff Stelling asked me if I could fill in for him on a weird gig in Paris. A new channel called Eurosport.

Off I flew – and the first person I met there was the amazing David Duffield. He walked into the office and shouted with a chuckling roar: 'MORNING, CAMPERS!!!!' I had found a new friend and a new home. You know the rest.

The cycling season is a remarkable thing, and these days it covers much of the planet for much of the time. There is more racing than ever before, and via GCN+ you can enjoy the action from anywhere there is an internet signal. Yet there is nothing quite like actually being there, drinking it in.

Wherever you live there will be a race nearby and there is no reason why you should not get involved. You see, cycling is a way of life – it's been my life – and I know that to live it you have to get off your backside (even though it's a sit-down sport).

Yes, to fully appreciate this crazy majestic intoxicating world of cycling, you have to be there in person.

Hopefully a time will come when watching the racing with me yammering at you will not be enough. You will simply have to go and experience it for yourself, live and on site. And I hope you do.

This book will give you a template to plan your very own personal calendar. Cycle racing is not just about Alpe d'Huez and the Champs-Élysées. There are a thousand events, other than the Tour de France both on and off the official calendar. So start assembling your own season. I have. My best ever. It's in your hands right now.

Sean Kelly once said to me: 'What you take away from cycling is a sore arse and a million memories.' The man is a genius and doesn't even know it.

I hope you enjoy my memories.

CK xx

CYCLING LEXICON

Sticky Bottle: An extended hold of a water bottle offered up from the team car while it accelerates – thereby propelling the cyclist at a pace to regain time lost due to a racing incident.

JANUARY

ONE

GRAND PRIX LA MARSEILLAISE
GANGSTER DASH

The rooftop observers watched me run for my life. I was sprinting.

By the time I reached the midway point of the bridge, the assassins were charging me down. I heard the gunfire before the cars, and turned to see them speeding along Boulevard de la République towards Pont d'Issy. They were travelling at such a rate that all four vehicles slammed into the bridge ramp so hard they nearly got airborne. And still the machine-guns blared – *ratatatatatat!* – matched by the rotor chatter of the helicopters.

I looked back to see the cross-flashes exiting from the Uzi barrels. It was terrifying; I was done for.

I knew I had no chance of making it over cleanly, so I slowed to a walk as the gunfire stopped and the cars, one white and three black, cruised past. At the end of the bridge they made a U-turn and came back my way slowly.

One of the black cars crawled past me and a Japanese guy hanging out of the passenger side window with his machine gun shouted what was clearly an obscenity at me. I had royally screwed up their little game; quite a big game actually. But hey, I was late for work. Due on-air in 20 minutes for goodness' sake!

Half an hour earlier, I had been stopped trying to move a barrier. 'Arêttez!! Vous ne passez pas . . . ARÊTTEZ!'

What looked like a combat-hippy was standing by the obstruction. She wasn't happy.

'I need to get to work. How long will the bridge be closed?' I asked.

'I don't know, who knows such things? It is art. For art you must wait . . .'

What I had just stumbled into was a film shoot. The bridge over the Seine to Boulogne-Billancourt in Paris was closed. The Eurosport offices were on the other side and in a short while I was due to be commentating. This was not good.

As I looked around, I could tell this movie was a big budget affair. Cameras on rooftops, one helicopter filming another helicopter and more combat-hippies guarding roads to the bridge; all radios linked to the director's team.

'Lots of money flying around here. What's the film?'

'*Taxi 2*,' she said with a tone that added *please shut up*.

'Ahhhh, I saw the first one. Shot in Marseille, wasn't it?'

'Oui, chez moi.'

'I know Marseille: I love the Grand Prix.'

'Le quoi?'

'Un course de cyclisme. Pour les sprinteurs.'

'Phuff . . . Not as fast as this,' she said.

That was our conversation closed for the moment. But time was ticking and my programme was going to go ahead, with or without me. Negotiations were not going well.

'Look, I have to get to work.'

'Well, we 'av to film, so you must wait.'

'For goodness' sake, call your team and ask them when this scene is going ahead. It will take me no more than five minutes to get clear. I am a television commentator at Eurosport over there and my race begins shortly. Please!!'

She scowled at me before wandering off a few paces and thumbing the radio. She grudgingly asked if I could pass. Holding her earpiece, she headed back my way. It was obvious from her expression that this was not going to be good news.

'You must wait.'

I gave it another five minutes before I hit sod-it mode.

Over the barrier I clambered and started running.

'*Noooon!!!!!!*' shouted the combat-hippy just as her radio crackled: 'Action!'

I don't know how many blank bullets they had on set, but they must've used most of them in the next 90 seconds or so.

Of course, *they* could reload and go again . . . *I* could not. I had only one take available to me. It's a bike race – and what could be more important than that?

Clearly plenty of folk felt differently.

As the cars made their way back to the starting position, I cleared the bridge to be met by another art student with a radio. He began his speech from a distance as I approached. 'You 'av just ruined a very expensive take. Do you realise what you 'av done? You 'av —'

'Piss off . . . Thank you!' I barged past.

The crowd watching was much happier, hoping to see the whole sequence again. The bored drivers in the cars, backed up in the traffic jam, less so.

Taxi 2 came out the following March in 2000 and was a huge hit. Somewhere on a cutting room floor is the famous lost sequence simply marked 'fat bloke running – please cut or frame out'.

The original movie *Taxi* was filmed on the hilly streets of Marseille. The premise is a guy who runs a souped-up taxi that is entirely illegal but used in honourable missions to help people running late and in need of a great deal of speed. It showcased the edgy but fun nature of the ancient city perfectly.

The film naturally highlighted the majestic folds of a place that lies upon a semicircle of limestone hills tumbling towards the shoreline. A better venue for a sequence of car chases you will be hard pushed to find. The same applies to the bike race.

Marseille rests upon the Étoile Chain of mountains that head off northwards towards Montagne Sainte-Victoire and Aix-en-Provence, a more snooty rival for 'capital of the region' status. But Marseille is *much* more interesting. It has the Grand Prix, after all.

The race began in 1980 and immediately came to mark the start of the European cycling season. Since then a couple of other races have butted in on the calendar a week or so earlier, but for most in France, and particularly for most of the world's top durable quick men, this is where the season begins. It is also the opening round of the highly competitive and brilliant Coupe de France series. These are the finest regional French races brought together in a calendar, with a championship table and great kudos to the overall champion. Open to cyclists of all nations but founded upon the best races in France, it is spectacular. The GP La Marseillaise is the opener, and very special. The racing is always competitive; often bordering on brutal.

Run over a distance of around 180km (112 miles), it may not be particularly long, but there are virtually no flat roads. We are not talking real mountains here, yet there are so many hills to take on that there is a gain of around 3000m (9840ft) of altitude on the average edition. This makes it properly selective by the end, and it will have shaken the will of many pure sprinters by the time the course heads home for a reduced sprint among the hardest of fast men. You can't help but love it.

The Col de la Gineste has often been chosen as the final climb. It's not the toughest, having a gradient of only around 3% over 7.5km (4.6 miles) – but how this is attacked is what makes the difference. It's usually a frantic finalé. Over the top of this last peak there remains around 11.5km (6.8 miles) to the finish next to the Stade Vélodrome football stadium. Built in the 1930s, the old velodrome surrounding the pitch was eventually taken over by seating tribunes and disappeared. Good that the race finishes here to remind everyone that the world's greatest sport is on bikes.

The peloton is usually made up of a vast array of the world's finest quick hard men. And there have been many occasions where French riders have had to hand over the coveted trophy to those dropping in from abroad. But just as in the national anthem of the same name, they are always ready to come back fighting. A stanza from the fourth verse seems appropriate:

> If they fall, our young heroes,
> Will be produced anew from the soil,
> Ready to join the fight against you!

It is an amazing race and well worth a visit . . . but I'll be honest with you, I have not had the most comfortable relationship with Marseille over the years. It all began when I was a young traveller, just 17 years of age and found myself a little confused in the city's main bus terminal. I saw a driver with his elbow hanging out of his open cab window and wandered over. He knew I was there but didn't acknowledge me standing just below him and carried on smoking. Gathering myself, I asked in perfectly acceptable French: 'Excuse me, sir, where do I find the bus to Toulon?'

He took a moment to remove the tab from his lips. Then blew a jet of cigarette smoke at the windscreen he was staring out of and said coldly: 'Je ne parle pas Anglais.'

I walked around the front of the bus to see the destination card above the still smoking driver. It read: TOULON.

I went to Menton instead.

Marseille is a remarkable place founded in 600 BCE by the Greeks. It is one of the oldest continuously inhabited cities on earth.

For centuries Marseille has had cultural and economic links to the Middle East, North Africa, Asia and, of course, the entire Mediterranean. The Brits have been here a while too: for both good and ill.

In these parts, the action in the port of Mers-el-Kébir still resonates. After the Fall of France, in June 1940, the British government feared that the ships of the French Navy would fall into Nazi hands. Repeated requests that the fleet should sail for the French West Indies and out of reach, or alternatively place itself under British control, were ignored. Admiral Darlan was convinced by Nazi assurances that his fleet would remain under his orders. Finally, Churchill ordered the destruction of vessels based in the French Algerian port of Mers-el-Kébir. The action took place on 3 July, 1940.

Most of the crew on board the cruisers and battleships destroyed by the British that day were from Marseille and Toulon. There are memorials to the 1300 sailors who lost their lives that terrible afternoon. Churchill called it 'the most hateful decision, the most unnatural and painful in which I have ever been concerned.'

The people of France were, of course, outraged. In the rest of occupied Europe there was more understanding. Britain was now alone in the war against Hitler and clearly going to fight on. The attack revived Anglophobia, particularly in the Mediterranean ports, and such sentiments can still crop up in Marseille. So beware. If it bothers you, just say you're Irish. You'll have a ball.

Roads down towards the harbour descend in steps. At every junction on your journey, you will find bars and cafés of increasing bawdiness. This place rocks – and if you don't roll with it, you will not enjoy yourself. So get immersed. You can find cuisine from all points of the Mediterranean. In a month you can enjoy a different meal at every sitting, in surroundings that will leave you both energised and a little exhausted. It is almost illegal to get bored in this city. It is always on the go; particularly on race day. Magically so.

CARLTON COMMENTARY

'Like an overcooked piece of spaghetti dropped onto the floor.'
An extreme winding mountain road

TWO

LA TROPICALE AMISSA BONGO
THE FRIDGE RACE

Now, I'm rarely intimidated by the size of anyone; I'm a pretty big guy myself, a fact that I'm often reminded of at cycling functions when people get a look at me for the first time. 'You're a lot bigger than I expected' is what I hear a lot. I get it, I'm a commentator and thus, in the way of the TV world, I function out of vision. My job is to dress for the action without necessarily having to dress for the occasion. It's the talent in the studio who have the make-up and the honed everything – bodies, teeth, hair, tailoring . . . Except Sir Bradley Wiggins, of course. He can do what the hell he likes; he's Sir Brad.

So, because the sight of me is a rarity, people have often created a picture of me in their minds. It's a vision that may well be wide of the mark, and which is based entirely on the tone of my voice. A vision of a man somewhere between *Media Perso-nali-d* and, I like to think, *George Clooney*. Thus, upon catching sight of me there can be a bit of a stall. I'm often found shaking the hand of someone looking straight through my eyes into the universe beyond with a fixed smile as they hit Control-Alt-Delete. This reset can take a few moments, meaning the handshake goes on for some time.

'Are you alright?' I ask. The handshake continues.

'Yeeeees. You are not – not what I thought you'd look like.'

Still shaking hands. 'Bit big?'

'Bigger than I thought.'

On one occasion a confused fan's handshake slowed to a halt, even as they kept a nervous grip of my hand, which had long since gone limp, desperate for release. For a few seconds we stood there holding hands, looking at each other. Then came the post-hypnosis, *back in the room* moment and my hand was urgently released, like an unexpectedly hot spoon.

So . . . I am wary of sizing someone up in advance.

Sean Kelly and I had been invited to meet the race organiser of the Amissa Bongo, a race with a name that summons up images of a wistful percussionist trapped on a desert island without his favourite instrument. But that's just my mind for you.

We were on the Tour de France and had been called by the organisers, who had a special guest keen to meet one of the cycling greats. Their goal was to persuade Kelly to come to the race in Gabon the following January. The only reason I went along was because I was driving. 'This might get a little boozy,' said Sean. 'Best get your orange juice head on.'

It was the night of the Galibier stage. We were high in the mountains and found ourselves in the very old quarter of a mountain town. The dark damp streets were too narrow for cars, so we parked up and walked carefully over smooth, ancient and uneven cobbles that seemed to be struggling to escape.

'That's the place,' whispered Kelly with a little trepidation. There before us was a single-storey log cabin, the shallow roof of which spread so wide it almost touched the ground. The walls of the ancient place were black with age. The small, shuttered windows barely glimmered amber in the gloom. It had a dug-out porch area and steps down to a very short door as if they'd accidentally built the front door facing the hillside. The night was foggy, like an episode of *Hammer House of Horror*. This was Baskerville Manor. No howling dog in the distance, but there should have been.

'In we go,' said Kelly with the sigh of a condemned man. 'And mind your head; you'll need it later.' We ducked down and entered.

At first I thought the fog had drifted indoors, but the rich, treacly smell of Havana cigars said otherwise. In the corner by the fire were our hosts. There was no one else in the place. The gentle ting of a delicate mantle clock told us it was midnight.

Suddenly, laughter, the silence smashed by an expertly delivered punchline. The table was in uproar. From pin quiet to party at the flip of a joke. Not on us, you understand.

We approached anonymously until someone shouted: 'Kelly!' and they all struggled enthusiastically to their feet to greet him, knocking a few glasses over in their haste.

Mayhem ensued – the usual smorgasbord of 'Champion . . . Grand Champion . . . Monsieur Paris–Nice . . . Le Roi . . . ' – while I stood there in amazement. I was expecting the Amissa Bongo race organiser to be in the shape of, say, Daniel Teklehaimanot, the Eritrean Champion, or perhaps Amanuel Ghebreigzabhier, Ethiopia's All African Road and Time Trial Champion. But this, taking up the whole of one side of a table set for eight, this was not what I expected at all.

This was a man mountain – whose voice matched his size. 'AND WHO IS THIS?' he boomed.

Sean, bearing the weight of his admirer's arms like a bad scarf: 'That's Carlton Kirby.'

'WELCOME! WELCOME, MY FRIEND! COGNAC, PLUS COGNAC POUR LES MESSIEURS.'

And so it began. A long night of me sitting slightly off stage as they bellowed at Sean, feted him and tried to woo the poor man into agreeing to attend the upcoming race.

'C'EST UN FÊTE MAGNIFIQUE,' the organiser roared again before leaning in with a deeply conspiratorial soft tone. 'Le cyclisme naturellement, mais aussi, il y a de la musique, beaucoup de bière. Et des jolies filles!!!!' Then rolling back in his chair, bellowing: 'OUI! BEAUCOUP DE JOLIES FILLES!'

It was quite a sight. But, I noted, Sean's grin was now slightly fixed. He was nodding a lot but his eyes, when they caught mine, signalled: *Get me outta here.*

Naturally I tried on several occasions to offer a light: 'Well, we must be going now, there's a big stage to prepare for.'

The only reply was: 'NON! RESTE ICI! PLUS COGNAC!'

It took a long time and many repeated promises, mostly hollow, before we were finally allowed to escape. 'Yes, yes, we are definitely coming. We'll be there alright. Yes, sure thing. Righty ho! All the best. Yep, see you in January!'

We got to bed around 5 a.m.

Our planned 'quick drink with an African race chap' turned out to be something very different. The night, like our African host, turned out to be far, far bigger than expected. So is the Amissa Bongo.

Want a ride in the sunshine in January? Don't want to go all the way to Australia? *Welcome to Gabon! Home of African Cycling,* says the poster. And it's not fibbing.

These days all the continents of the world have a World Tour race – except for the biggest, Africa. But it's only a matter of time before the UCI will grant such status to one of the already impressive roster of races. The Tour of Rwanda is probably the favourite to be granted this elevation first, and close behind will be the wonderful Tour de Fasso or maybe one of the great races in South Africa. That said, since 2006 the race with the best roster of superstar riders on the mighty continent has been the Tropicale Amissa Bongo.

In 2005 the President of Gabon, Omar Bongo, decided that there needed to be a race to reflect his nation's ambition. And so it was that the father of this young and beautiful country decided to name the event after his young and beautiful daughter, Amissa. A year later it duly became one of the select few races on the calendar to carry a person's name. Sure, such race titles usually reflect a great of the sport: the Cadel Evans Ocean Race, the Coppi e Bartali or the now defunct Grand Prix Eddy Merckx. Well, now we had the Amissa Bongo. And yes, you're right: Amissa Bongo herself didn't know much about cycling, but that's OK.

Gabon was not exactly what you'd call a cycling hub. National TV billed it as a festival on two wheels. But the organisers had a head start on other African nations: the name showed they had presidential approval; their colonial past gave them great connections with the French Cycling Union and close connections with A.S.O., organisers of the Tour de France; and the French-speaking population loved the famed voice of Daniel Mangeas, the renowned Tour de France podium caller. All this plus that short flight time from Europe and an amazingly pleasant winter climate. The race became an instant hit.

Sure, you would have been hard pushed to find a Gabonese rider in the early editions, but plenty of Africa's star riders from other nations did come along for the fun of it – and so indeed did some top European World Tour riders, mainly from French teams. It was quite a party from the very start.

It's a race of seven stages run at high pace through a mostly flat or gently rolling tropical landscape. One for the quick men then, but punchy too: crosswinds play a part as the peloton emerges from heavy jungle, merging into magnificent open planes and is then later tested over some grippy hills. Sumptuous. No wonder stars of the sport are drawn to it. Sprint great André Greipel lists the Amissa Bongo as one of his favourite events.

Each day the riders head towards an enormous party at the destination town. There is a carnival going on and all kinds of informal support events. Small flyers are posted on lampposts announcing these competitions. I remember a *free-style cycling race* around town with *no rules* except *First home wins: A FRIDGE!* The race was simply brutal, yet highly entertaining. Kicking, laughing, slapping, barging – you name it, it was happening in this *anything goes* minor classic.

What must have been 300 riders turned up. They were screamed off the start by a man with a megaphone: 'Trois. Deux. Un. ALLEZ!!'

About 300 nutters of all ages started running with their bikes before leaping aboard and pedaling like crazy. These were mostly fixed, single-gear iron cycles, often with different-sized wheels, but who cared? It was magnificent mayhem.

It took about five minutes for everyone to disappear. Then, after around 15 minutes, they were back. With around 15 riders in the front group, the final corner beckoned, the finish line only 20m (65ft) beyond that sharp left-hander. The approach speed was impressive, and there was a lot of commitment – but, sadly, not much talent. The inevitable pile-up caused a collective sharp intake of breath and cries of anguish from the crowd as the riders careered into the open yard of a truck repair shop. The man on the loud hailer was in a frenzy. 'OH, NON! NON, NON, NON, NON, *NON!*'

Out of the fog of war a skinny young lad wearing a shirt that must have once been white was first to remount. He crossed the line and immediately disappeared into the mob of cheering fans, feted quite rightly like the hero he most certainly was. On the orange-box podium he got his fridge. Like his shirt, it was very second-hand. Nobody minded at all.

The first Amissa Bongo, run in 2006, was won by Finland's Jussi Veikkanen. Since then, it has grown into the African race with the most prestigious roster of riders. This status is largely due to the attendance from the beginning of the Française des Jeux team, who decided not to bother going all the way to Oz for winter racing. Other French teams followed suit, including Arkéa–Samsic, Direct Énergie and Delko–Marseille. The Amissa Bongo got a sprinkling of Tour de France superstar riders, while the athletes themselves could then turn up at the start of the World and European Tours in February, lightly toasted and race ready. Everyone's a winner – except for the Australian races, which the French teams now ignore.

Over the years African stars have started making the headlines in Gabon. In 2014 Eritrea's Natnael Berhane, riding for Cofidis, held off Luis León Sánchez over seven gruelling stages to send the continent's press into a frenzy. Four years later, Rwanda's Joseph Areruya did it again for Africa.

This is the world's biggest continent. Yet despite the fact that the land mass of the UK can fit inside the borders of, say, Algeria almost 10 times, we still think of it, at least in cycling terms, as rather small. Well, it most certainly is not. With its 54 countries (and additional dependencies) now engaging in cycling as a sport, Africa is destined to build an enormous presence going forward. And races like the Amissa Bongo (bless her) are part of the foundations.

CYCLING LEXICON

Burger: A round friction burn injury, often visible on the hip area, due to torn kit.

FEBRUARY

THREE

TOUR OF QATAR
DANGEROUS CARGO

So it turned out not to be a nasty boil after all.

Desert Adventure: Be at one with nature under the stars, said the tempting flyer at the check-in desk of my five-star Doha hotel.

I'll have a bit of that, I thought to myself. Little did I know I was now on a path that would lead to something having a bit of me.

For the moment we hadn't met; in fact, sand spiders don't meet much at all. They can survive six months or so before taking blood from whatever animal happens to wander by; camels, usually. Camel spider is another name for them and a better sobriquet perhaps than 'snacker of men'.

I was three days ahead of the racing at this desert sprint fest/classics tune-up. An inevitable highway stage race across this unfeasibly flat, occasionally gusty, oil and gas super-producer nation.

Qatar has the world's richest local population. I say 'local' because most of the inhabitants are itinerant contract workers who are startlingly less well off. The Qataris themselves are extremely wealthy and were happy to spend a few riyals on a sporting contest such as ours. These petrodollars made the event, by any measure, rather generous. Nobody was complaining at spending 10 days in a five-star luxury hotel bedecked in gold, scarlet and green. It was quite the experience. A bit like being holed up in a treasure cave. Bling was the thing.

I slipped into my onyx bath and turned off the golden swan's head (actually the mixer tap).

As I lay in a gently bobbing cloud of bubble-bath foam, it all felt rather familiar. You see this humble cycling commentator started his career long ago writing feature pieces for *Middle East Money*, a business magazine for the region. My column was called 'How to Spend It', a title later adopted by other publications. My job was to investigate luxury on behalf of our wealthy or aspirant readers. I'd travelled extensively in this part of the world, so I was thinking to myself as I bathed: *This hotel is a bit like those in Oman. Oh, and Bahrain. And Abu Dhabi. And Saudi. And Kuwait. And . . . this is bollocks.* I clambered out of the bath, stepped into the adjoining cubicle and hit the Body Dry button. It was an impressive system and clearly cost far more than a simple towel. Completely dry, I knotted the world's heaviest luxury bathrobe and shuffled into a pair of slippers that looked like trophies from a Yeti hunt.

As I flopped into my pony skin armchair, I pondered the leaflet. Right now, the chance to escape all this opulence and find out a bit more about Qatar before the race began, seemed like a very good idea. I called reception to ask how much.

'Mr Kirby, it is all part of your Sultan Package. There will be no charge. What size are you?' My momentary silence produced the explanation: ' . . . for the clothes and equipment.'

This sounded intriguing. Knowing that sizing varies depending on which part of the world I'm in, I understood this question needed to be treated with caution. If the items are made for Bangladesh, then I am a 4XL; and such items may still pinch. In Germany I am a humble XL. So I said: 'I'm the same size as your security guard.'

'Ah, Rhami, the man at the scanner?'

'Yes, that's him,' I answered without adding: *the one who takes far too long patting you down.*

'You are a 2XL, Mr Kirby . . . We go up to 8XL.'

A Toyota Land Cruiser pulled up at 4 p.m. It was white. They are all white. To distinguish each car from one another they carry spectacular swirling gold geometric patterns with Arabic calligraphy. Each are apparently unique to the owner. I have no idea what mine said but it was clearly a Desert Adventure vehicle as the smiling staff, of whom there were three, made clear as they bounced out in matching logoed polo shirts. They were making a fuss of me.

With an enthusiastic 'Please, please sir, please', I was ushered into the back seat.

I realised I would have to do very little on this magic carpet ride into the wilderness. My bags were stowed next to a cardboard trunk marked Sultan Kirby and I settled into the quilted leather seat next to a fixed-grinning guide.

'Very nice to see you, sir, very nice. Where are you from?'

'London.'

'Oh very nice, very nice. But very WET. Where we go now is very dry. VERY DRY. It is the desert, sir. . . Very deserted.'

'Thank you, I'm looking forward to it.'

'Manchester United is not in London, sir.'

'No.'

'I like Manchester, sir.'

'Have you been there?'

'No, sir.'

Thankfully this adventure was not about conversation.

That night I lay in a cosy 'General Authority of Customs: State of Qatar' sleeping bag looking at the start list for this 2015 Tour of Qatar. It was a more than impressive roster with a mix of superstars whose plan was: 1. to back up the fast classics boys; 2. maybe have a pop themselves; and 3. warm the bones in February on a series of loop stages that brought them home every afternoon in time for a dip in the pool. Same bedroom every night, and if the day went well for you, then so much the better. If it didn't, there was always a luxury spa to help you forget.

The riders' list bettered most races on the season calendar: Kittel, Cancellara, Boonen, Valverde, Bouhanni, Terpstra, Sagan, Gilbert, Van Avermaet, Kristoff, Boassen Hagen, Demare, Wiggins, Sam Bennett . . . and on it went.

Then I checked the route maps. Erm . . . flat. Yep, that's it.

If there is anywhere flatter on this earth, then it's likely being used to play billiards. Qatar was, of course, once a huge tropical jungle that had emerged from the sea. Over millennia it had mulched down into a massive pile of vegetation that, rather handily for our now wealthy locals, turned itself into vast oil fields. This is the very commodity that has helped power the world and, of course, accelerate our negative impact upon it. And just when exploration techniques meant they could now calculate when it would all one day run out, the Qataris went and discovered the biggest gas field on the planet as well.

Now, when you have plenty of cash and a largely empty and near perfectly flat country, you tend to build highways straight to the places you want to go. It means there is not much diversion along the way. No, the main feature is wind. And this is useful for riders practising ahead of the classics season. Famously the World Championships came to Qatar in 2016 and the course had just one significant turn, smack in the middle of it. I remember it was a right-hander way out in the desert. A junction of two highways. A strong, westerly tailwind approach and crosswind exit. It was the only damned feature on a day that ran for 257.3km (159.8 miles). The men's race took close to five and three quarter hours to complete. Sagan beat Cav' at the line to take the second of his hat-trick of world titles.

Despite the 21-rider break that contested the finalé, it was possibly the biggest non-event in World Championship history. The venue wasn't right for this. Too hot by far, meaning the streets were largely empty and many a rider had their challenge ended by having to stop to throw up. Sunstroke and heat exhaustion were rife.

On that *loooooong* day in the desert, my work consisted mainly of flimflam with a frenzy on top, which sounds like the name of a fruit cocktail (of which there are plenty in the juice bars of the megamall in town). Alcohol is tougher to find in Qatar, as visiting football supporters will have discovered at the World Cup as they sat sulking in their air-conditioned stadium seats. Fans may also have met a police force with very big sticks. Cheers!

The Tour of Qatar died after the World Championships. There was no 2017 edition. And for that we must be grateful. Although if ever I wish to remember the race I can always pop along to Sheffield University Medical School, where students on the Diploma in Tropical Medicine and Health (Short Course) still wonder at Cyril the sand spider, who sits in a jar on a shelf. Cyril and I go back a few years.

In February 2015 the view of the universe was drawing into sharp focus as the fire embered down to a gentle glow. I was as relaxed as could be, having enjoyed a fabulous chicken biryani washed down with mango juice. Knowing the roster of riders very well and having no mountains, hills or indeed much else to be bothered researching, I lay there in cosy comfort while drifting along the short road to unconsciousness by idly looking for shooting stars and cruising satellites. I have never felt more at peace or more solitary. But I did have company that night, inside my sleeping bag . . . and he was peckish.

The next day I arrived in the commentary box limping. What looked like a huge boil had come up on my right calf. The Italian sound engineer gave up squeezing it when I yelped, then sprayed some iodine on it before dressing it with gauze and a bandage. The throbbing lasted about two days. The swelling took a week to go. The scar? I still have the scar.

The race? Not terribly memorable. A series of shortish loops before running into town for each finalé, almost entirely ignored by the locals. The sprinting was entertaining enough, but the memory of them didn't linger. Then again the star riders got in some useful, early season Ks.

Once back in the UK, I decided to visit my folks in Sheffield and took along the luxury eiderdown sleeping bag I had been kindly allowed to keep after my desert excursion. I thought it might be useful when the grandchildren visited. But over the next few months everyone who stayed over at my parents' house developed the same lesions I had found in Qatar. And then my mum found Cyril. Who turned out to be female. And who now had a family, all living together in a permanently warm airing cupboard high on a hill overlooking Sheffield.

It's probably fair to say that she panicked a bit when she noticed them backing into the dusty shadows behind the unlagged copper imersion heater. The 999 call operator was very kind. And the University team came in silver suits to take our friends away.

If you must visit Qatar, do pay a visit to the megamall. There you will marvel at the Love Bridge where young couples queue up to have pictures taken. It features a waterfall not even 2m (6ft) high pouring into what looks like a goldfish pond. It's surrounded by AstroTurf and plastic flowers. There is a bridge over the little lake upon which the lovers stand. Behind them is a painted backdrop of an Alpine scene. If their friends taking the pictures get it just right, then the pair can look like they are somewhere else entirely. I suggest you follow their dreams . . . elsewhere is good. But if you do go: check for spiders.

CYCLING LEXICON

Puppy Paws: A now banned aero position whereby riders rested their forearms on the bars with their hands hanging loose.

FOUR

VOLTA AO ALGARVE
'FREE OLLY!'

Apparently you can indeed get arrested for buying an octopus. This depends on how you buy it, of course, and I am not talking about breaking CITES regulations here. Just about your regular European Blue that features at the higher end of menus in and around the Med.

Now, I like to think of it as a mere misunderstanding, but the locals saw things otherwise. The common cephalopod I bought was just your regular fare destined to end up in a casserole. But here was the rub: I wasn't supposed to buy it. I had no right.

One hot afternoon in August I had wandered into the Tavira fish market after hearing the skiffle-patter of the auctioneer. I was back in town after an enjoyable week in late February covering the Volta Algarve. Marcel Kittel won the sprint into the harbour in 2016, a year when the roster of riders for this terrific race was the equal of any grand tour. Contador, Cancellara, Gerraint Thomas, Tony Martin, Urán, Roglič, Greipel, Pinot . . . you get the idea.

It had been a glorious 19°C (66°F) as we headed towards March; still needed a cardy. Now, here in mid-August, it was a hammering 38° (100°). Yep, my knees were out on display . . . that's how hot it was.

Standing at the back of the tiled auction hall crowd in my shorts and flip-flops was a nice place to be. The outside heat was quickly forgotten among the piles of crushed ice being liberally shovelled onto the newly sold boxes of fish before they were dragged outside with a flurry of grapple hooks and squeaky wellies by workmen squinting away mouth-held cigarette smoke.

The fish market in Tavira is a hectic place, just along the quayside from the tourist ferry that chugs its way over the lagoon to the spectacular sandy Praia. I was billeted at the Mares Residential, a villa turned guest house with a restaurant boasting 'the freshest fish in town'. A big brag, to be honest, with so many harbourside restaurants equally as close to the busy fish market.

So there I was people-watching as the (mostly dead) creatures of the deep were being bid for. The fish were still, but the crabs, lobsters and crayfish were not; their maker waiting to meet them in a kitchen not far from this place. Until then they survived in a gently tumbling pile; claws made safe with bright red elastic bands; bodies softly crackling as they wriggled and wrestled each other upon their bed of ice.

And then my moment came. One of those odd occasions where I reacted to something so instinctively that I couldn't even call it impulsive. That would suggest a moment's thought . . . and my hand shot up without any such a thing.

A round earthenware pot had been presented to a general hush. Into the pot was poured a deeply saline solution from which the creature needed to escape. It was as if a fire had been thrown into the pot. Out plopped a beautiful deep purple octopus. They kept a hose on him, or her, while it flailed and searched for salvation in the square glass tank. There was no escape. Not yet.

The bidding was ferocious at first, but quickly settled into a battle between two equally round men who were clearly not fishermen. They were buyers for the restaurants.

Now, I don't forget much and I recalled a conversation with Eurosport reporter Ashley House about the sentience of the octopus. It's why Ash won't eat these amazing creatures. According to him, the octopus is a remarkably complex being that, like us, possesses the ability to feel pain and experience fear. Indeed, this higher level of consciousness has been recognised officially by the UK Government. No such news had reached Portugal where they merrily poked the creature as the bidding progressed. I was filled with a sense of pity.

So it was that as the auctioneer raised the pen he was using as a mini gavel on his clipboard, my hand involuntarily shot up.

'*Aaaaaand* SOLD!'

To me! Oh.

I clearly wasn't ready for this. I wasn't part of this gang. For a start, I had no bidding paddle. I didn't have a flat cap or a fag in my mouth either. The auctioneer pointed my way and the crowd parted as puzzled faces turned to look at me. There was silence . . . then uproar.

What I had just done, and was soon to be found guilty of, was to interrupt an auction for licensed and registered bidders – of which I was clearly not one. This was being explained by the five people nearest to me, all speaking at the same time. In Portuguese. They were barrelling around me, getting more and more agitated, until an unfeasibly small lady took my hand and led me over to a hatch in a wall, where I was asked to sign various documents.

I was asked to pay first my annual dues as a registered monger, then a fee to take part in the auction and then the price of the octopus I had just bought. And, it turned out, there was also a fee to the stevedore who would drag the box with the creature in it to any waiting vehicle that had a licence to park in the trade area. Not one of mine.

'Look, this is all getting a bit silly,' I said to nobody in particular.

Then I got a tap on the shoulder from a man who was clearly in authority. The Port Authority to be precise.

'What are you doin'?'

'Erm . . . buying an octopus?' I offered apologetically.

About £140 lighter, I was allowed to leave with my octopus and a police caution.

A small crowd watched as I carried my rather expensive new friend in a heavy-duty plastic bag down a small flight of stone steps where the gently bumping fishing boats were tethered. A couple of the onlookers shook their heads and exchanged baffled comments as I let my rather expensive friend go. The octopus seemed to pour itself down the last green steps and disappeared into the harbour.

'They have feelings apparently!' I called back by way of explanation. Nobody was interested.

The Algarve is the heartbeat of the Portuguese economy. Sure, there is the fabulous capital, Lisbon, halfway up the Atlantic coast and the amazing Port wine estates. There is a thriving garment industry as well, but it is tourism that is the big money generator and the Algarve is where it is at.

There is the Tour of Portugal or Volta a Portugal em Bicicleta, which gets around the nation smartly between the Tour de France and La Vuelta. But it is the Tour of the Algarve that is the bigger draw. The late February calendar slot helps generate a spectacular roster. It's perfect if you don't want to travel to the Middle East to test early season form and also if you like fish. Just the best fish. Did I mention the fish?

I like Portugal. A lot. And they like the Brits too. Our mutual history goes back a long way – the first ever international alliance. The Anglo-Portuguese Treaty was signed between the Kingdoms of England and Portugal back in 1373. Of course, 650 years ago we had a common enemy: Spain.

It was pretty much the same in 2016 for Geraint Thomas, Alex Dowsett and Ian Stannard along with Tiago Machado, Nelson Oliveira, and André Cardoso . . . All on nodding terms as they tried to get the better of Alberto Contador, Louis León Sánchez and Joaquim Rodríguez among the stars of other nations. Portugal really does like to beat Spain.

Lasting five days, this perfectly formed race has made it a mission to offer something to every kind of rider. The classics boys get a shout, the sprinters too. With two days of serious gradients, including the iconic Alto do Malhão, the climbers can have fun too. And just to make sure the mountain monkeys don't run away with it, the Grand Tour GC men have a time trial thrown in for good measure.

A quick glance at the start sheet helps you know this race is big. And since the Middle East early season races began to implode a little, the shine has returned along with the sun to Portugal. There are far worse places to spend a February than in and around the Algarve. It is stunningly beautiful.

The 2022 edition turned out to be something special from somebody very special. The search for the next Eddy Merckx was declared over by none other than Eddy Merckx. It's Slovenia's Tadej Pogačar apparently. This despite a couple of claims coming from closer to Eddy's home in the form of either the hugely impressive Wout van Aert or perhaps the five years younger and mightily precocious Vuelta winner Remco Evenopoel. The more junior of these two superstars did take a knock to his march towards greatness – partly due to a terrible accident at Lombardia in 2020 where he crashed off a bridge into a ravine, but also due in no small part to his sheer cockiness and his willingness to express his belief that he should have been the one supported at the 2021 World Championships and not Wout van Aert. 'I had the legs to win it . . . and everyone knew it.'

It seemed a fair claim when you looked at his form shortly afterwards at the opening of the 2022 season. It started in earnest with runner-up spot in Valenciana behind GC big hitter Aleksandr Vlasov; a result closely followed by victory for Remco in the Algarve. The season ending spectacularly in Spain.

This is a race where you find the old and the new in so many ways. Stars on the wane and those on the rise from all disciplines. If you want good stage racing in a compact form, look no further. Capital of the region is Faro, a place many simply fly into before hiring a car at the airport and heading off along the coast. Well, don't be so hasty. Faro is terrific and worth a stayover. The harbour is charming and its sandspit beach a delight. The Atlantic crashes into Portugal just to the west of the port city, creating huge orange sandstone stacks and cliffs as a backdrop to sandy coves where you can rest up from the impressive surf.

Inland you find the barren lands of the cork farms of the Montado where these hardy trees periodically give up half of their bark in a form of rotation farming that has kept a modest economy, which covers a million hectares, going for generations. It's a way of life sadly threatened by the global penny-pinching move towards plastic corks or, even worse, screw tops. Pedants will bang on about natural cork spoil rates as an excuse . . . but it's just about saving money. So go and see this UNESCO World Heritage nature reserve while you can. It's stunning but don't sit too long; those are vultures circling above you. Seriously.

My advice is to book yourself a no-luggage bargain flight and wear your oldest clothes. When you land, simply head into Faro city and marvel at the bargain prices in the boutiques and clothes shops. Buy a new outfit. Bin the old one. Buy a bag and fill it with more new stuff. Then head off, box-fresh, to follow one of the friendliest races there is on the calendar. Take the coast train. It's just amazing to waft along the shoreline to the inevitable seaside starts and stage ends that pepper the race. You'll get close to your heroes and discover a few new ones to worship. All crammed into five days of fun in the much-needed February sun.

As for food: Cataplana is lovely. It's basically a casserole cooked in a copper dish with a lid. Think of a hearty broth with a tomato, onion and pepper base. There is garlic and tarragon along with white wine and chouriço sausage in there too. You can choose either chicken, pork or fish versions . . .. and if you are a heartless bastard, you can order one with a once-sentient octopus: equally delicious (don't tell Ash).

CARLTON COMMENTARY

'He's pedalling squares.'
Struggling uphill

MARCH

FIVE

STRADE BIANCHE
FROZEN PIZZA

'Hi, Olga – yeah, I know, it's so miserable. We've got driving sleet here in Norfolk. Carlton is really grumpy; just staring forlornly through the window. If this goes on much longer, I'll have to let him back in.'

This is my wife Steph's favourite joke. When the weather is bad, she calls friends up just to be able to reel it off. Bless her.

Back in 2012 I was looking north forlornly at the sunny side of the square in Sienna. One of the planet's most beguiling views. But I was in the fridge, trapped at a rudimentary commentary position which appeared to have been constructed from wallpaper pasting tables. We were in the shady half, with temperatures around 12°C (54°F) and a wind chill that magnified this: downwards. Gusts that would create a tailwind finalé blew along the finish straight, having been captured by the buildings. Anything not nailed down or plugged in was getting lively on the desk as we set up. Using lip mics, both Dan Lloyd and I were struggling to keep hold of our notes during sound checks. Or at least I was as I shivered. Somehow Dan had managed to source a quilted jacket.

'They didn't have your size, mate' was his answer to my raised eyebrows. I'm good at the forlorn look; it comes naturally.

Sienna can be cold. It never looks like that in any pictures of the place. Electric blue skies are always the backdrop to the majestic Torre del Mangia. Built as a lookout tower and bell house in just 10 years in the mid 1300s, it sits on the south-eastern corner of the Piazza del Campo next to the Palazzo Pubblico (which sounds far better than 'Town Hall').

This was 600 years before the advent of heavy-lifting pneumatics and other power tools; you wonder how they did it. But back then, architecture itself was designed to be mind-blowing, the idea being to subjugate by rendering those you wish to control or defeat in awe of your cleverness. Do this, and you are already ahead of the game. Churches and warships were always made to impress. Same with this citadel.

The engineers back in the day were most concerned about the heat of summer. So all the important stuff was built on the south side in the shade facing north. Well, things have changed. Air con arrived and suddenly all year round the best place to be was on the opposite side . . . in the sun. So the prime real estate on this square shifted from our side to the other.

Naturally in the spring this sun trap is a magnet, so all the chi-chi restaurants were abuzz with those basking in the sun; teasingly, just over 90m (295ft) away from us.

The Stampa, or press room, was housed in the old town hall. From here, the cables to power us ran directly outside where we sat, out in the open, just after the finish line and the makeshift podium. We were being tortured by the cold and gullying wind but also by every wanker basking opposite as they got on with the job of emerging from winter. I watched enviously as we went on with our technical prep while making shiver-scribbled notes and listening to race radio. Live transmission was still 90 minutes away.

Opposite me, like unboxed tortoises emerging from hibernation, moving slowly, they were taking their time over lunch, bedecked in the latest sunglasses and fancy jumpers, sleeves rolled up to the elbow in the spring sunshine. You know, rubbing it in.

Finally, we were told we had 40 minutes before joining the race live.

'Let's g-grab a pizzz-za, Dan,' I stuttered.

'Sure!' said Mr Survival Coat.

As we emerged into the sunshine, my spectacles misted over.

Finally we arrived in front of a brass-framed menu. I stood within my own cloud of dry ice.

'I can't see a thing, Dan. Is that pink note the specials?'

'No, mate. It says they're fully booked.'

The only place with any space was back over in the shade in the south-western corner. We pushed though the old glazed doors and entered . . . heaven. There can only have been half a dozen customers, but it was cosy as you like with a big, ancient, wood-burning oven a glowing dome of redemption.

'Prego!' said the lady, guiding us to a chunky wooden table and handing us paper menus.

There were no questions. She zipped off and returned with orders for another table. What passed us were the most amazing pizzas I have seen outside of Napoli.

'We've come home,' I murmured.

'We got here first,' said our friends from RAI.

I rubbed my specs clear to find Alessandro merrily tucking in. Cheeks full and smiling as he chomped.

'This place is the best,' he said through a mouthful. 'The oldest and the best. You see, in the days before air conditioning –'

'I know, Ally. Just enjoy your food, my friend.'

And we enjoyed ours. Less than half the price of the sunny side too. Perfect.

The name of the gem of a place? Pizzeria Spadaforte. If you go to the race and want to find it, simply imagine the riders continuing straight on, beyond the finish line. They would crash directly into the place.

Do feel free to ignore the sunny yet packed La Costa. It's aptly named.

Strade Bianche is an amazing race full of drama and beauty and always featuring a start list rammed with stars. Some say it is the greatest classic of them all. It has everything: the best course, run at the best time of year, with the best racing towards the best finalé on the planet.

It has everything except cycling history. And since 2007 it has been busily creating it.

There has been racing in Piazza del Campo since 1590. Bullfighting had been outlawed and they had to think of something. So instead of killing the beasts they came up with *bufalate*: racing buffalo bareback. I know, bit naff. As you can imagine, despite the raucous enthusiasm, the racing wasn't as dramatic as hoped, so they began *asinate*: donkey racing. They were getting there.

Finally in 1663 they came up with the modern Palio. A bareback horse race with riders representing one of 17 societies, or *contrade*, each with their own colours and traditions. These *contrade* are of varying size and have each enjoyed different levels of success over the centuries. But one thing they all have in common is fanatical support. The noise and colour of the spectacle is something all should witness. It is as decadent as anything Venice might offer, mixed with the raucous support of an Inter vs AC Milan derby and as rough as a game of Calcio Storico in Florence. Just go.

Then, getting on for 350 years later, someone had the very good idea of having a bike race climb the narrow winding streets up to the citadel and finish in the famous Piazza. Thank you, Lord.

The first Strade Bianche took place in 2007. Immediately it was a hit. Of course it was. A rolling route with a gain of nearly 4000 m (13120ft) of altitude crammed into just 186km (116 miles). There is virtually no flat ground to play with, providing multiple attack points along the way. So it's impossible to settle into a rhythm. Then factor in the 11 sectors of white gravel roads accounting for 63km (39 miles) of a route that ultimately leads to one of the world's most beautiful squares. All these things combine to bring us a race of glorious mayhem. I, and many others, just love it.

The idea of mixing a race up with sectors made of pounded white marble spill was a stroke of genius. These are what give the race its name, Strade Bianche, and also its unique character. The cheapest way of paving country roads in this region is to use the rubble and gravel from the marble mines and cutting houses that pepper the area. These are where your lovely kitchen surfaces come from – and for centuries the spill from this process has been pounded into the earth to give farmers the tracks they needed to get around their humble estates.

Naturally, asphalt has begun to take over, meaning the strade bianche have become a rarity. Thank heaven, then, for the success of this amazing race. It means that, rather like the cobbled byways of northern France and Belgium borders, these now scarce and unstable surfaces are being preserved for racing and our enjoyment. And no matter the weather, it's a real challenge.

If it's dry, the riders and support vehicles kick up an enormous dust cloud that settles onto sweaty bodies, turning riders into what looks like a B-movie: *The Racing Dead*.

The Giro d'Italia famously visited the course in 2010. It was an epic run to Montalcino, with Cadel Evans leading home a field of dancing statues: the rain left the entire peloton looking like a plasterer's radio by the end. We had to rely on physical recognition of rider style because no numbers were visible; even picking out team colours was near impossible. The Giro came back to play in 2021, where young Swiss rider Mauro Schmid took his first Grand Tour stage win.

But it is as a stand-alone classic that Strade Bianche thrives and beguiles. It sits as an amazing entreé into the season, coming as it does just before Tirreno–Adriatico and Paris–Nice and two weeks ahead of the Monument Milano–Sanremo.

Perhaps because of its unpredictable terrain, it is hard to fathom the kind of rider who might win. Classics specialists naturally, but puncheurs or even Grand Tour stars can have fun. Tadej Pogačar came home 7th when trying it for the first time in 2021. He came back in 2022 and won.

Yet apart from the raw talent always found in the start list, the main attributes required of any winner seem to be a mix of both toughness and unpredictability. Let nobody know your plan. And let nobody catch you when you go for it.

Julian Alaphilippe did this beautifully in 2019. The tracking shots of him moving along the blade of a huge hillside spur I can never forget. Clear of the pack, he and Jacob Fuglsang formed a two-up attack to pressure Wout van Aert, who was dropped from the break. With the peloton closing, the Dutchman bridged back but at a cost. On the steep streets of Sienna, Alaphillippe launched, taking the best lines through the tight turns towards Il Campo and the finish line to win by two seconds ahead of the Dane. Wout van Aert won in 2020 and fellow cycle-cross god Mathieu van der Poel triumphed in 2021.

But my favourite winner was the amazing Fabian Cancellara, the only rider to win this amazing race three times. Back on that cold, cold day he warmed my heart, not just for his performance but also because it turns out this great man, who must have met a thousand journalists and commentators in what was a remarkable career, never forgets a face.

It was a difficult interview, if only due to my shivering.

'Fabian, a fa- . . . fa- . . . fa-'

'Flipping freezing, Carlton?' he asked, kindly avoiding an oath while trying to help.

'No, fa- . . . fa- . . . fantastic d- . . . day.'

'Yes, it was,' and away he went. What a pro.

This race should be a Monument. One day I think it will be. It may take another 60 years or so for the pedants to allow this, but it will happen. So it's too early just yet, but one day they will erect a statue to the founders of this race. They should place it directly outside the Town Hall in memory of that cold afternoon in 2012 when the first statue appeared. Holding a lip mic. Frozen solid.

CYCLING LEXICON

On the Rivet: A single hammered rivet on the nose of old school leather saddles. Leaning forwards racing puts your body on this rivet.

SIX

TIRRENO–ADRIATICO
BOULDER BAG

Massi Adamo is a genius. Pure and simple. The man can turn a long day of racing into a highlights package that actually gives you an expanded view of what has gone on. Less is more when Massi is in charge.

He is a producer like no other because along with the genius comes a joyful nature that is frankly unheard of among those who emerge from the dungeons that are edit suites. His friendly demeanour is disabling. This has a downside in that he can ask for favours that would earn anyone else a simple *piss off*. Just small things; but annoying. Massi gets away with such requests because you know full well that if it were you asking the same favour of your colleagues, only Massi would say: 'Sure, no problem.' So when he asks, you say yes. No matter how annoying.

'Hey, guys! Can you take my bag to the hotel for me? I'll see you there later, I'm eating with the crew!'

Now, a little detail is needed here. Dan Lloyd and I had been given a 'car' for the Tirreno Adriatico. This vehicle was a Fiat 500 Grande. Believe me there is nothing *grande* about it. The boot will accept a hard-boiled egg before becoming difficult to shut.

Massi's bag was . . . ENORMOUS! What I like to call a Texas Wallet, seen at international airports, the bag of choice for American tourists 'doing'

Europe. You know the thing. Metre and a half tall, fat and on wheels. I had a pizza delivery person like that once. Anyway, his bag:

'Bloody hell, Massi, what have you got in this thing?'

Turns out that Massi's 'life scatter' away from his work extends to his packing. Basically he has three weeks of clothes in there. So, no need to wash anything. 'After this I got to go to Moto GP and then home to Suzanna.' Poor Suzanna.

By the final week of his stint, the smell from this bright red case will approach toxic as the percentage of dirty clothes outnumbers the clean stuff.

Anyway, because it was Massi, we hulked it onto the back of the car. It was heavy. I mean really heavy. Massi laughed from the open door of the edit truck as we struggled. 'Aaaaw, thanks guys.'

I was now straining alone to get it onto the back seat. Dan Lloyd watched on, frowning with hands on twiggy hips. 'What have you got in there, Massi?!'

I spluttered: 'Yeah, Mass, how heavy can underwear be?'

It only just fitted in on its side and completely obscured the rear view. Dan was not pleased. 'Right, let's go . . . it's three hours to the hotel. Maybe four.'

We got to our mountaintop residence after dark. Very dark. Up there on that clear moonless night, it was the definition of quiet. As we stepped out of the car, a crunch of ice underfoot told a story about our altitude.

We wobbled to the back of the vehicle like this was our first time on skates.

It took us a while to check in. Lots of slipping and sliding followed by the usual passport confiscation and tick-box questionnaire beloved of Italian hotels. And then . . . finally . . . we had to deal with Massi's bag.

I fell only once during the extraction exercise. But to any casual observer I must've looked like I was trying out for a place on a Rhythmic Gymnastics Olympic team. Every limb was busy trying to maintain balance.

Once out of the car, the scarlet monolith stood there mocking us. 'What the hell is in there?' asked Dan.

'I dunno, let's have a look.'

I laid the bag down and unzipped it. It was solid jumble sale inside. Just clothes and his bathroom stuff. But lots of it. The case was made of heavy non-rip fabric.

'Is there any space left in there?' asked Dan.

What? Why? Then I noted Dan's smirk. This meant devilment. 'And you are thinking what precisely?'

'Oh, you know . . . why don't we make it even heavier? Give him a taste of this shit when he gets to pick it up from reception.'

Nothing more was said as we hunted for a rock.

The boulder of granite we found was the size of a regulation football. But it weighed a ton. We decided to brave the bottom of his bag where the dirty stuff was. We wrapped it in a Kylie T-shirt (I know!) and just about managed to extract enough space to accept our lumpy friend.

Zipped up, you wouldn't know a thing. But lifting it? Oh my.

We carried Massi's case together for fear of destroying the wheels on the gravelly path. Up the steps to reception, we grunted and wheezed, leaving it upright behind the counter. Time for a beer.

Greg and Kathy LeMond were there in the open lounge, next to a roaring fire. We joined them and shot the breeze about the day and, of course, divulged our tease. Kathy thought this hilarious but promised to say nothing.

Two hours later Massi was dropped off by the production crew. They'd had another of their big nights. Thirty of them block-book restaurants as soon as the route map of a race is announced. They then agree a fee for a five-course meal with wine, lots of wine. Massi was flush-faced, full and very merry.

'Hey, guys! How's it going? Thanks for taking my bag –' *burp!* '– There's no way it would've fitted in our car.'

'Mass, your bag is the heaviest thing in Luggage Land. I mean it weighs a ton!' I said.

Dan had a glint in his eye and raised a glass to hide his mirth. 'Yeah, fuckin heavy,' he called into his beer.

'Oh, come on, guys. You are big boys now. It's not that bad.'

'It is, Massi. It's very, VERY heavy.'

Kathy LeMond joined in: 'Sure looked heavy, Massi, when they brought it in.' Greg chuckled.

Massi gave us all a tipsy confused look of comedic pity while wagging a drunken finger at us. 'You people . . . heh! Anyway, weaklings, I'm going to bed. 'Av a good night. I'll see you in the morning.'

With that, he went for his bag. It didn't move.

You could see his mind recalibrating. He was thinking, but it was a slow process. He tried again.

The grab strap at the top end of the suitcase strained against its stitching, the fibreglass frame complained as it deformed. The caster wheels had failed in their housing and were now locked solid.

Despite his stupor, Massi was determined to show that our protests were mere exaggeration. He dragged his load to the foot of the stairs. It was a terrible sound as the jammed wheels gouged out distress lines into the reception's floorboards.

'Told you, Massi!' I called over.

'Rabbeesh!' he offered.

He needed a minute per stair as he finally disappeared up and around the corner.

It took Massi three days to find the rock.

'Yooooo bloodee wankaz . . .' was his battle cry that breakfast.

Nothing more needed to be said.

———

Springtime, and all is well with the cycling world. For the pros the early season races have been dealt with. The season shakedown is near complete and the top dogs are approaching their racing best. Time, then, to tighten everything up and go racing proper with some serious stages, not too many, and quality opposition, hopefully not in as good a shape as you are. It's early spring and the season is getting serious.

France, meanwhile, is busy having a troubled time with shocking weather and grumpy locals at a race ironically called The Race to the Sun. Paris–Nice is often run without any sun at all. Particularly over the last few editions, it has been a miserably wet affair. Professional riders go out in all weathers, as you know. It's their job. No rider actually likes riding in shocking conditions; those who welcome cold and rain are simply of the understanding that there are others in the peloton who are likely to suffer more. It's a sustainability factor: if you can stand the weather, you have a good chance of success. This has nothing to do with liking the rain and cold. Nobody does.

So, what is the alternative? Italy. Nice will have more rain, sleet and grumpiness because its end point is much further north than most of Italy. If you are a pro rider and you have the choice, surely it's far better to head for a place already busy emerging from hibernation with its own magnificent spring stage race, the Tirreno–Adriatico.

Instead of running north to south as the French equivalent does, the Tirreno–Adriatico goes west to east, notably from the Mediterranean coast, or Tirreno at the top of the shin of the Italian boot, heading cross-country to the calf on the Adriatic coast, or Adriatico. It's a spectacular race and – *I say this very quietly* – it is my favourite race of the whole season. I love it.

There are several reasons for my fondness of the Race Between the Two Seas. Primarily, of course, it is springtime in the most beautiful country on Planet Earth. This delight is then magnified by the fact that as a northern European, and very much on the blue-white spectrum of skin tone, I look half decent coming out of winter. It's the time of year when people of my pallor look like they are thriving. Italians do not. They emerge from the darker months looking a bit worse for wear. They are waiting for tannin. I find it's a very brief window of sartorial advantage when I reckon I look better than most of my pals from Italy. (Don't you worry too much on their behalf: this window is a very small one.)

It is at this race where the butterflies appear. To be honest, by the end of it, I'm feeling a bit ugly on the café terrace of San Benedetto del Tronto. After eight days of racing, Italy is looking disgracefully fantastic. Sunglasses on, jacket sleeves pushed up to just below the elbow (they still do this), sitting quietly, arms splayed resting on other chairbacks while a sockless ankle peeps out from a Gucci loafer as it rests on a knee. Confident, with faces turned towards the sun, they quietly bask; leaving me to ponder the indelible impression that their life is rather bloody wonderful . . .

Still, so is the racing.

Without getting too dewy-eyed with nostalgia, 2013 was the year that shocked the French. Paris–Nice had a problem: the roster of riders heading to the Tirreno–Adriatico had never been more impressive. In no particular order, the greats included: Cavendish, Greipel, Cancellara, Sagan, Degenkolb, Van Avermaet, Rodríguez, Froome, Nibali, Contador, Evans . . . and on it went. The list was remarkable. Paris–Nice had . . . well, let's just say Richie didn't have too much trouble winning into Nice that year. The very best of cycling had gone for pizza, not baguette.

I remember the shock at the Paris studios of Eurosport. They couldn't fathom it. They had believed that France would be supreme for all time and that the three jewels of the cycling crown theirs to keep: the finest Grand Tour, Classic and Stage race were theirs. Or were they? Sure, Le Tour is without equal and you might argue about Paris–Roubaix vs Flanders, but here was Paris–Nice whose supremacy was now clearly in decline. 'Paris–Nice beaten? By Italy? *Noooooooon. C'est pas vrai!*' Well, the start list said it was très vrai indeed.

The announcement of the race roster was mildly tectonic. The Tirreno–Adriatico had not only by far the better start list, but quite frankly the best roster of any race that year – including *all* the Grand Tours. It was phenomenal and a credit to the work of the finest race organiser there ever was: Michele Acquarone. His masterful management of the entire RCS portfolio was paying big dividends. His Middle East races were kicking Spain out of early calendar supremacy. The Giro was clearly reinvigorated under his stewardship, and apparently dead races like Roma Maxima were suddenly alive and kicking. But it was at this Tirenno–Adriatico that his magic cycle tree bore the heaviest fruit.

Acquarone was a man Mark Cavendish described thus: 'He's a riders' man. He listens to us, really listens to us. Properly, ya know. I like 'im a lot.' High praise indeed.

Back in 1966, the Beatles began recording *Sgt. Pepper's*. There had never been an album quite like it. Over in Italy the first Tirenno–Adriatico was born. Even now there is no race quite like it.

So much is crammed into this amazing week. Geography is its friend. No other race has so much varied terrain in such close proximity. Transfers are remarkably short simply because everything you could possibly want is so close at hand. We have coastal flats naturally, but the hills are right there like a theatre curtain screening the drama to come.

Meanwhile, looming almost dead centre of this cross-country extravaganza, you have the Gran Sasso, the mighty peak of the Appenines. It dominates the landscape and we play with its slopes just for fun – and sometimes for torture.

So whether it is Sagan winning up the slope into Chieti and beating his own teammate Vincenzo Nibali, or John Degenkolb blasting the opposition to smithereens next to the ancient cave city of Matera, you have grippy finishes. At altitude there is Chris Froome thriving up to Prati di Tivo on the Gran Sasso itself. There's Tony Martin showing off in the time trial, Mark Cavendish doing his thing – or indeed, doing the unexpected – like nailing it in the Team Time trial to take the lead of the race in the opener. It's where the stars often exceed their own billing with some unexpectedly memorable performances. The kind of efforts that you might think would only be found in a Grand Tour. But think again: it is here you'll find them. This race seems to offer riders a freedom to go for it. To be unafraid of strategic mistakes. To test both your opponents and yourself. To know where you are as the season's racing gets serious. It's brilliant to witness.

They cram a lot into this race and have done since its inception back in 1966. It has always been a great race. The list of winners proves that. It's a blizzard of greats: Pogačar, Roglič, Quintana, Van Avermaet, Contador, Nibali, Evans, Scarponi, Cancellara, Moser, De Vlaeminck . . .. and many more stars besides. Eddy Merckx perhaps the exception that proves the rule.

But it was the race of 2013 that turned a great race into an amazing one. It was this year that the Tirreno–Adriatico moved ahead of Paris–Nice in so many ways. Since then the Italians have had the advantage. It has been a huge star magnet.

Sure, Paris–Nice has battled its way back into contention. If riders could, they would probably like to ride both – but the calendar says no. So, if you have to choose? Well, huge transfers and stinky weather count for a lot at this part of the season. Grand Tour racing legs are what everyone wants to test, not how well you can sleep after a massive coach journey in a hailstorm. Yes, I know snowstorms are not uncommon in the Apennines. But I also know the sun will be out tomorrow.

So why should you love Tirreno–Adriatico this much? Well it's easy to get around, but even more important than that, it's easy to get close to the stars. Perhaps because Italy is just waking up, the race seems always to surprise a nation still obsessing about football in March – Champions League time. It's like Italy are waiting for Milan–Sanremo to truly believe in spring and cycling. So, if you do make the trip, you will find yourselves very close to the action and close to your heroes. You will bag a good spot at the barriers of the finish line. You will be within chatting range, possibly on your own, talking to the likes of Chris Froome as he warms up or down. 'Good day, Chris?' you might venture. He'll nod, breathless and sweating, before looking over to a staff member who'll then look at you and wave a finger across his face while shaking his head. *No more questions* is the gesture. But at least you got to try.

You might then share a hotel breakfast with your idols and ask starstruck questions of Peter Sagan: 'Bacon, Peter, are you sure?'

You'll get some sort of reply. As you know, he sounds like a hornet trapped in a jam jar. So it could be: 'Yes, I love bacon, the king of breakfasts' or 'I eat what I eat, that's the way it is' or 'Food, yeah, you need it.'

Any of these are Saganic answers, but you won't be sure as you don't speak Wasp.

Cycling fans have a magnificent gift in that you can get closer to the stars in action than in any other sport. Yes, you can touch them as you run alongside, but please don't. What the Tirreno–Adriatico also does wonderfully is allow you to share the riders' lives as they travel around. The hotels are not full; everyone is just a few notches down stress-wise. They are as relaxed as can be in competition. The sun is out, food fantastic, racing brilliant. It's always a star-studded start list. Transfers are short, good hotels aplenty, you can annoy your heroes at breakfast. And there's a rock in your suitcase. All in all, this race is, perhaps unexpectedly, amazingly fun to be at . . . unless it's you with the boulder.

CARLTON COMMENTARY

'He couldn't look more threatening if he had a lantern gland on his head and lived in the deep.'
André Greipel on full charge

SEVEN

MILANO-SANREMO
LA PRIMA HURTY!!

I really like heavy rain. Best of all the sound of it when I'm tucked up warm in bed. I also love cities when it's pouring down, particularly at night when you will likely have the streets all to yourself. And in places where rain is not so common you can feel a bit like Charlton Heston in the film *The Omega Man*. He was the sole human survivor of a global pandemic. Sure, he had some fun breaking into car showrooms and generally getting into a party mood. Until it hit him. The solitude, that is. It was all very dark.

I was in a bit of a party mood as well in 2017. I was back in Sanremo a couple of days before the riders would set off from Milan. An evening storm moved in over our bit of the Mediterranean, so that Thursday everyone was moving around in taxis while I decided to walk to dinner. I was completely alone in the downpour, having taken the most direct route past all the boutiques where cars are banned.

I'd set off at a brisk pace, leaving my friends waiting for their cabs in the hotel lobby. I was in a hurry, having bragged I'd beat them all to the restaurant. So I marched completely alone through drenched streets. I was as happy as Charlton Heston. Until it hit me. The bench, that is.

The pain was literally breathtaking. There was lightning everywhere – but only in my head. I almost blacked out. And all because some urban designer had decided to plant a solid, granite-like, flat-top bench (with, I admit, beautifully chamfered edges) right in the middle of the precinct. It was made of exactly the same stone as the pavement, so in the rain the bench was virtually invisible. It was also made for children to sit outside a rather expensive toy shop. The top of the bench stood no more than 35cm (14 inches) off the ground. You know, about shin height for a grown-up.

Though I didn't know it yet, I'd just broken my right leg.

I rolled about in the burbling gully for a good three or four minutes before I could gather myself. The breath came back to me in short pants. I'd gone down hard.

So, yes, I was wet when I limped into the trattoria.

'CAAAARLTONI!' exclaimed Roberto. 'The lifeguards are not on duty until June, you should not be swimming!' The place erupted.

I can tell you, the 'Smash Your Leg In Diet' is brilliant. You hardly eat a thing.

I can also tell you that codeine is a brain-fogger but does knock out much of the pain; well, just enough to get through a good few hours of commentating. Kind of. I was taking tablets like Smarties. I'm not sure it was my finest work.

Most of my words came from the top of very full lungs. Like bursts of gunfire as I fought the discomfort.

'Dan –' short breath '– who won last year, mate?'

'Arnaud Démare, you backed him.'

'Oh, yeah – 66 to 1 – I remember now –' *gasp* '– crash with Gaviria –' *pant* '– shagged it for the other quick men.'

Dan paused, like the adult in charge, before cautioning: 'You know, we *are* on air, Carlton!'

'Oh, yeah – sorry about that – anyway –' *breath hold* '– back to today –'

For many, the cycling season is not really off and underway until Milan–Sanremo. It is, of course, the opening Monument of the season and brings together a supremely talented roster that represents most wings of the cycling peloton. It doesn't matter what kind of specialist you are, there is a chance to thrive in this one. Grand Tour winners, sprinters, classics gods – they all have a chance.

The fans certainly get their money's worth as well: it is extremely long, at 291km (181 miles) in its most common form. The fatigue this distance generates among even the very best riders makes it extremely unpredictable.

The peloton heads south along the Po Valley across the Milanese industrial plane towards the coastal casino town of Sanremo. Beautiful the destination certainly is, but the early part of the journey can sometimes be a bit bleak and most of what we drive past are either industrial estates with vast factories or mega-farms of still brown muddy fields just starting to turn green with the first shoots of spring. La Prima Verde.

And like the season itself the race seems to leave winter behind on its run to the Mediterranean. Gradually the world occupied by the riders becomes more beautiful. Greener it gets on the approach, in expectation of the longed-for cliffs of the coast.

It takes 142km (88 miles) of mostly pan-flat racing before a gradual rise reaches the top of the Passo del Turchino and runs down towards the water. It's cathartic.

Suddenly everything is different. The light changes as the sea reflects the sky and the race, like the scenery explodes.

As if to soften us all up, the Tre Capi arrive. Three humble peaks that at any other time would be rather benign. Not now, not with 234km (145 miles) already in the legs. One after the other, they pound the peloton and then *boom!* Il Cipressa – a launchpad for the brave or the mad.

Time for a gang fight, and everyone left is invited. Sprinters take on puncheurs take on Grand Tour contenders. If this were a barroom brawl, even the piano player would be jabbing away. And if anyone does manage to crawl out from under the pile of bodies, how do you bring such a breaker back? Everyone is battered by now.

The number of riders who have anything left depends entirely on how the day has gone. It could be a solo, a select group or a bunch. Yet whatever form the front of the race takes, it will get broken down further on the Poggio.

There are now just 10km (6 miles) to go as the climb intensifies. This is no parlour game. Attack after attack from the near exhausted rage on. If there is anything left in the account, now is the time to spend it. Over the top we come, weaving down past the newly fragrant gardens and greenhouses of the flower growers and into town.

And how this drama ends is anyone's guess. Solo, cat and mouse, small breakaway, quick men, hard men, GC men – who knows? But whoever has just one more functioning sinew than the rest . . . will win on Via Roma.

It doesn't matter how good you are. Milan–Sanremo has no respect for a rider's palmarès. You can be on the best of form and not triumph. Previous winners might be expected to have a battle plan. Such forethought means little.

There was a six-year gap between Sean Kelly's two wins. The first in 1986 was a three-up sprint with Greg LeMond and Mario Beccia. A pack of 30 broken men came home 23 seconds later.

But Sean's second win in 1992 was spectacularly different. Moreno Argentin was away, having attacked the remaining field on the Poggio. With so much talent still left, nobody wanted to chase for fear of guiding another big name to victory. So Argentin got a margin. Then, over the top, Kelly went for it. At this point, so deep into his career, he had been written off as a potential winner – and the group hesitated. As for Kelly, he knew any chance for him depended on a high degree of risk-taking on the run home. Every corner of the descent, he was on the limit. Faster than anyone, he bridged to Argentin at the flamme rouge.

Argentin forlornly tried to get Sean to take a turn with the pack closing fast. This was the best game of bluff in the Irishman's career. He opened his mouth wide to look like he was in oxygen deficit – all the while weaving enough to give Argentin a view of those closing in. Argentin, more fearful of those behind than the apparently exhausted Kelly, kept pacing.

Then, with moments to spare, Kelly's mouth snapped shut into a grimace and he launched. Argentin was beaten at the line by a bike length. The pack of 26 mobbed the line just 3 seconds later. Wow!

Sean has said that this was his greatest day. So unexpected was it that even he was in thrall of the moment. And his helmet, the worst-looking lid to ever grace a man's head, like a sea turtle nesting on him, couldn't spoil things either. He didn't care. His famous celebration – double fists to the sky – was seen for the last glorious time at a classic. Monumental.

That was 30 years ago. Since then, there have been so many memorable editions. I loved calling home the Mark Cavendish photo finish win in 2009. The great man was annoyed after watching the replay, apparently. I couldn't be sure who'd won. Mark knew alright. Doing it for the pure sprinters.

Then, in 2013, Gerald Ciolek sent Africa's team MTN Qhubeka into a frenzy with one of the most surprising wins, timing his finish to perfection and beating Peter Sagan and Fabian Cancellara among a group of the Magnificent Seven. You might have expected Ciolek to place at the back. But no, every dog has its day. Even an underdog. Wonderful!

2018 saw a stunning solo from Vincenzo Nibali, who reminded us that Grand Tour winners can have some fun here too. The crowd went nuts for the first Italian winner since Pozzato 12 years before.

So, how to enjoy yourself? Fly into Nice just over the border, where you will have a choice: hire a car or take the train. Do the latter; the coastal railway is lovely. It fuddles along the cliffs past the stunning Menton, which is well worth a stop-off if you are in the area. Then cross the border into Sanremo itself. You have left behind the snooty end of France, and Monte Carlo, to enter a more proletarian version of a casino town on the Italian side. More pizza than Lobster Thermidor, and all the better for it. You can head back to Monaco for pampering. Here even the Grand Hotel Des Anglais is not as expensive as you might think. Just like the race itself, you should not be surprised to be surprised. Best pizza in town? No competition: Club 64 on Via Giuseppe Verdi, five minutes from the finish line.

The Milan–Sanremo has at its heart a magnificent unpredictability. Even the best riders can be blindsided at any time. As Sean Kelly once told me: 'Whatever you are prepared for, be sure to prepare for something else.'

Everyone who wins Milan–Sanremo will always count their blessings – and indeed every victory has an element of good fortune about it. This in no way diminishes the achievement of winning this most optimistic of races. At the start there is nothing but good wishes between the riders. The season is young and there to be enjoyed. They may, of course, feel different at the end of the drama, but it's springtime for goodness' sake! Let's look forward to the next edition and wish everyone the very best of luck. Or, as they say in the theatre: 'Break a Leg!'

CYCLING LEXICON

Chewing the handlebars: Suffering.

EIGHT

VOLTA A CATALUNYA
THE LONGEST WALK

Bloody map! It was raining gobs of sleet and clearly I was no longer worthy of my old Cub Scouts rank of Sixer. My map was falling to bits in my hands and I was in trouble.

It had been five hours since I left the sunshine-dappled town of Prades to take on the biggest Catalan mountain, the Pic du Canigou. I was walking because this Pyrenean trail was said to be too rough to ride. My bike was locked at the campsite on the valley floor, where I'd spent a very uncomfortable night after my air mattress punctured. I had no repair kit. I also had no plastic map sleeve and I was wearing a Peter Storm waterproof cagoule (it wasn't). I also had rather diminished map-reading skills, which is why I found myself wet, cold, grumpy and not a little scared. The rain began just about when the metalled road ran out.

There are extreme weather refuges up here on this amazing mountain. These are strictly for emergency use only – not for idiots who can't fathom a whole load of grid lines converging to indicate a tectonic heavenward spike of rock. This numpty had reckoned it looked like a jolly jaunt as the crow flies. Well, there were no flying crows because there were no trees. I pushed on alone on a mountain that other people, more clued-up, were avoiding due to the predicted bad weather. A winter storm in May? It happens.

I should have known better; it's not like I had an excuse. I could have checked for free, thanks to Météo-France. This service is amazing: it provides military grade information, to anyone who wants it. Indeed, it was these fine folk who predicted on French radio and TV that a hurricane would hit the UK on the night of 15 October, 1987.

Meanwhile, back in Blighty, Michael Fish was presenting the weather and was in quite a jolly mood: 'Earlier on today apparently, a woman rang the BBC and said she'd heard that there's a hurricane on the way; well, if you're watching, don't worry, there isn't. I had a peep at the radar just a little while ago' . . . and on he went, offering the kind lady who'd called in from Jersey some comfort. That night the hurricane smashed its way across northern France and southern England. Described as a 'weather bomb', with gusts of around 200km/h (124mph), it was famously destructive. Afterwards major improvements to atmospheric observation, computer modelling and the training of forecasters were announced. In other words, the Brits, like the lady in Jersey, would listen to Météo-France from then on. Well, some Brits never learn, so here I was, two years later, alone on a desperately cold and wet mountain with quite a few hours to go before I got back to any comfort. It was only mid-afternoon but it was getting dark.

The Pic du Canigou is a sacred mountain to Catalans. A week or so before midsummer night, families from France and Spain head onto its majestic slopes carrying bundles of twigs that contain handwritten wishes and prayers. In memory of their ancestors, this is the Troubade and it begins around St John's Day in mid-June. Then, on the night of the solstice, these hopeful pyres are lit. It's a spectacular display, turning the already beautiful Canigou into a sparkling diamanté giant overlooking the Mediterranean. I'll be honest, it's just about the most spiritual thing you can see. I get misty-eyed each time I think of it.

Well, mist was very much my problem now. It was creeping into my jaunt and getting denser. Soon I was in a full-blown, snowy storm-cloud and my visibility was down to about 5m (16ft). I couldn't go up any higher and descending was dangerous too. So I made my way carefully along a track that skirted the incline. Little did I know I was traversing the mountain. I did this for what seemed like hours.

And, yes, dammit, at some point, I began to cry. A kindly and concerned local man made a beeline towards the sound I was making. Turns out Oscar had just come up from Vernet-les-Bains on his Suzuki dirt bike to put his sheep back in the barn. He heard my whimpering and found me crawling down a rocky slope to the path that led to his field.

'Aidez moi,' I sobbed. And he did.

We jiggled back down and he dropped me at the campsite.

'But this is not my campsite! Where are we?'

'Vernet-les-Bains, monsieur.'

'But I need to be in Prades. I came up from Prades!'

He thought I was delirious. What ensued was a long and protracted negotiation; he wanted to take me to hospital.

I finally persuaded him that all I needed was a place to stay the night before making my way down to Prades in the morning. He dropped me at a hotel that he described as 'très sympa pour un Alpiniste'. And it was.

The hotel was perched on the westerly slopes of this spa town. It was old and tall, squeezed in among a terrace of candy-coloured shops and houses. It boasted just one star, which at that moment meant heaven.

I struggled through the unlocked half of a narrow, Art Nouveau double door into a beautifully tiled reception area where the owner sat behind the desk with the back of his balding head just visible over the counter. He was watching the news. They were reporting floods in the valleys.

'Oui!?' he said without turning around.

'Avez-vous une chambre pour ce soir, monsieur?'

Still watching TV, he pointed to a series of hooks, all with numbered keys hanging upon them.

'Certainment, monsieur. Combien?'

'C'est juste pour moi.'

He finally eased himself out of his seat and took a key before turning to catch sight of me for the first time.

'Mon dieu!' he exclaimed, taking half a step backwards. Then more sympathetically: 'Oh là là là là!'

He asked where I had come in from. 'From Prades, over the Pic,' I told him. I may well have played this one up a bit; I hadn't actually crested the Canigou, but I certainly must've looked like I'd completed the task.

He then called through to the small bar at the rear which overlooked the mountains beyond. 'This guy's just come over the Pic!!!' Two old boys turned with eyes squinting from the rising smoke of their cigarettes to give me some approving noises and gentle hand-on-knee applause.

The owner then turned back to the key hooks and selected a different room. One I had clearly earned.

'Come with me,' he said, 'You need a room with a bath.'

It was early evening and the storm was clearing. I disrobed to find my room had a spectacular view. Its double doors led to a small balcony, below which the mountain fell away steeply. My bed was blessed with no footboard, the curse of any tall chap. Its starched sheets and blankets looked just perfect.

To my dismay, however, I found no bath. Just a sink in the corner. I opened the door a little to locate the corridor communal facility but still no bathroom. *Oh, well,* I thought and ran hot water into the sink.

While this was going on there was a bit of a commotion from the stairwell. I didn't investigate but it sounded like heavy lifting. Lots of puffing and banging about.

Just as my steaming sink was full there was a knock at the door. 'C'est Bernard. Votre bain monsieur.' I hid my modesty with a towel and opened the door to find my friend standing behind half a barrel. He gave a beaming 'ta-dah' kind of look and rolled it in past me. He laid it to rest halfway through the open windows onto the balconette. Still smiling and saying nothing, he went into the corridor toilet and ran what looked like a fire hose back to the barrel. 'Cinq minutes!' announced Bernie Le Bain and left. I sat on the edge of the bed watching the steam rise out of the demi-cask. Sure enough, five minutes later he was back, carrying a small milking stool and some enormous towels. 'Call down when you are finished,' he said. And he was gone.

I sat with my nostrils hovering over the warm suds, smiling out to infinity and as relaxed as you could ever imagine. It was one of those rare times when you really don't want to nod off and dream because the reality is so lovely. So you hold yourself in near slumber with half-closed eyes giving you a soft focus, widescreen view of heaven.

About 40 minutes of blissful meditation passed before a gentle wrap on the door told me it was time up. The water was indeed cooling in the early evening chill.

As I let Bernie in, he clearly had a plan. 'Allez!' he called, I thought just to himself, but when he got to the barrel he took hold of it and looked back at me. 'Aide moi,' he demanded with a grin. Together we simply tipped the water out off the lip of the balcony. 'Like the monks used to do,' said my friend. The steam from our impromptu waterfall wafted back up past the balcony doors as he closed them. 'Will you eat with us tonight?' he enquired. 'Cassoulet.'

I didn't hesitate: 'Oui, merci beaucoup!'

My footsteps on the tiled floor announced my arrival into the dining room, empty save for Bernard, who was watching a terrible TV panel discussion about sod all, so beloved of French channels. Bernard lent over from a table set for two and simply switched the plug off at the wall.

'My wife has prepared a cassoulet for us. We don't serve dinner usually; we are just bed and breakfast except on Tuesday lunchtimes when we have, er . . . cassoulet.'

On the table was a tin bowl overflowing with chopped-up baguette and a huge, two-litre carafe of red wine. We were already hammering into both when Claudine backed out of the kitchen doors carrying a battered cauldron of magnificence. Bizarrely she was dressed for a night out, wearing hat, scarf and gloves. She kissed two fingers of her right hand and dabbed them on Bernard's head. Then she blew an air kiss at me and with a lyrical *Bon appétit* she was gone.

This was manna and the view was heavenly. We didn't say much.

We ate slowly as we pondered the storm that had driven me here. It had now passed over, but its underbelly hung over the horizon and was being illuminated in a spectacular display of purples and carmine red, the reflection of which put Bernie and me in a soft pink spotlight.

After a while we had entered the land of tipsy, and whatever emotional guards we had were now down.

He didn't look over at me when he said with a gulp: 'C'est magnifique, ça!' To which I could only whisper: 'Oui . . .'

There used to be a race known as the Vuelta a los Pirineos by Spanish Catalans and Tour des Pyrénées by their French brothers. It ran as part of the European Tour from 1995 to 2010. Daniel Fleeman, twice a British National Hill Climb Champion, won it in 2008.

These days you will see the Canigou as the Tour de France passes by in the valleys. Too tough to play with, I guess.

Meanwhile, just a handful of Ks away on the other side of the Canigou, the Volta a Catalunya plays its own game and occasionally crosses the modern border between France and Spain – a divide deemed entirely imaginary by any proud Catalan.

For me this race is a prize in the Calendar. I've called some beauties too. 2016 was a classic edition, with a start list that featured three Grand Tour champions: Froome vs Contador vs Quintana. Joining them, the recent Paris–Nice winner Geraint Thomas and the defending Catalunya champion Richie Porte of BMC.

A 25-year-old Nairo Quintana looked like the real deal for the season. Froome and Contador were busy marking each other out in a scenario I was more than familiar with: 'They're staring each other into the abyss here!' I commented at the time.

The fourth day was the Queen stage up to Port Ainé. Out front was a 10-rider superbreak including Philippe Gilbert, Thomas De Gendt, Laurens ten Dam, Ben Swift and Peter Weening. Late on Wout Poels, Nieve, Gesink and Miguel Ángel López and Dan Martin, attacked from the peloton. Tejay van Garderen got involved too as did Porte, Quintana and late on Contador. As you can tell from this roster of superstars, it was quite a day. Froome didn't have the legs to follow and Contador blew his chances by chasing everything that moved. But when Quintana attacked the gap to De Gendt up front, all the greats fell away in the Colombian's wake.

De Gendt won that dramatic day, but it was the young Quintana who blew away everyone who mattered for the title. And what names they were: the best on earth at the time. He secured a race lead that he never lost. Such was the confidence boost to Nairo that he went on to win Romandie and La Vuelta that year. He took his third Tour de France podium as well. Watching Quintana in 2016 was amazing. The high peaks of the Pyrenees had never looked so easy.

First run in 1911, the Tour of Catalunya is the oldest race in all of Spain. La Vuelta came 24 years later. Indeed Catalunya is the world's fourth oldest stage race, predated only by the Tour de France in 1903, the Tour of Belgium in 1908 and the Giro d'Italia in 1909.

The list of winners underscores its prestige, with names like Merckx, Anquetil, Gimondi, Thévenet, Moser, Kelly and Jalabert joining all the Spanish greats.

Catalans are quite a people, with their own language and culture dating back to an ancient principality from medieval times trapped between the three kingdoms of France, Aragon and Valencia and bordered by the Mediterranean to the East. It once included Roussillon in France and the island of Majorca as well.

Towering over all of Catalunya is the Canigou. It was long believed to be the highest peak in the entire Pyrenees, in part because of a freakish weather phenomenon involving light refraction in early February and at the end of October. During these times, if the weather is good, the Canigou can be seen at sunset from Marseille some 250km (160 miles) away across the Gulf of Lion. It's big.

If you want the challenge of riding it, you will need a mountain bike. It's not for the faint of heart. If you would like to retrace my steps, there is a trail from Prades at around 340m (1115ft) above sea level and climbs up towards the peak at 2690m (8825ft). So an altitude gain of 2350m – but in just 25km (16 miles). That's mad. It gives an average gradient of 9.2% – but the opening 9km (5.6 miles) are just 2%, which means you'll be hitting inclines to write home about (when your hands stop trembling). We are talking sections of, wait for it, 39.2%. And there is even one section called La Cheminée du Canigou, which is just 99m (325ft) long but is 50.3%. Meaning that every metre of elevation gain exceeds distance travelled on the map. In other words, you go up a metre before you have moved a metre as the crow flies. That's just weird.

Alternatively, you can take on some smaller tests for softies instead. You know, like Col d'Aspin, Col d'Aubisque, Col de Portet, Hautacam, Tourmalet . . . easier stuff.

I'm often asked what the difference is between the Alps and the Pyrenees. I always reply: 'In the Pyrenees you are never that far away from a sandwich.' I'm not being greedy; what I mean is that these more southerly mountains are tough but they are inhabited. Beautifully so. The Alps are magnificent, but rather bleak. In the borderland between France and Spain you have thriving towns and villages, each with a distinctive feel. At the western end of the range, you have the Basques. To the east, the Catalans. These are ancient proud cultures with warm welcomes and hearty cuisine built to bring joy to any who venture there. In particular, as a cyclist, you will be among friends. They are rightly proud of their history in our great sport. They like their mountaineers too.

I kept in touch with Bernard for a couple of years before his hotel closed, but I felt I never really got to thank Oscar properly for rescuing me. Each year when we go racing in the area, I think of them fondly. So that's two Catalans with a place in my heart. They just happened to be from the French side of the Pic du Canigou.

CARLTON COMMENTARY

'He's clean around the corners and tidying this race up.
I bet his middle name is Henry.'
Describing Gavin Hoover, American track star

APRIL

NINE

TOUR DE LANGKAWI
FAST AND FURIOUS

We hadn't noticed the helicopters tracking us. We were too busy concentrating on the road. We were travelling at the very limits of what our brown Daewoo saloon could manage. I have never, not even on the German autobahn, travelled so consistently fast. In traffic. Bloody hell.

Sitting in the front seat next to the driver was the sagely Brian Venner. A man not so much shaped by cycling as hewn by it. For years Brian, in partnership with Caroline Vickery has headed one of the world's finest TV sports production companies Vsquared. Brian had been everywhere and done most things around the world of cycling, so I thought this explained his apparent calm in the face of a situation that seemed like a near-death experience to me. As the cars, trucks, pandanus trees, wandering dogs, overhead bridges and visions of my happy childhood flashed by, Brian remained calm in his front seat.

'You alright back there, dear boy?'

I responded with a kind of squeak.

Brian put down the production notes he was thumbing through and turned around. 'You don't look too jolly. Driver, might we knock it down a notch or two? We have a worrier . . .'

The speed began to ebb naturally on the slope up to the crest of a motorway bridge. Up ahead, over the brow of our asphalt hill, there was a threatening red glow to the sky. It looked like Satan was a bit pissed off that he might have to wait a little longer for his guests.

Over the top, we were greeted by the biggest welcoming party you can imagine.

As is so often the case in countries like Malaysia, the cities are often the very definition of hyper-development. Kuala Lumpur, or simply 'KL' as Brian called it, is a case in point. Yet despite the rush to modernise, some things stay charmingly old fashioned. And so it was with the traffic management lights set up by the police: cooking oil tins with thick cotton wadding wicks, forming a burning diversion to the side of the road. But there were no cars in this fiery channel. Not yet.

At the front entrance to this pyro-tunnel stood guards holding emergency powder flares. Then the head demon emerged, out of the scarlet smoke that served to emphasise the seriousness of the situation. We knew he was important because he had a big torch.

Our friend, who turned out to be in the National Guard, shone a beam through the smoke right at us. The light then began to describe the path we were meant to take towards the armed guards 100m (328ft) up ahead at the barrier.

Brian is an experienced man. He's solid. The kind of person who has seen it all. He oozes calm. But sometimes the cheeky schoolboy that controls his soul escapes. 'Ooooh!' It was the sort of noise you might use in a playground to show you are entirely unfazed by a threat from an upstart bully.

It broke the tension immediately. Our driver now carried the smirk of a confident man. Threat levels were clearly being marked down to minimal – at least, by those in the front seats. Meanwhile, on the back seat, I was checking my trousers.

We drove down the cloudy tunnel of flame at walking pace with the officer in charge strolling alongside like a big game hunter proud of the giant cat he'd just bagged.

We came to a stop in a circle of regular flashing electric beacons.

The pre-fight staring match between our driver and the sergeant outside was ended by a loud knock from the officer's torch on the glass.

'Give it to him,' said Brian.

Without taking his eyes off his opponent the driver reached into the breast pocket inside his jacket. The officer drew his gun.

I don't speak Malay but even if I did it would've been a challenge to keep up. There was a lot of fast talking going on now, the verbals coming mainly from the policemen. I didn't need a translation.

Our driver was not armed. Slowly a letter was removed and proffered.

The document was opened and read. A few words were then exchanged in far quieter tones. Calm ensued. The officer then thumbed his radio and explained the situation to someone.

'What's happening, Brian?'

'Dear chap, we are part of a sporting event of global significance as far as the Ministry of the Interior is concerned. This race will go well. It always does. And we are the magicians that make it happen. So we have, not to put too fine a point on it, diplomatic immunity to help us avoid any trouble. You know, parking fines and so on. That said, we may well have stretched it a bit far this time . . . let's see.'

The officer had gone for a little circular walk in the smoke. When he got back to us, he simply handed the letter back and nodded. The lights were moved and we were on our way.

As we left, with the smell of powder flares still lingering, Brian wearily pointed out a police helicopter with rotors unwinding to a stop.

'Well . . . they've spent some money on us tonight, chaps.'

Langkawi is an island off the coast of Malaysia, close to the border with Thailand. It is exceptionally beautiful. A tropical paradise: waterfalls running into mirror-like pools, rainforest-covered mountains, beaches of sand as soft as milled flour, and tropical reefs easy to explore as they reach into the shallows of seawater so clear it is almost invisible.

For years this place was the destination for what was effectively the tour of Malaysia. Some big names added it to their list of favourite destinations. If a cold Northern European emerging from winter needs an event at the opposite end of the comfort spectrum, then Langkawi is that place.

The inaugural Tour de Langkawi was in 1996, the fruit of a sporting master plan of the former prime minister Mahathir Mohammad. It was instantly Asia's richest race, the prize money totalling over £100,000.

Starting on the beautiful island of Langkawi, it rapidly drew an international roster. Its format was also very much part of the appeal. Beautiful country roads with impressive highways and the high ground of the magnificent Genting Highlands. It was an instant hit with some of the world's best teams.

The event went through several incarnations over the years, running between 8 and 10 stages and latterly being run entirely on the mainland.

Sure, it's had bumps in the road as well. After about a decade of racing, a new sports minister decided the event should feature more riders from the region and suggested a quota on foreigners. Some teams didn't take kindly to the suggestion and looked elsewhere for their hot weather training during the European winter. About that time the Middle East offered an alternative that was almost jet lag-free. The start list suffered in Langkawi.

One sports minister sacked and a charm offensive later, we were back on track. The race was simply too good an event to ignore, even with its rivals making headway. Of the many gems Langkawi has to offer, its place in the calendar is the pearl. It comes a little later in the season than some of its rivals and thus offers a gift to those who wish to delay hitting peak form. This suits two types of riders: the elderly or, to put it more kindly, the highly experienced veteran, whose form window has begun to narrow with age and needs to be targeted specifically; and secondly, but most significantly, the new kids on the block who need nurturing a bit and for whom a full-on packed calendar is neither wanted nor wise. As a result, you get a phenomenal race where the old hands guide the new stars.

And wow, what new stars we have had at this amazing event!

2015 saw Aussie super sprinter Caleb Ewan get his pro career off the mark with wins in Malaysia for Orica–GreenEDGE. It was not the first time we found ourselves asking 'Who is this kid?'

In 2016 a certain Miguel Ángel López emerged to win the big climbing day for Astana – and, of course, went on to light up the mountains of Europe in a fantastic breakthrough season.

Then 2017 brought us a skinny waif with the power of a mountain lion in 19-year-old Egan Bernal. Another great find, unveiled by Androni owner Gianni Savio. The Sky chequebook has never opened faster. Two years later he was Tour de France champion. That year's future Grand Tour stage winners Ben O'Connor and Fausto Masnada and a teenage Sergio Higuita also raced.

The old boys had their triumphs too. Andrea Guardini, for example, amassed a total stage tally of 24 at the race from 2011 to 2018. Fair to say, he liked it.

This is a race of contrasts, one that bizarrely favours both pure sprinters and the best climbers. There is nothing in between; certainly, no time trial. They tried it once and didn't like it. Slim pickings for rouleurs too.

Sprint or climb – that's your lot. Mostly flat roads give way to a dirty great big climbing day in the middle of the race. Sprinters get to show off for much of the race, but the overall title goes to a climber.

And the racing is always a delight. So, if you want an entrée into the future of cycling and are pondering who will be the next star to show up, you'll probably find them here. In essence, a team manager who wants to try a few things without breaking their precious cargo, either new or antique, knows that the best place to do this is away from Paris–Nice or the Tirreno–Adriatico in a gentler environment without the pesky confidence knock of a time trial. Veterans and youngsters love it.

And we love watching them.

CYCLING LEXICON

Fred: Cycling newbie with hairy legs and baggy kit.
Poor bike handling skills.

TEN

TOUR OF FLANDERS
DRINKS ALL RONDE?

It's a grey, drizzly spring day and you are at a bus stop. You catch the eye of a soon-to-be fellow passenger and your opening gambit is: 'Oi-oi . . . de panne bink-bank wevelgem dvars doors vlaanderen de ronde, eh?' Then a hopeful thumbs up.

If the person you are talking to says: 'What the hell are you on about?', you are not in Belgium. If they lean in, put a hand upon your shoulder and say something along the lines of 'Devolder, he's back', then you are in Belgium. And you will both very much know what the hell you are taking about.

This is Flanders – and that means it's FESTIVAL TIME!

Burble, burble . . . burble . . . . . . BURBLE! Uproarious laughter. *Burble, burble . . . burble! . . . Oooooh Kay.*

I was standing outside the Wiggle Honda camper van parked at a corner of the central square in Oudenarde, home of the Ronde finish since 2012. I was gazing at the amazing athlete that is Rochelle Gilmore, who was standing on tiptoes, holding the van's door frame for support. She was the last of those able to attend this meeting with the Grand Vizier: Sean Kelly.

He was giving a pep talk.

The Team Bus was so packed that the sound was being deadened by all the bodies. All I could hear was a muffled burble with a feint Irish burr. Kelly was imparting the wisdom of a man who'd finished the Tour of Flanders as runner-up on three occasions and who remains irked that he never won it. What wisdom he was offering I cannot tell you, but it was clearly captivating. There was a final burst of applause, led by Rochelle and her thanks to the great man, who then wrestled his way out. As he emerged, he called back: 'Just be sure you win the bloody thing!'

'TOO RIGHT!' shouted Rochelle to her team.

'You OK, Sean?' I asked as he flattened his hair and straightened his clothes.

'It was hot as hell in there. Time for a quick meeting, I reckon!' This is Kelly code for a swift half; something always to be met with a grin.

Off we set towards a favoured bar in the corner of the square which looked to be packed. We got about a couple of metres along our beeline before: 'Hey Sean! Come and join us' and 'Quick selfie, Sean? It's for my mother who's sick at home' and 'Mr Kelly, remember me? I was the guy who handed the hamper to Phil Liggett in that handicap race back home. I was the one with the hat. You remember, Sean, the orange hat!?' And on it went. Mobbed he was.

In these situations, Sean is a paragon of politeness . . . he pushes on but keeps smiling and nodding. You'd expect this smile to set like stone into a near grimace, but it is genuine. You see, Sean Kelly is a happy cycling god in this heartland of the sport, with believers in his thrall. He could say anything – 'Excuse me, excuse me, I have a meeting to get to' – and the response from the faithful might be: 'Sean spoke to me . . . *Spoke . . . to ME!*'

Honestly, in this place, Kelly could tell someone to piss off and they would be overjoyed.

So we battled on through the throng heading to a bar that had a doorman of sorts keeping a handle on who was going in. It turned out he was the brother of the owner, who was serving beers at the taps.

I peered through the doorway over Sean's head. There wasn't a particularly strict entry policy because it was really full inside, perhaps just below the level where the windows might burst. But then I started to recognise more and more faces and suddenly understood the star quality of those favoured guests. It was astounding: a collection of kings.

The security guard was doing his job and so was the face of Kelly. A sound wave had announced his arrival and our doorman friend called over the inside throng towards the bar: 'Can you take two more?'

The owner looked over, saw Kelly and said: 'Just him!'

As he turned to say ta-ta, Sean saw my disappointment and sympathy prevailed. He shouted back to the owner: 'THERE ARE TWO OF US . . . TWO!' A moment of kindness never forgotten.

With a nod from the boss, we entered this amazing distillation of cycling giants. It was like a mega-club of my heroes. Everybody knew each other, and they were having one hell of a party. I couldn't believe it: Greg LeMond was sharing a gag with Jens Voigt. Three Planckaerts – Wally, Willy and Eddy! 'You wait your whole life for a Planckaert and then three come at once,' I said. Nobody laughed; not at my gag anyway. These gods were too busy having fun. Track legend Patrick Sercu turned around and handed Sean a beer.

'Where's Merckx?' asked Sean.

'Gone for a piss!' said Sercu. 'You've got his beer!'

Sean roared with laughter. As relaxed as I've ever seen him. Everybody in this place, save for this humble reporter, was a hero and there was no edge to any of the conversations. They were free to talk without a care. It was a privilege to witness.

If everyone was having fun, the bar owner's mirth was halted in an instant when someone called out something that was met with a huge cheer. Clearly, though, what was said did not go down very well with the owner. Not one little bit. He flipped three busy taps to vertical. Beer pouring halted, he stalked out.

'What's that all about, Sean?'

Sean, smirking, finished a gulp of the old amber and said: 'Some eejit wanted a round of drinks on the house. Your man's not happy at all.'

Then another shout went out: 'Has anyone seen Eddy's beer!?'

It was time to go to work.

The Tour of Flanders – or, more properly, Ronde van Vlaanderen, or simply De Ronde – was born in 1913. This was bad timing. They managed just one run before the First World War went and spoiled the idea. The fields of Flanders saw the most brutal fighting of the conflict. But like the famous poppies that continued to flower, the race was back on at the first opportunity. The first major event after the Armistice.

The race ran between the two Western Provinces of Flanders, from Ghent to Mariakerke on the outskirts. A looping course remains today, keeping the action close to the fans who famously hotfoot it over the often muddy fields to catch multiple views of the battle.

The first edition ran for 330km (205 miles) on heavy iron bikes clattering over poor country roads – pitted dirt, gravel, broken uneven cobbles. Apart from the obvious hazards, an extra worry for the organiser, Karel Van Wijnendaele, was the possibility of ducks, from the pond that was circled by the wooden velodrome where the race would finish. They were shot.

This was a humble start for what is now a massive jewel in the cycling crown. Ticket sales from the velodrome were disappointing, even with a bowl of duck casserole included in the price. The funds collected barely covered half the prize money.

These days, the winner of De Ronde can expect to cover the average race distance of 260km (162 miles) in around 6 hours. In 1913 the 25-year-old Paul Deman won from a 6-rider sprint after 12 hours aboard his heavy metal steed. The following year, he won the 1914 Bordeaux–Paris.

And then the war broke out, and Paul Deman was the natural choice for the Belgian resistance who needed a fast bike to smuggle documents over borders. He was, of course, captured by those cunning Germans, who chased him down on a motorcycle. The day the war ended, he was awaiting execution in Leuven. Naturally he became a national hero . . .

The race was restored in 1919, and had soon established itself as the most important race of the season in Flanders. Then cycling went international, and in 1948 the first season-long competition was announced: the Challenge Desgrange-Colombo. Until then Flanders had been run on the same day as Milan-Sanremo, but Flanders now had its own date and immediately drew a huge entry list of 265, including 50 cyclists who were not Belgian. From then on, there was no stopping its rise to prominence. It became a superstar playground. By the 1970s the race had achieved legendary status. Eddy Merckx took his second win wearing the World Champion's rainbow bands. The bitter rivalry between Freddy Maertens and Roger De Vlaeminck captured everyone's attention.

In the '80s Adrie van der Poel made it seven wins – the fifth of those in a four-up sprint that saw Kelly second . . . again.

Tom Boonen, Fabian Cancellara, Peter Sagan, Philippe Gilbert . . . on it goes. It's an amazing list, but one man for me stands out: Stijn Devolder.

In 2013 the word was out that Devolder was in stunning form. The 'old' man had won Flanders twice before, back in 2008 and 2009. Many were saying his best years were now behind him. But news scouts were reporting that he was ready to go for it again and had all the numbers to back him up. I certainly believed it was possible – and so did most of my well-informed Belgian contacts. He was 34 years old.

Some racing days can be heavenly. On those occasions troubles seem to belong to others. When that happens, it must look and feel like victory is your destiny. Everything goes smoothly and victory turns out to be a forgone conclusion. Well, on this day in Flanders, for Stijn Devolder just about everything went wrong.

If there was a crash to be had, Devolder was in it. There were punctures, he was taken off the road by an out-of-control rider, he crashed into those who fell in front of him . . . and every single time he picked himself up and battled tooth and nail to get back into the fray up front. It was as amazing to witness as it was heartbreaking. (I'd backed him at 80–1.)

This was surely the last chance for the great man to win once more – and it wasn't to be. His amazing form was confirmed a few weeks later when he lived up to my predictions and became Belgian Road Champion; a title ranked in that nation as highly as any World Championship.

Such heartbreak, yet a little poetry too perhaps. After we finished our commentary Sean was keen to get out and mingle. It was crowded at the podium area just beyond the finish, but I had another duty. Walking back down the course the latecomers were still pushing on home . . . and finally, there he was. Stijn, about to finish 58th.

I don't know if he recalls the welcome he got that day. If he had glanced to his right at about the '150 m to go' marker he would have seen me applauding . . . and cheering . . . and crying. Quite simply I was in awe of the man. (I had of course also just lost £800.)

CYCLING LEXICON

Chain Ring Tattoo: Marks left by an oily chain following a crash.

ELEVEN

SCHELDEPRIJS
SIZE ISN'T EVERYTHING

The waiter looked mildly irked and was clearly in a hurry to move on. To be fair, the early evening rush had begun for those who'd had too light a lunch while watching the big race. We felt lucky to have a seat.

My Belgian friend Eric van Hoorick had a question about the buttered veal he'd just ordered. You could see the waiter was in a hurry. He was already standing sideways-on to us and pointing at a customer nearby in a *Be with you in a minute* sort of way. He was on his marks, getting set, but couldn't go until Eric's question was sorted.

The result of this mild impatience meant that the waiter was offering all the right answers, but to entirely different questions, in a vain attempt to move on. I was mildly amused, to say the least.

'How –' was all Eric managed to air before the staccato reply: 'It is pan seared and then grilled.'

Eric tried again: 'No, I mean how –'

Our waiter was still pointing at the other customer who was himself pointing at the menu to mark his choice while waiting for our culinary fencing match to end. 'It is lightly coated in herbs and butter,' he said.

Eric was now smiling in an apologetic way, eyebrows raised up in the middle in a supplicant's appeal for mercy. 'No, I just want to know –'

'From the morning market, fresh,' explained the waiter in a *What now, FFS!?* kind of way.

The next hopeful customer watched on forlornly, his elbows now on the menu, arms in a triangle as he rested his chin upon his crossed hands. He bore the vacancy of a bored child idly watching kittens wrestle. His cheeks billowed slightly before his lips released the mild *pff* of surrender. He was hungry. So was Eric.

Eric decided to end his tussle by refusing to be interrupted again. He took a breath and fired it out: 'How big is it? What size is the *veal?*'

The waiter stiffened; stopped pointing at our more obedient rival; drum-jabbed his pencil twice on his notebook; and uttered with disdain: 'It is big enough!'

Eric was now laughing, which didn't help.

Our man grabbed our menus, slotted them under his arm and stalked off to the sound of our neighbour's forlorn 'S'il vous plaît, monsieur!' as he crashed through the kitchen doors.

'Glad I ordered the burger,' I offered.

When it came, Eric's veal looked exceptional and he tucked in. For the record, my burger was OK, nothing to write home about – unlike the great race we'd enjoyed earlier.

We were in Schoten, a small town just six miles from the centre of Antwerp, close to the Netherlands border and home to, wait for it, the oldest race in Flanders: the Scheldeprijs.

Since 1907 this remarkable contest has changed only modestly. History pours out of it in conversation with the locals. Be in no doubt it has a hugely important place in the racing calendar if – and only if – you are quick. The sprinting fraternity call it: 'The Decider!'

It is here the fast men of the peloton seek the answer to that age-old argument: *Who is the best in a 'proper sprinters' race?* Welcome to the Scheldeprijs.

You'll often hear the final day of the Tour de France described as the Sprinters' World Championship Final. But that's a little off-target for a number of reasons, primarily the fact that teams contesting Le Tour do not usually attend with a squad designed to support their quick men. If those fast-legged souls manage to survive the mountains and time trials en route to the finalé, then surely teammates' tired minds and legs will line up in support of their rocket man one last time before everyone goes home.

But on Le Tour many of the best sprinters will be either absent from the original start list or will simply not make it through the mountains to the Champs-Élysées. And if they do get to Stage 21 of the Grande Boucle, they'll be hobbled by the efforts of an unrivalled three-week endurance test.

Which is why it's at the Scheldeprijs that sprinters find their arena. As a result the fast-men's roster for this great jewel of a race is always stunning. Put simply: If you are quick, you are here.

So packed with sprinting elite is the start list that some teams arrive with two, three or even four real chances to win. It's remarkable.

The 2022 race was set to be a classic. Huge names back to their best and, after the lockdown years, a fascinating tussle between the young guns and the veterans. Couple that with terrible rainy weather and strong winds, and we were set for a spectacle.

Pre-race discussions centred on how those with longer careers behind them might effectively bounce back stronger after the guaranteed isolation caused by the pandemic. The logic was that old pros know how to train alone. They also have the discipline to follow a rigorous training schedule without supervision. Basically, they know the formula for success and will stick to it without a coach. No need of a mentor for the old dogs.

The younger puppies, however, have that magic ingredient of possessing little or no fear. They carry belief in their mental musettes. It may be misguided but it plays a major part in any bunch sprint scenario.

It was all coming together like a perfect storm . . . until it fell apart.

You see, as commentators, we base our assumptions about riders on tangible data and results. But it is impossible to account for strategy. And sometimes choices made by teams and riders out on the course count for so much more than power.

Mind over matter . . . if you don't mind, it doesn't matter.

Or rather, if you don't use your mind, it will matter. And so it was that the favourite team of all, Quick-Step Alpha Vinyl, with the resurgent Fabio Jakobsen, misfired spectacularly on a stage where they usually excel. Ahh crosswinds! Favourite status ended up in the bin as they went rolling backwards in the storm both metaphorical and literal.

The day – and the peloton – exploded. Strategies were shredded and in the end we had that rarest of things here: a solo victory. The winner was an old beast, Alexander Kristoff. In his long career he had never won a sprint race alone. I still don't know how he did it, and I called the race home. In the end it was all about being ready and willing to take that chance – and he did.

Over the last 60km (37 miles), he was so agressive. There were groups all over the course. Feathering his effort within the leading sextet while doing enough to maintain a gap on other favourites. And then, having just enough left in the tank to attack from a perfect distance . . . far enough out to dispirit the chase and close enough to the line to make it work. It needed brawn, brain, belief and brutality. The Viking had it all.

This solo victory turned out to be the exception that proved the rule at the Scheldeprijs. The 2022 finish was a rarity in an amazing race that usually ends as fast food for hungry sprinters. What we got was still a feast. And how big was it for the veteran winner? Kristoff's broad grin on the rostrum said it all. After a long spell of thin results, this, just like Eric's veal, was big enough to satisfy.

CARLTON COMMENTARY

'On paper, Dumoulin should win . . . but paper is highly flammable.'
At the 2015 Vuelta, which Aru won

TWELVE

AMSTEL GOLD RACE
DISCUS T'ING

'Balance. It's as important as flair and sustained power numbers . . . you see, when you're sprinting on the track, you'd better have it all . . . I remember back in the day, when blah won the blah de blah . . .'

I'll be honest with you, I'd switched off. The man standing in front of me was Frank Kramer, a man who knew virtually nothing about cycling. Now, I liked Frank, I liked him a lot. A former top-flight footballer and latterly an occasional commentator on Eurosport, he was fun to be around. But he was a man with an opinion on just about everything, and right now, those opinions were not lighting up my evening.

Besides, those opinions were being largely drowned out by the band in the far corner of our spectacular barge, which had been transformed into a floating party vessel and duly rented by the organisers of the Amstel Gold Race. Cycling was the theme, jazz was the music and booze was the order of the night. Amstel beer mainly.

As Frank jabbered on, I was looking right past his ear towards the lady who was apparently in charge of this swanky entertainment vessel. She was extremely striking and yet also strangely familiar.

That's Ria Stalman, I thought to myself. *I'm sure of it.* And it was. I pushed past Frank to say hello.

'What the hell are you doing here?' I asked.

'Welcome to my boat, Carlton!'

'Wow, Ria, you remember me! You look so —' I searched for the right word, '– different!'

Ria Stalman was a gold medal-winning discus superstar of the 1984 Los Angeles Olympic Games. When our paths crossed in the early '90s, she was still in competition shape: big and powerful.

'I'm a bit smaller these days,' she explained. 'I've trained down. And now I have a new life. Welcome aboard! Beer or champagne?'

To be honest, I'd always thought her a bit daunting; she had a *not to be messed with* air about her. I thought she could easily have worked the doors of any Amsterdam night club. But now? Well, here she was transformed. Or maybe I mean I was transformed. Now that I felt less threatened, I found her strikingly beautiful. (OK, go ahead, roll your eyes, raise your eyebrows. Whatever.)

Frank ambled up. 'Who's this, then?' he asked with a wink, through a blizzard of vol-au-vent crumbs.

'I see you found the buffet, Frank,' sighed Ria, brushing off bits of filo pastry from her blouse.

'It's Ria!' I exclaimed half-turning, 'I haven't seen her in ages.'

Frank knew full well who she was but kept the tease going. 'She's too small to be Ria Stalman. No way at all. Stalman is massive. A beast. An Amazon.'

Ria's eyes met Frank's. 'Would you like a coffee?' she asked eventually.

'Not until you show us who you really are. Come on, how can you be Ria Stalman? Prove it!'

Now I don't know if this is a regular thing between them or not, but what followed next just blew me away.

Ria picked up a full ashtray and emptied it into a bin. Wiped it and then checked it over. It was one of those large pub ashtrays you used to find in bars, designed to accommodate a full night of smoking. About as big as a dinner plate, printed with the Amstel Beer logo, it must have weighed a kilo or more.

With her back to the door, she bowed towards us and then, in a movement of sheer power and grace, span outside onto the steering deck and, in a turn and a half, released the ashtray.

It flew what must have been over 50m (165ft). It described a perfect arc before smashing in the middle of a small traffic island.

It's weird when you experience elite athleticism away from the normal theatres of sport. Other-worldly. I stood there with my mouth open, still looking into the air; replaying what I had just seen; trying to understand.

'OK, you are Ria Stalman,' laughed Frank.

Ria smiled as she pushed past us to attend to other guests.

'That was amazing!' I said.

'She sure is,' said Frank.

I think he might have been just a little bit in love with Ria. And at that moment I think I was too.

Yes, the unexpectedly spectacular is a wonderful thing . . . Welcome to the Amstel Gold Race.

Considering the amount of cycling success achieved by Dutch riders over the years, it's perhaps a little odd that they have so few major races in the country. *Well, it's a bit flat*, you say. And that's true, and you may think that any race in the Netherlands would be one solely for sprinters at the end of a boring day riding past windmills, tulips and polytunnels. Well, think again, my friend, because if ever there was an exception to the *flat land racing is boring* rule, then the Amstel Gold Race is just that.

There *are* climbs in Holland. OK, not many, but the ones they do have will be used again and again and again. Oh, and again.

If you look at the map of the Amstel Gold Race, it looks like a yard-long piece of spaghetti, overcooked and then dropped onto the only part of a map with a few hills on it. It's a tangled mess with so many crossovers you'd think the peloton might just catch its own tail. But who cares if spaghetti Bolognese is a disorderly dish? It can also be a meal to savour.

The Amstel Gold is that dish: tasty, if a bit messy. It's also very testy: 35 hills over a run of around 265km (165 miles).

It's best described as a festival of hills and crashes, skirmishes and all-out war; all played out on winding narrow roads and lumpy terrain. It's perfect for what the French call *puncheurs*, which is a fabulous bit of Franglais. And what a punch-up you always get. Metaphorically, I'm talking; not necessarily inside the Amstel Tent.

Ahhhh, the Amstel Tent!

How, asked the organisers, can we sell tickets to a cycling race that is free to anyone who wants to go and see it? Fans can just turn up at the roadside and watch their heroes whizz by, and pay nothing but their bus fare. Such a freebie gets even better on a multi-circuit race as the fans get to see them come past regularly. Even more fun can be had if you know a few back roads and can nip over to Loop 3, a kilometre away (barely more than half a mile).

Organisers decided that the answer to the eternal question *How to ticket cycling?* was to give the fans something to keep them glued to the spot. Beer. Oh, and stamppot. One session of this combination could see a grizzly bear safely through hibernation.

Stamppot is the Dutch equivalent of Britain's bubble and squeak. It was originally the leftovers of a larger meal combined to avoid waste. It has now become a dish in its own right. Basically, it's all the bits of veg uneaten from the Sunday roast mixed with mashed potatoes, mustard and a little vegetable stock. To enhance the large blob on your paper plate, simply stick in a sausage or two and maybe a dollop of sauerkraut to the side, and you are good to go . . . to sleep. It's like central heating for your tummy.

So they chucked in a circuit or five past the Amstel Tent. *A fiver to get in and all you can drink* is not an offer many Dutchmen, or thirsty Englishmen for that matter, can easily turn down. We've occasionally lost a cameraman to such temptation. 'Where's Steve, anyone?'

We'd sent him off to film some colour in the Happy Tent, and he wasn't seen again until after the live transmission. We found him in the production truck, 'recharging his batteries' behind the graphics machine. The snores gave him away.

The Amstel Gold Race is wonderful.

Now, the Netherlands may have been a little late to the party in cycling terms. The first Dutch winner of the Tour de France was Jan Janssen in 1968. Their neighbour, Belgium, first achieved that feat in 1912. Belgium, of course, has many races, notably in the Ardennes area. Seems like hundreds of them, with quite a few of high renown (as you well know).

Clearly somebody thought that this was an imbalance which needed to be levelled out a bit. Not just in sporting terms, but because right here was an opportunity to sell beer.

Usually when you think of the late '60s in the Netherlands, many hemp-based images spring to mind. Thank heavens, then, that just before the nation lost itself in a bohemian cloud, somebody got their shit together and organised the Amstel Gold Race.

So it was that just one year before the Summer of Love, Holland had a race to reckon with. Though not without a bumpy start. The first edition was almost cancelled due to arguments about road closures – and more. The Dutch do love an argument, so there was quite a bit of negativity out there, lots of 'What's the point?' from the moody elderly; 'It's a Belgian game' from the sporting press; and 'Hey man, I'd rather just chill' from the early hippies.

No surprise that the early winners were Belgians, among them Eddy Merckx, who won twice. But then came along Jan Raas, who cheered the home crowd. His five wins made this a source of national pride and finally in 1989 the race became part of the then World Cup calendar. It has never looked back.

So here it is, now established as the first of the three Ardennes Classics. Narrow testy roads leading to steep hills with famous climbs such as the Cauberg, Kruisberg, Eyserbosweg and Keutenberg. A race with over 4000m (13,100ft) of altitude gain. In Holland!

'How can this be?' you ask.

Well, take a trip to the Amstel Gold Race and find out. The racing is frantic. Positioning is everything and the approaches to the climbs crowded and nervous. Teams want to be first onto those hills and leading on the descents. Every team's race director will be screaming in the riders' radio earpieces: *'Get to the front!'* – but they can't all fit. Crashes are common. It's great viewing, and the beer's not bad either.

It's well worth the trip.

CARLTON COMMENTARY

'He flies up hills in much the same way that breeze blocks don't.'
Peter Sagan climbing well

THIRTEEN

PARIS–ROUBAIX
OH SUGAR!!

'Aaah!! Carlton!! DO NOT . . . MOVE . . . A MUSCLE!!!!'

And I didn't.

It was clear from the tone of the man high above me that I was in trouble. And I certainly was.

Working at La Biscuiterie Rouger in northern France was not fun at the best of times but, to be honest, it was boring rather than dangerous. Until now.

I still had no idea just how much peril I was in, but the clearly serious situation was soon to be carefully and precisely explained to me by Alphonse, the foreman, whose silhouette I could make out through the clouds of sugar dust at the hatch of the hopper.

'What the hell are you doing with that shovel?'

'Moving sugar . . . like you told me.'

An hour earlier I had no idea how short a straw I'd just drawn. Asked if I'd like a break from the baking heat of the waffle ovens, I gratefully accepted a job that I soon realised nobody else wanted to do. I should have spotted the mirth of the oven ladies as I left. They knew.

I was to climb the outside ladder of a huge, 30m (98ft) sugar hopper, open one of the four hatches on the domed roof and descend down an inside ladder to the bottom of this enormous metal tube that had been cooking in the summer heat for hours. It was punishing in there: hotter even than my job removing stuck waffles from the cast-iron jaws of the biscuit factory oven plates.

At the foot of the hopper was a bank of perhaps a ton of sugar that could not be drawn off because the huge screw at the foot of my metal prison had snapped in half.

My job was to shovel the sugar mound sitting on the dead half of the screw onto the functioning half that was still attached to the motor. So far, so good. Less good, to my mind, was the battered brass shovel I had been given to complete the task: the handle was broken.

Sweat poured off me as I toiled and my right hand began to blister. Added to my discomfort was the sugar dust kicked up by my digging. It stuck to my sweating face and hands, turning me into a syrup-coated version of myself. I was getting heavier too as my damp clothes soaked up the sugar cloud. It was sweet hell. I've never been more uncomfortable.

Finally the blister popped and blood spilled onto the white stuff. *I've had just about enough of this shit.* I climbed back up the inside of the hopper, emerging into the cooler air high above ground. Immediately my clothes got stiffer as the sugar started to set.

Once I reached ground level, the hunt began for a better spade. I found a nice shiny steel one near the stores and grumpily returned to my task, asking myself: *Why the hell didn't he give me a decent spade in the first place? Prick.*

After about another 20 minutes, Alphonse the foreman was screaming his warnings.

'LISTEN TO ME *VEEEEEERY* CAREFULLY OR WE WILL BOTH DIE . . . DO YOU UNDERSTAND?'

I stood there like an alabaster statue.

'OK . . . These things up here are not just doors; they are blast vents. If your nice shiny spade causes a spark, it will ignite the sugar dust and we will go off like a bomb. That's why I gave you the brass shovel. It does not spark. Do you understand?'

'Yes,' I said, frozen, knee deep in sugar.

'Good. Now I am going to open all these vents to try and air the cylinder and then you are going to climb *veeeeeery* carefully up the ladder while making sure that spade does not touch anything. Am I clear?'

'Yes . . . sorry . . . I didn't know . . . blisters, you see.'

'Shut up and just do what I've told you or we'll both be in hell before you know it.'

After what seemed an age, the view above me cleared and I was finally allowed to take on the short climb towards safety. I have never taken so long to make an ascent. Step by step with more than mild peril at hand.

When I reached Alphonse, he took the shovel and dropped it to the ground below. He was whimpering with relief and anger.

'You have never heard of silo explosions, have you? he said.

'No.'

He put a fatherly hand on my shoulder and softly murmured: 'I should have been more clear. Just use the brass shovel next time.' He could see I was in a bit of shock and thought he should keep an eye on me. 'Why don't you join me for some lunch?'

———

As was the custom in France, school children and factory workers had a generous lunch break, enabling them to return home to share a midday meal as a family. The working day starts earlier and ends later to accommodate this.

I found myself waiting at a table for my friend's son to return and marvelled at what seemed to be a cycling shrine with photos and newspaper cuttings and various race souvenirs. But one picture fascinated me. It was the cover of *L'Equipe* from years ago. It featured two riders, but one had a huge red cross drawn in thick pen over him. Mesmerised, I asked about it.

What followed was a potted history of Alphonse's favourite race, Paris–Roubaix, and his deep indignation at the scandal surrounding the only declared joint winners of the Hell of The North.

Northern France had suffered more than most regions during the Second World War. Back in 1949 the conflict was something to try and forget about, but international rivalries remained strong; occasionally toxic.

French rider André Mahé was robbed of a clear victory into the famous velodrome after a race steward misdirected the leading three riders in the break. Heading away from the entrance to this cycling shrine, one of the three, Jacques Moujica, punctured on the terrible back roads they found themselves on. But the margin remained significant enough to the chasers that Mahé and Frans Leenen still had a chance of victory. They doubled back and entered the velodrome on the opposite side of the track. Mahé beat Leenen to take the win. The pair duly did the lap of honour as Moujica crossed the line 3rd. There was then even enough time to accept bouquets and head into the famous showers before the chasing peloton arrived to apparently decide the minor places.

The reduced bunch duly entered the velodrome and Serse Coppi, brother of the hugely successful cycling god Fausto, crossed the line in 4th place. But the race was far from over.

All seemed well until word of the misdirection of the three podium winners began to circulate. Fausto Coppi sensed a chance to help his brother and appealed the result on the grounds that the correct route had not been followed by the declared top three riders. All hell broke loose.

The Federations got involved. The Belgian Federation backed the Italian Federation's protest and the judges then changed their minds. Coppi was declared the winner. France went mad.

The French Federation protested to the UCI, who told everyone to calm down. Four months later the result was declared void with no winner. All three federations went mad.

There was an explosion in the French, Italian and Belgian press. Thus it became Item One on the agenda of the UCI's post-season conference that November. Nobody was happy. After much debate and not a little beer and wine, a compromise emerged from the smoke-filled dining room. For the first and only time in its history Paris–Roubaix had joint winners: André Mahé and Serse Coppi.

It was the biggest win in the career of Serse. Mahé was gutted and maintained, right until his death in 2010 at the age of 90, that it was to Fausto's shame that he had used his superstar status to make sure his far less successful brother added something major to his sparse palmarès.

———

Ever since my lovely lunch with Alphonse, I have followed the results and reports of the Paris–Roubaix closely. And when I eventually had the great fortune to work on the amazing race it was with huge pleasure and excitement that I found myself on the road to the Roubaix velodrome in the good company of the great Sean Kelly, who won the Hell of the North on two occasions in 1984 and '86. My enthusiasm was not, however, matched by The King. On my debut he looked as grumpy as could be.

'You OK, Sean? Looking forward to revisiting the old velodrome?'

'I most certainly am not,' he declared. 'It's bloody freezing. The only thing certain to come out of that cursed place is piles! Sitting on them bloody concrete press benches.'

I wasn't sure if he was joking at first, but his mood was set and carried onto the air in commentary. As we approached the first cobbled sector, I asked him how punishing the surface was to race upon. He took a moment, his eyes narrowed and then he said the most considered sentence I have ever heard him utter: 'I'll tell you one thing: me prostate took one hell of a beating on that stuff.'

I was dumbstruck. A few empty dead-air seconds ticked by before Sean filled the silence.

'I was pissin' blood after.'

Desperate to smooth things out for the viewers, I chipped in with forced good cheer:

'Sooo . . . more than a bit rough on the old undercarriage is what you are saying.'

'Certainly was,' he replied blankly. We got away with it.

Paris–Roubaix is a monster of an event. I've mentioned many times over the years that it's hard to love the finish town itself but easy to get enchanted by the race. It is truly remarkable.

If you are going to attend, do your homework and don't get sucked into a managed event unless you are sure about the organisers. There are some great ones out there. But some bad ones too and they seem to focus on the bigger events like Paris–Roubaix. As Sean says: 'There are a lot of people in this world who can help you open your wallet.' So take care.

There are no sectors more popular than Arenberg or Carrefour de L'Arbre, but you will have to get there early. Very early. So if you have a choice, it's worth taking time to find out about a few other 'little gem' sectors out there – and the link roads that will help you jump between them.

I know you all have gps on your phones these days, but a good old paper map is worth buying because the most detailed of these carry the farm tracks and unpaved byways that you will need. Such lanes often don't make it onto your electronic maps. The Blue IGN map, Code 2504E is the one you want. Each centimetre square covers just 250m. You will find all the short cuts you need. Job done.

Why not start at the beginning? Troisvilles is the opening challenge and given No. 27 in the hit parade countdown. No gentle introductions here. If riders get it just a little wrong on entry, they face disaster. A much bigger road brings you to its entry point which is gently sloped downwards. This makes for a great deal of speed generated, adding to an already high pace which was set in the panic to get onto the cobbles up front to avoid getting caught out by any crashes ahead. It stretches over 2.2km (1.6 miles) and pitches up into a climb towards the end. Go there and be scared.

If you want something a little more explosive, then Beuvry-la-Forêt to Orchies is worth a punt. The cobbles are set in loose gravel and mud, so if it's raining things get a little unstable under the wheels. A distance just shy of 1.5km (0.9 mile) means it gets a 3-star rating. Just 100m (328ft) more and it would be a 4-star. So it's worth a look.

And finally Champhin-en-Pévèle. While the crowds are up the road waiting at Carrefour de L'Arbre, be clever and go here instead. This is one of those sectors with huge cobbles. All cut by those sentenced to hard labour in centuries past. Their work is our playground. The big blocks give way to smaller cobbles during a bend, so making the surface variable. Nobody likes to ride this variation. It changes back to big blocks again towards the end. The block changes also affect the crown on the road – sometimes high, sometimes flatter. There are puddles too on wet days just to keep you fascinated for the 1.8km (1.1 miles) of its length. This is sector 5 on the countdown. It's a 4-star test too!

Everyone knows the roads to Roubaix are fraught with danger. It is a magnificently tortuous route that thrills and entertains the viewer and is both dreaded and respected by all who contest it. It's a race where there is so much to consider and the smallest mistake by yourself or a rider or a spectator – or, as we know, even a race official – can lead to disaster. So take great care.

As my friend Alphonse said to me all those years ago: 'In Roubaix, like in life: get a little thing wrong, and it can blow up into something very serious. Now get back into that hopper with your shitty brass spade and we will say no more about it.'

CYCLING LEXICON

DFL: Dead Fucking Last. Different from DNS (Did Not Start) or DNF (Did Not Finish).

FOURTEEN

RED HOOK CITY CRIT
'GO HOOKERS!!'

I was in town for the Corner House Grand Prix Presented by Van Dessel Cycles Princeton, NJ. (Americans do make the most of their event titles.)

'I'm here for the CHGPPBVDCPNJ,' I said, by way of amusing myself, when engaged by an over-cheery ice-cream seller's *Hi, how are you!*

You could tell by the fixed smile and dead eyes he didn't get me.

'The race,' I offered.

'Oh wow! Awesome! You have a great day.' With that he moved on. Later I saw him chatting to another vendor and gesturing my way. I was having fun.

As you'd expect from a university town, Princeton has a lively cycling scene with criteriums running throughout the year. It's busy. Down the road from Princeton the Rockleigh Crit is a perfect example of how local club enthusiasts can produce something extraordinary. They recently celebrated their 25th anniversary. Indeed, you might think New Jersey to be a unique hotbed of the sport, but it's the same all over the United States.

American racing does not have Tour de France kind of recognition, and its major races have had a habit of getting into financial trouble – but rest assured, this nation does cycling very well indeed. The cycling market in the States is said to have been worth around $9.5 billion in 2021. OK, that is not too much bigger than the United Kingdom's at £6.4 billion ($7.9 billion), but the UK market might be saturating while the US market is widely predicted to grow at $9 billion per year for some time to come. It's on the up, just like the crop of young riders making waves on the World Tour, topped off currently by the fabulous 'Durango Fandango' Sepp Kuss who dances up mountains for Jumbo–Visma and UAE Team Emirates' 'Phoenix Firebrand' Brandon McNulty. Yes, I made those nicknames up – and I'm sticking with them. America has a wave of talent coming through and it's down to a hugely active racing scene that just happens to be a bit different to Europe.

The CHGPPBVDCPNJ was a fantastic day of racing in Princeton, one of several events throughout the year that seem to upset nobody at all. By that, I mean road closures are completely accepted without grumbles and a carnival atmosphere descends onto the course, making everyone feel welcome. It's a scene replicated throughout the nation perhaps a thousand times a year across all disciplines of our wonderful sport.

You can choose to contest or spectate at Downhill, Dual Slalom, Four-Cross, Super D, Enduro, Cross-Country (XC), Short Track XC, Ultra-Endurance, BMX, Stunt riding – and we haven't mentioned City Crits or straight up Time Trials and Road Racing. Perhaps therein lies the problem. There is so much choice the scene perhaps self-dilutes. Are potential stars distracted or spread too thinly? I don't know. What I do know is the scene is amazingly diverse and, most importantly, fun.

Naturally, competition extends well beyond the course boundary. Every criterium is seemingly determined to outdo any other you might think of attending and sometimes this enthusiasm for the unique can spill over into . . . maybe a bit of madness?

Enter the amazing Red Hook Crit series. How about a tight city circuit with plenty of crazy turns and a stacked field of high achievers? Then make them compete on fixie bikes . . . with no brakes.

It's a *come and have a go if you think you're hard enough* kind of vibe but without deliberate violence. Though violence there can be. It's hugely entertaining.

Crashes? Guaranteed.

Full on dramatic racing? Hell, yeah!

Isn't this just a bit crazy?

'Quite possibly, but everyone seems to love it.' That's organiser and founder of Red Hook David Trimble being interviewed.

Are you going for world domination with this format?

'Already done that!'

. . . and he has.

Casey Lloyd won the inaugural Red Hook 2008! A woman beating the guys brilliantly. Over the next eight years it grew and grew with star names from the pro ranks giving top amateurs a chance to measure themselves against the best. By 2014 it had turned into a magnificent world series with men's and women's races in Milan, Barcelona and, of course, Brooklyn New York.

America sending a race series over to Europe! Who'd have thought? Well, remember it's over a century since America finessed endurance racing in Madison Square Garden and sent it back over the water as Madison Racing. The event has now vaulted from the Six Day Scene into the Olympics and World Championships . . .

Forty-five countries took part in the 2015 Red Hook opening round in Brooklyn with races two and three following in Barcelona and London and then the season finalé in Milan.

The Brooklyn course is on the dockside area where the cruise ships usually hook up. Hence the name. It is designed for both mayhem and entertainment with 10 turns crammed into a lap of just 1.3km (0.8 miles).

The race length is also tight at just 26 laps or 30km (18.6 miles). Couple all this with the carnival atmosphere, the foodie outlets, music systems and beer tents all moshing together beautifully with the action, and you have what can only be described as 'one hell of a cycling party'.

At each round 250 riders attempt to qualify. The best 85 make the main race and the rest then run an 18-lap Last Chance Race, with the first 10 getting to ride on. That's a total of 95 fixed gear bikes making the main event. All fast. All determined. They can't possibly all stay upright. And they don't. Lapped riders are out. It is quite simply a magnificent battle of attrition. Just wow!

If you have never been to one, and you have the choice, head over to the original in Brooklyn. You will not be disappointed.

Red Hook Racing is the biggest global race series in the world for fixed gear criterium racing. Perhaps an Olympic event of the future? I'm certainly up for it. Thank you, America. I'm hooked.

CARLTON COMMENTARY

'Dan Martin looks like he's suffering . . . but he always does; even when he comes down for breakfast.'

FIFTEEN

LIÈGE–BASTOGNE–LIÈGE
KABOOM!!

Coffee morning on Crimicar Lane, Sheffield in the late 1960s followed the classic pattern for the time.

At 11 o'clock on a Thursday, five housewife friends could be found around a dining room table at No. 164 with a plate of biscuits arranged in a perfect flower shape set upon a plain white cloth. Instant coffee with milk was the drink; no messing around.

Today, if you want such a drink, you'll have to ask someone with designer everything, including attitude, for a Black Americano, extra hot with a dash of milk, full fat, cold, not steamed. All in their smallest cup which will be called something stupid like 'tall' or 'demi-grande'.

Back in 1968, all this was called: a cup of coffee.

The only thing to decide upon was how many sugars. 'Two and a half please,' said Mary. She was odd.

'Please help yourself to a biscuit, ladies . . . how are your other halves?'

Aaaand they were off. Gentle as you like; each taking their turn to lead as the others sipped and listened. All was well on that late April day until . . . the bombshell.

In bounced the hostess's five-year-old daughter, off school after a tonsillectomy. She marched straight up to the oldest guest, Ruth, and stared at her intently.

'What are you doing, Deborah?' asked her mum.

'She's only got one face, Mummy. You said she had two!'

In any collective endeavour, there has to be an accord because without it nothing gets done. It will come to an end, nothing lasts forever. But who will destroy it? Who is the Deborah in the breakaway pack? Well, if Kelly was involved, it'd likely be him asking the questions. An old school, no nonsense hard man, happy to be awkward. And when his legs were good, very few had to answer to him.

'At Liège my first race was against my teammates. All of us wanted to be in the breakaway. If you made it up the road, then your teammates would have to back off into the pack and wait their turn if we got caught.'

To be fair Sean was usually in the right place at the wrong time for his opponents. There are clips out there where the name Kelly from a finish line announcer produces an audible sigh from fans of opponents as it becomes clear that their heroes will have a huge fight on their hands with Sean for company.

The great man won many races, many of them in tortuous conditions. But one of his favourites he describes as 'a beautiful race'. Quite the compliment for The Old Lady, La Grande Dame or La Doyenne as it is variously known.

Liège–Bastogne–Liège is the oldest of all the five Monuments and has two phases: the opening half of the classic is flatter, mainly highway, run south from Liège to Bastogne – and then back again. The return leg is different, on more uneven meandering country roads with some climbs, which arrive back at the departure city after more than 250km (155 miles) of hard racing.

Back in 1892 there were no motorcars to speak of. Daimler and Maybach, later to become Mercedes, sold their first car that year. But there were bicycles. And they were the preserve of the very rich. At the time even a decent penknife was a luxury purchase for the average person. So to see a bunch of blokes with waxed moustaches and straw boaters pedalling along the broken roads of Belgium must have been quite a rare and wondrous sight. This was a long time ago – the country of Belgium in its current form had only been established 60 years earlier.

The chaps and their trusty machines with solid rubber tyres can't have realised they were pioneers, but the Cycling Club of Liège were a determined crew and decided they would have a weekend race from Spa in the Ardennes down to the Luxembourg border. The Belgian press got involved and everyone was getting a bit excited. Nothing like this had happened before. It was to be the birth of the first classic Monument.

On the planning recce the organisers stopped shy of their target and had some lunch in Bastogne. As the beers flowed – and there are plenty of those in these parts – somebody realised time was getting on and declared: 'Sod it, let's go home.' Or something like that. And the route was made. Well, almost. It is not, after all, called Spa–Bastogne–Spa.

The first race gathered so much press attention that the mayor of Liège wanted to know why the race was not run from the home of the Liegeoise club that had organised it. Nobody could think of a suitable reason why not, so the Liège–Bastogne–Liège was formed.

So could we now assume that the route was now set in stone? Absolutely not.

Belgium is a nation of just over 11 million people . . . and 30 million opinions. Nobody can decide anything without having a damn good argument about it. Usually over a few beers. Did I mention the beers? As a result the race has had quite a few amendments over the years with the main bone of contention being the positioning of the Côte de la Redoute. Purists believe, quite rightly in my opinion, that it should always be the final test before the run for home. This has not always been the case: the organisers have tried to make the race appeal variously to the classics men whose spring season is just drawing to a close, and the Grand Tour stars whose season is just about to wake up.

So yes, the face of the race has changed many times over the years. Yet the combination of climbs and distance is not lost on the very best cyclists on the planet. It is where Classic Superstars do battle with GT gods for our entertainment.

If you are going to go, why not head for the turning point of the race in Bastogne itself? There you can try one of the four dishes of the day at what sounds like the only dining eatery in town: Le Restaurant. There is more than one. It is known locally as L'Ancienne Gare, the Old Station. If it's available I can recommend the Onglet de boeuf flambé au whisky + frites. It really is a cow's tongue – but don't think about it too much, and you will be delighted. As it was the only restaurant in town, it must surely have hosted the organisers of this amazing race back in the day . . . you know, before cars, aircraft, social media, two world wars, political correctness, cheese string, bullshit. Thankfully beer has been around since 5000 BC. So do as they did: Take some time to kick back and have a ponder. Then make your way back home. You can do Luxembourg another day.

'I always felt at home at this race. Always enjoyed the day. Not like the shitty racing in Flanders and Roubaix where you can tangle with some idiot getting it wrong in front of ya.'

It's not PR speak. But Sean is dead right. And if you don't fancy the Mud and Guts racing of the cobbled classics, go for something different. But don't you go thinking it must be a gentler affair . . . it is most certainly not. This area has always been a battleground. The many tank memorials along the route attest to that. And whenever Kelly got involved we just had to wait for the bomb to go off. Sean Kelly won The Old Lady twice, both from a breakaway.

1989 was one of those days when the A-Teams would arrive with several options. The PDM team had a strong lineup. As such, it was hard to know who to plan for. A free pass to have a go was on the breakfast table. Everyone murmured about their chances as the cheese and jam baguettes went down. Some declared they didn't fancy it; others said they had good legs. Sean Kelly kept quiet. *Say nothing, do plenty* was his way.

The overcast but dry day saw Pedro Delgado of Toshiba, Reynolds-Banesto's star Fabrice Philipot and Kelly go clear on one of the early climbs of the return leg. On the race-defining Côte de la Redoute, there were four upfront after Australian Phil Anderson of TVM bridged over. It was a narrow gap at high pace with a fracturing peloton who would regroup on a mild long descent. The bunch was a significant star-studded chase of around 30 and included Stephen Roche, Robert Millar, Tony Rominger, Laurent Fignon and Miguel Induráin.

Into town came the four front runners with only a 16-second lead and 5km (3.1 miles) remaining. Still exchanging nicely until just before a left turn with 200m (656ft) to go. TVM's Phil Anderson decided he had to go long. Having been beaten by Kelly at this race in 1984, the Australian wanted to shake him off. The pack were almost upon the four when Sean countered, caught Anderson and pushed on for victory . . . His familiar double-air-punch celebration was seen from behind by 33 riders.

It wasn't the last Irish victory in the great race. The Old Lady smiled upon Dan Martin when he won spectacularly in 2013, but he was to find out just how fickle she could be the following year.

Martin's Garmin–Sharp team had done an amazing job for him throughout the day – raining attacks on the peloton and protecting him in the climbs. Then it was down to him to pay them back . . . And it looked a certain victory. But coming into the final corner the most bizarre incident occurred: Dan rolled over a pen dropped by a member of the public. At any other point on the course this would have meant nothing, but all the angles were right – or wrong – at the fateful moment. He lent into the last bend before the line just clear of Simon Gerrans, Alejandro Valverde and Michal Kwiatkowski. Then hit the pen. It rolled under his front wheel which slipped from under him. He got Bic'd!

Despite all the climbs, so intense was the racing that day and so compact the field, Dan ended up 1 minute 37 seconds down . . . in 39th place. At the time, there was talk of him grounding a pedal? He did not. Perhaps there was oil on the road? Nobody else suffered; the road was clean. A fan's picture later showed the white pen responsible. A bizarre moment. Nasty. Dan said he was crying before he hit the ground.

Professional racing can bring to the fore a raft of emotions. Anger and disappointment are there for all to experience even within the most successful careers. The best riders can use such setbacks to push them on. Dan Martin may have felt the spite of La Doyenne that day, but he went on to win Il Lombardia at the season's end.

Back in 1989, Sean Kelly was not messing around in the break.

'By then in my career I'd already won a lot. But you always want more. I'd also had too many bloody podiums the previous season for my liking. Second and third place is no good to anybody. I was a little bit upset about that. So I used my anger that day.'

Sean Kelly has a wonderfully understated way of talking about the aggressive determination that is a vital ingredient of a succesful racing career. It sure was difficult to get around Sean when he was 'a little bit angry'.

No nonsense. No messing around. Honest . . . When he was racing, Sean Kelly had just the one face. Hard.

CARLTON COMMENTARY

'Arriving like a Zeppelin in the night.'
The threat of John Degenkolb moving smoothly to the front of a sprint

MAY

SIXTEEN

TOUR DE ROMANDIE
ROBOT WARS

'Et voilà, monsieur, l'addition!' The waiter delivered this on a fly-by to another table at the burger bar on the shore of Lake Geneva, or Lac Léman or Lake Leman (German, Genfersee) . . . Oh FFS: the large body of water with a single spout fountain they are all very proud of in these parts.

I wasn't in a great mood. And I was about to get grumpier. The bill took a bit of rudimentary maths for me to translate into pounds sterling. This being 1987 the figure I came up with was. . . a bit of a shock. I had just finished a burger. Not at a fancy hotel. In a burger bar. And it came to £22. Back then in the UK you could go to a Stranglers concert and still have change for a pint and two burgers. I'd done that the previous Thursday and they were great. The Stranglers, not the burgers.

I was a bit dazed. And I didn't mean to get audible, but the Yorkshire Battle Cry just burst out of me: 'HOW much!!!????'

Welcome to Switzerland. Or more specifically Romandy, or Romandie (French), Welschland (German), or even more bizarrely Romanda (Romansh). Take your pick, it's the same place. Yet despite all their differences, in all these languages the numbers mean the same thing: expensive.

After the Second World War, Europe and much of the world had beaten itself up quite a bit. It had not been cheap knocking seven bells out of each other, and most Western economies were broken. Neither winners nor losers had very much budget left over to be spent on running large sporting events.

Of course, Switzerland was in far better financial shape having been neutral during the war. All sides needed somewhere to keep their cash safe during the conflict, so the Swiss held everybody's coats and wallets for them as the big scrap kicked off.

When it was all over, Confoederatio Helvetica (that explains the CH on Swiss number plates) was one of the few places to emerge from the conflict rather well. So in May 1947, as if to throw a party for the poor kids in the neighbourhood, the world was invited to a new stage race: the first Tour de Romandie. The world duly said a whimpering 'thank you' as everyone tried to move on.

There was German spoken at the start line. Swiss-German speakers, or as my German colleagues call them, German 'squeakers'. The French are equally amused by the tone of the Swiss version of their mother tongue. Likewise Italian-Swiss sounds rather different. I guess the closest way of describing it would be Geordie or Liverpudlian accents in English. As my wider family are from Liverpool and my wife's originally from Newcastle, we like to call it lyrical, warm; jaunty even. Others may tease – at best.

Anyway, it seems Switzerland has often been the butt of jokes from those next door. The Swiss rise above it. Anyway, Romandie was just a nice way of showing the world that conflict is probably best invoked in a sporting context. So Switzerland, or rather the Romandie region, effectively gave everyone their coats back and said: 'Right then, let's all shake hands, shall we, and get on with the rest of our lives . . . there we are . . . that's better, isn't it?' And it was. And is.

And this largely French-speaking part of Switzerland gave the world one of the finest stage races we have known.

Switzerland does, of course, have another stage race and perhaps one far more easily recognised as coming from the land of triangular chocolate: Le Tour de Suisse (The Tour of Switzerland). This race began in 1933 and happily continued racing through the opening years of the war as if the distant sounds from over the mountains were only thunder. They did take a break from 1943 to the war's end, as it was all getting a bit serious over the borders and who knew what might happen?

As you well know, Switzerland is full of mountains. Bizarrely, though, the Tour of Switzerland is not a race that plays too much with the high ground. Historically the lives of the Swiss were spent in the valleys away from harsher altitudes. So that race stays largely in the valleys visiting the towns and cities. It is Romandie that takes us on a hike up to the sky – and, to my mind, is all the better for it. Of the two races it is easily the most dramatic and brings with it a fantastic series of vistas that you will find in the glossiest of your cycling magazines.

Romandie is stunning. And so is the start list. And that is because of the nature of the course. It offers just about everything a Grand Tour will throw at a rider – in a more compact form. There is a time trial, mountains, and rouleur/ puncheur stages aplenty. As a result it was thought for many years to be the perfect build-up to the Giro d'Italia that came directly after.

But times and training methods change. It was once the habit to have a long build-up of racing almost to the front door of the season's opening Grand Tour. Racing, not training, was seen as the ultimate prep for star athletes. No longer is this the case. As training methods changed and regimes became far more scientific, targeted and effective, the need to race right up to the start of the Giro ebbed away . . . and so did the star quality of the start list.

But they came back.

There was a new fashion for a far longer gap between racing and a Grand Tour. With the exponential rise in data-driven training plans there has, over the past decade and a half, been a habit of sending riders to altitude and onto intense sessions of interval workouts in front of men in white lab coats and clipboards. (OK, beach gear and ipads; I'm old. Be kind.) So training, not racing, is now the way to get ready for the big ones.

Suddenly, and without moving its place in the calendar, Romandie went from being the once favoured Giro prep race to being part of the new longer approach programme towards the Tour de France itself. So the stars came 'home' and the race found new life.

A look at the winners over the last 12 years or so tells you all you need to know: Valverde, Evans (twice), Wiggins, Froome (twice), Quintana, Porte, Thomas, Roglič (twice). You get the idea.

———

All very successful, then. Like the horology business that puts the finest watches on the wrists of the world. Everything in Switzerland works like clockwork. Even some of the people.

I arrived at the front of my hotel high on the hill overlooking Lake Geneva and left the lights flashing on my car. There were warning signs everywhere which clearly detailed the penalties for stopping just about anywhere without the right pass. I dashed into reception where a young-ish chap dressed like a much older man was waiting for me. Hair: centre parting. Glasses: rimless, so thin they were barely visible. Cardigan: burnt orange corduroy trousers. 'Ve haff been expecting you, Mr Bond,' he didn't say.

I spoke first. Kind of. 'Hello, I have a res –'

'Your name is Mr Carlton and you are wiz us for three nights.'

'Yes, that's right. My car is –'

'You will park your car in ze underbay. You will use ze lift. This will cost 15 francs per day.'

'Righty ho. And how –'

'You will drive 8 metres further on. Your car is pointing in the correct direction. There you will follow ze lift unt instructions on ze control unit. Please!' With that he handed me my room key.

'Thank y –'

'You are welcome.'

It was a bit like talking to a machine. It made for good practice. Back in the driving seat, I approached a sheet metal door just to the left of the hotel reception. 'I reckon that's at least nine metres, you arse,' I mumbled in faux conversation with the hotel robot.

'Select language', instructed the speaker. I did. A slightly more meaningful chat ensued. At least, the lift machine voice was a little more soothing. American English, of course, in that candy-coated telephone option-tree tone. I immediately assumed the taped message was an air hostess called Susan.

'Your lift is on its way,' she said.

'Thank you, Susan,' I couldn't help but reply.

'Please prepare to enter the lift. The doors will open in 10 seconds.'

They did. Ten seconds exactly; I counted them down.

'Please drive slowly towards the green light. When it turns red, stop!'

'I will. Thank you.'

The door to the garage lift slid open, and in I went.

'Goodbye.'

'Bye, Susan. Thanks for the chat.'

The door slid shut behind me and we were on our way. Down.

There was a sign on the wall which read: *Your journey will take two minutes. Should you need help, please press the emergency button on the left.*

I started my stopwatch on the Omega Speedmaster my dear wife had bought me. This was the first time I had ever used the function. I was disappointed to find that the trip to the basement parking lot took two minutes. Exactly.

This place is weird, I thought. It got worse.

Back at reception, mein freund said barely a word to me that was not an instruction. Taking a white pen, he opened a leaflet and began pointing.

'Here is a map. You are here. Ze tram to the lake is here. Breakfast is from 7.30 and will finish at 9.30.'

Yep, I was already missing Susan.

The next day I went to the press centre, run by a Dutch chap. He supplied me with all the right badges and a race road-book. 'Is it just me,' I began, 'or are the Swiss around here just a bit –'

'Odd?' he offered.

I nodded.

'They are a bit special. They mean no harm. I've been here for 12 years and I am just about accepted. Tolerated, really. Don't let it trouble you. It's normal.'

So I stopped worrying about it. But I have to say, I have never felt so lonely in the company of others as I did on this race. The crew, like everyone, barely said a word to me. And they were not quiet folk. Not at all. After the race the producers, director, editors, commentators of all the local languages, piled into the VIP area and had a few drinks. My badges did not allow access.

I checked into my hotel each night to find I had always been booked into places separate from the television team. I spent the entire race alone. And nobody gave a damn. Weird.

Everything, of course, worked precisely to time. The racing was brilliant and one of my favourite riders, Rohan Dennis, had a fab run in the leader's jersey for a few days, which cheered me up no end.

The penultimate stage ended on top of a mountain. I looked on as the entire race caravan left for Lausanne. I watched them go from my humble hotel where I was the only guest. It stood on the now empty mountain where the ski season had ended a few weeks prior. Absolutely nothing else was open. Apparently there was a big dinner party down by the lake about two hours' drive away. My badge said 'no'. I was used to this by then.

You'd think with all the success of the Tour de Romandie it would be a jolly affair. Well, it is. But only for the Swiss themselves. It's really hard to break into the tight social bond they have with each other.

There is a term for the people who once lived in the high-altitude, remote hamlets of Switzerland. It translates as 'ladder pullers'. So remote were they that no roads led to their dwellings. Access was via long ladders up the mountainside. At night they would pull these up for security, cutting themselves off from the world. I think the Swiss like this notion; they use it metaphorically. They mean no harm.

Switzerland and particularly Romandie has a lot going for it. It is a stunningly beautiful and impressive race. If you are going, don't expect too much conversation, but do get ready for a few breathtaking moments: The views and the racing obviously, but also the price of a burger. *How* much!?

A lot.

CYCLING LEXICON

Floating: Apparently effortless riding. Good legs, good bike, good day.

SEVENTEEN

TOUR DE YORKSHIRE
WHERE'S THE DONKEY?

The newsroom at BBC Look North was a busy place. The first morning bulletin had been written by me at around 5.30 a.m. ready for the first programme at 6.00. The usual fare of council funding decisions, sheep on motorways and objections to a country and western themed pub from a noise abatement group. The Yorkshire side of the Pennines tended to have news that was a lot less 'stabby' than the news bulletins to the west of the hills. By 9.30 I was looking forward to breakfast in the canteen, but waiting at my desk was a visitor: Mr Steven Grint from Accounts.

The week before, I had produced a great piece on a couple of youngsters who had secured the rights to some 1950s' rock and roll numbers and put them together into a catchy party mix. Calling themselves Jive Bunny, they hit No. 1 in the charts. But Steven wasn't here to talk about that. His concern centred on my item: Proposed Wind Farm. Lots of windy locations in the UK wanted to be considered. In the end it went to Delabole in Cornwall. Anyway, Steven didn't look happy. He launched at me in his best nasal tone. He wanted answers.

'Just a quick question regarding your expenses from last Thursday,' he began as he put on his reading specs and continued in a moderately raised tone: 'It says here: *Donkey £40*. What on earth did you need a donkey for?'

'There was no road access and we had a lot of kit to carry up the hills, so we hired a donkey.'

'Right. Where is the hire agreement? And for how long was the arrangement? Did you get an insurance waiver and what was included? A handler? I need more information.'

At this point it was all getting a little complicated, so I thought I'd move things on a little quicker by coming at it from another angle.

'Why don't we just say we didn't actually hire it? We bought it. Cash. A simple country transaction, you might say. Will that do?'

'No, it most certainly will not! Saying you bought the donkey . . . cash?'

'Yep.'

'Well, then, the question presents itself: Where is this donkey now? It's now considered BBC property. We need to know its whereabouts.'

'Ah! Well, why don't we just say it's dead?'

'DEAD!?'

'Look I'm trying to help here, Steve . . .'

'Mr Grint, if you don't mind. Until we have sorted this out.'

'OK, Mr Grint, let's just say it broke a leg in a ditch at the side of the road and . . . had to be shot.'

'Well, where is the veterinary bill for all this? And a police file number? They have to be informed of the death of such an animal.'

'Look, we gave a farmer £40 from the per diem fund to help us lug some kit up and down a Buttertubs hill . . . That's it.'

'Well, this is most irregular and I will have to deduct the funds from your crew's expenses.'

With that he left my desk, muttering all the while: 'Most irregular. Will not do at all . . . not . . . at . . . all.'

Steve was a refugee from Stevenage. He'd landed in God's Own County two decades previously and, despite never quite fitting in, had opted to stay. His regard for the practical versus the financial in this matter was clearly different to mine.

As far as I was concerned, I had simply got the job done without worrying too much about accounting for every little detail. Sadly it seems that for some folk, such details matter . . . a lot.

———

The Tour de Yorkshire was something very special indeed. The first running of the great race came two years after Gary Verity, head of the regional tourist authority, *Welcome to Yorkshire*, managed to persuade the Tour de France organisers A.S.O. to pick Yorkshire and not London as the site of the 2014 Grand Départ. The British government had backed the capital and even provided state funding for their rival bid. Gary Verity and his team ploughed on regardless, with all manner of guile and determination, to land the world's biggest annual sporting event.

The main thing in favour of Yorkshire was that Gary Verity, the no-nonsense straight-talking son of a hill farmer, and A.S.O. principal Christian Prudhomme got on exceptionally well together. Gary popped over to Paris and flooded Christian's mind with stunning pictures of the Yorkshire Dales and bamboozled him with stats about cycling use and local fans of the sport. Christian, of course, was also invited to London where he was given an appointment with the Minister of Sport and the London Mayor, Boris Johnson. It was, apparently, all a bit dry. After London he flew up to Leeds International Airport to be met by a colliery band playing 'La Marseillaise'. Like a state visit.

Prudhomme beamed and Verity, standing to attention, grinned back. They bonded instantly and together they achieved the seemingly near impossible: Yorkshire secured the 2014 Grand Départ. (The London Mayor wasn't happy.)

So the 2014 Tour de France duly came north – and it was magnificent. Yorkshire had spectacular weather to go with all the stunning hills and dales. Christian Prudhomme was deeply impressed. He began using the word *gorgeous* whenever he described the region. It was a joy to hear in a heavy French accent: 'York-shire ees – gour-gee-euse.'

And the multitude came to each of the Yorkshire stages. Every day there were hundreds of thousands, sometimes millions, lining the route; most of whom came on their bikes adding to the love affair. Pictures of my old favourite hills made it into cycling folklore. The charmingly named Côte de Buttertubs became a legendary image: thousands of bikes littering the hillsides as their owners roared on the peloton up the 15% gradients. It was as much a festival as a race.

The French media lapped it up too. My old friend and colleague Guillaume di Grazzia demanded to be educated in the strange tongue he had encountered. 'What means "Ay Up"?' he asked me.

I explained it was a greeting.

'Yes, but what strange etymology . . . I suppose it means: "Are you up"? That would make sense to me,' he said.

I let him have that one. I'd never thought of it before.

Two days later he came to me with a huge grin on his face before clearing his throat and declaring: 'You, my friend, are a complete WAZZOCK!' He was very pleased with himself.

But this 'Frorkshire' alliance did not end with the Tour de France. Christian Prudhomme wanted to come back. Of course he did. And whatever the A.S.O. wants, it usually gets. So it was that a plan was hatched to create a race around the glorious county. Just 10 months later Le Tour de Yorkshire was off and running as part of the UCI calendar. Amazing.

Considering it was from a standing start, the race was a remarkable success from the off. Big name teams attended with stars aplenty such as Bradley Wiggins, Marcel Kittel, Adam Yates and Tommy Voeckler. Likewise the course itself quickly established some classic elements borrowed from the Tour. The moors and the dales became familiar terrain and some of the finishes too. My favourite is the classic drop off the moors down to a finish along the seafront of

Scarborough. I used to holiday there as a kid and found that much remained the same, except for a distinct lack of seagulls on the cliffs where they used to roost. A series of council culls had seen them off. The council minutes didn't pull punches: 'They're crappin' ont' tourists an' their cars, an muggin' kiddies for their chips.' Apparently 80 such thefts in a year was too much. So in 2015 as the riders rounded the gentle cliff-backed left-hander to the finish line, the gulls' screeching was replaced by cheers from thousands of fans.

Tommy Voeckler, who'd brought joy and hope to France with his magnificent 10-day run in the yellow jersey back in 2011, was on fire. It was to be a typical move by the great man. Mugging a breakaway much like the seagulls relieving kids of their ice creams. At 38 years old, he turned it on for one last time. Like taking candy from babies.

The 196km (122-mile) run down from Middlesborough, cutting south-east through the dales, was a damp but fresh day. Team Sky set an infernal pace and shredded the peloton down to around 45 riders, Peter Kennaugh doing most of the work before his teammate Nicolas Roche attacked with 25km (15.5 miles) to go. Up the Harwood Dale climb he paced. Clearly this was a dangerous move.

Bridging over to the Irishman came Lotto Jumbo's Steven Kruijswijk and the French duo of Anthony Turgis of Cofidis and, of course, Voeckler himself in what I described as the Golden Doughnuts livery of Direct Energy. Look it up.

Now, whenever Tommy got himself in a break, he animated it wonderfully for the viewer. But his legendary exploits did not endear him to anyone sharing his bit of road in a break.

Once the breakaway was clear of the peloton, Tommy's agonising duly began. Grimacing while rolling all over the bike like he was pedalling squares. A man apparently dying a thousand deaths, on the limit. For those in the know it was like watching a fire drill in a retirement home for silent movie actors. Way over the top; but great entertainment. But you could never be absolutely sure. That was Tommy for you.

Breakaway companions often bought Tommy's act. Of course, there was always the chance he was indeed suffering, but surely not that much. He would skip turns at the front when he finally agreed to do his bit for the breakaway brothers. This would last varying lengths of time and often involve changes of pace as dramatic as his hanging tongue, breaking the rhythm of those around him. Then all of a sudden the tongue was back in his cheek and his eyes went from rolling up inside his head to pin-sharp focus.

Roche was wise to such antics and attacked the group first. Voeckler snapped from dead into the red in hot pursuit. Nobody else could go with them. Over Oliver's Mount they passed together, sharing the high-speed descent to the Scarborough seafront.

Then just as they shouldered the sea cliffs to their left Voeckler attacked to take the sprint home. 'The V-Bomber has blown them away,' I declared. Sadly a nickname too late in the man's career to stick. It was indeed Tommy's last stage win of an outstanding career. Such was the margin of victory, he took the Tour de Yorkshire title as well. Nico Roche was the runner-up.

A year later Tommy Voeckler retired to the commentary box in France. The Tour de Yorkshire lasted two more years until Covid struck. Team Ineos' Chris Lawless remains the defending Champion from 2019 after beating Greg Van Avermaet and Ireland's Eddie Dunbar in that final edition.

Now that COVID's grip has loosened will the Tour de Yorkshire be back any time soon? Sadly, it seems not. The steering committee was part of the Welcome to Yorkshire body responsible for tourism development – and headed by Gary Verity, as you know, certainly got the job done. It's estimated that more than 4 million people turned out to watch the Tour de France come by, and the scenes in Harrogate, Leeds and Sheffield bear this out. Gary was duly knighted – but then the accountants came calling.

Expenses were forensically analysed after concerns that public money had not been properly accounted for. Welcome to Yorkshire was funded by councils across the county, and they wanted to know precisely how their millions had been spent. A subsequent police investigation found no wrongdoing – but the stress was significant. Sir Gary resigned on health grounds. It was over. The race had lost its figurehead and driving force.

Since then, councils have stated that they will not again be funding the body that brought us the magnificent Tour de Yorkshire . . . so it seems that those beautiful racing days in May will be some time returning, if at all.

It was alleged that funds used for helicopters, limousines and the like were not detailed in the right way. But you know, sometimes you just have to get the job done, whether you have a receipt or not. A bit like me and my donkey.

Incidentally, UK Sport evaluated the impact of hosting the 2014 Grand Départ: an economic uplift of £102 million. As well as the many locals who enjoyed the party, there were 113,000 incoming visitors, who spent £24 million on accommodation alone. Thank you, Sir Gary.

CARLTON COMMENTARY

'Froome the bell tolls!'
The bell for the final lap on the Champs-Élysées
2013, 2015, 2016, 2017

EIGHTEEN

QUATRE JOURS DE DUNKERQUE
PULL THE OTHER ONE

'Je voudrais un . . . tire . . . teeyre. . . . teeeer?'

The word for a tyre in France is, of course, *pneu* – short for pneumatic, or air-filled. I did not know this at the time, but I did know I was upsetting the woman in this Abbeville fuel station.

The shock on her face was plain to see.

The more I insisted, the more shocked she became. As far as she was concerned, a mad Englishman had just pulled up in the middle of a downpour after dark just as she was about to lock up and was now standing here in front of the counter asking her for services she was not willing to supply. My panicky demeanour and clear sense of mild desperation weren't helping.

I'd punctured about a mile outside of Crécy and was in a bit of a state. It was raining heavily and my V6 injection Renault 25 was limping. It's a heavy car and much of the weight sits upfront where the engine lives. Being front-wheel drive, the poor flat tyre was now flapping on the rim about to disintegrate as I reached the forecourt of this forlorn garage on the outskirts of Abbeville in the Somme.

The woman remained polite. Probably more than I deserved. 'I can't help you, sir. This is a garage. The red light is for Michelin. Nothing more.'

YES! 'C'est ça! Un Michelin teeeer!'

Suddenly she became a bit calmer. She picked up an unfeasibly short pencil and on a scrap of newspaper drew a rudimentary picture of a tyre: 'Là!?' she asked.

Yes! 'Oui . . . ça!' I said with relief. 'A bleedin' tyre!'

'Ça c'est un pneu, monsieur. Un *tir* est un service entièrement différent. *Très* different.'

The penny finally dropped. 'Un tir' in French means 'a pull'. Oops! What followed was a series of apologies from me and plenty of smirking and shaking of the head from my new governess.

Profuse apologies accepted, she made a phone call.

I waited in the car about 20 minutes before a chap, ironically called Roger, arrived. He was most amused.

I stepped out into the downpour to be met with laughter. 'Evening, lover boy!' he said. 'We will get you underway in no time.' He rummaged in the back of his battered van and produced a rubber circle of salvation. 'Un pneu! UN PNEU,' he said triumphantly . . . and then spent the next 15 minutes chuckling away as he fitted it. Every now and then I heard him repeat to himself: 'Je voudrais un tir, madame!!!' followed by a snort and a long drawn-out wheeze as he tried to suppress his near overwhelming desire to roar with laughter.

I paid around £80 for this service. Apparently that's a lot for un tir in town at the back of the railway station . . . but entirely reasonable for a pneu.

The area of Pas-de-Calais and France Nord which borders Belgium is a playground of confusion at the best of times. This rather bleak place, sitting north of the Somme river, can't really decide what it is. The local patois is neither Flemish nor French, for a start.

For years people here have felt at one and the same time ignored and ridiculed by the rest of the French nation. The wider country it seems has never really had a handle on who or what these northern folk are like. Indeed since 1955, the Four Days of Dunkerque has been almost a metaphor for the region's lack of definition. For a start, it's run over six days at the moment, though it has also been as many as eight days of racing or as few as three. But the name has remained stubbornly the same: Le Quatre Jours de Dunkerque.

The Mayor of Raye-sur-Authie once explained to me: 'The title is famous. We cannot change it just because of a few extra days . . . or not . . . here and there'.

See what I mean?

The region is not the first on your list for a holiday. In fact, it's not on many French lists either. Most who hit the vast windy beaches of the North tend to be local or from just over the border with Belgium. And there perhaps lays the charm of this slightly dotty, ill-defined, unpredictable place. Those who know where to look do find treasure. And sometimes bombs.

Ten years after the Second World War, when most of the easy to find munitions had been cleared, it was deemed safe enough and financially viable to start racing. Yet still literally and metaphorically plenty of explosives lay beneath the surface.

I lived in Pas-de-Calais for seven years and during that time the local population voted, as they always had done, for the far left. All very proletarian. In fact, this was also their misfortune. With such an entrenched, near communist, political stance it was not worth any major political parties coming up north to campaign. It meant few favours were offered to an electorate so set in their ways. They didn't need bribing with goodies. So the roads were poor and so was the population.

Then, a bit like a smouldering bomb unearthed by a drain digger, there was an almighty bang! The entire region swung hard right to the Front National . . . Sacré Bleu, Blanc et Rouge!!!

The effect was seismic. Suddenly the great ignored were centre stage on those terrible French talk shows that blanket the old channels each evening, featuring hours of national soul-searching from a table of panellists holding unfeasibly large, brightly coloured microphones used as a comfort prop to hide behind. Talk Show Host: 'This is incredible! An area where resistance to fascism was most concentrated has now become . . . fasciste!?'

France was worried. So was Brussels.

BOOM! The money bomb was dropped on the entire region. Roads got better, buildings smartened up, cash poured into social infrastructure – and everything got a makeover. Even the tractors! Suddenly the place was awash with European funding and even the promenade in Dunkerque began to look . . . um . . . chi-chi.

So France put a comforting money-arm around the entire region; never again would it be so ignored. The Tour is now a regular visitor and the Four Days of Dunkerque a solid part of the national cycling scene with a roster of stars the envy of many other stage races sitting in front of the Grand Tour season. It is fantastic racing.

The battlefields of the Somme lie to the southern borders of the region and bring to mind those old grainy photographs of trench warfare where soldiers' startled eyes gleam like pearls in the filth. There is a lot of mud in these parts.

Where there's muck there's brass goes the saying, but the heavy clay loam here means only rather unfashionable root vegetables thrive on the vast plains. Farms are necessarily huge, the economies of scale essential to gain even a small margin from sugar beet, whose cabbage-like smell released from the processing plants hangs as a pall over the market towns like Hesdin. It's all a bit grim.

Yet cutting through the vast upper plains are gorgeous valleys like a string of gems leading to the coast. Village after village linked by rivers like the Authie, Îles, Maye, Canche, Liane and the Somme, all havens of beautiful tranquillity with chocolate box watermills and flower-bedecked châteaux, one of which belonged to the renowned designer Laura Ashley. She was renovating it until her untimely death after she fell down some stairs. And therein lies the rub. Among the gloom there is light, but even the bright bits have a dark side.

The village I lived in was smartly divided between those who had 'accommodated' the Germans and those who resisted. If you had an easier war playing Mein Host, you came out of it rather well. You might have become a mayor, for example, and during the war years were able to ensure the best communal land was farmed by your family and friends. Those who resisted, fared worse. The shadow of those times lasted into the late 1990s when those said to be 'too afraid to die' finally passed away to make an account of themselves to a higher being. The divide ran long and deep.

The four days of Dunkerque is a metaphor of division. Not everyone can thrive here. The excluded are climbers, GC men. They are either busy at the Giro or altitude training for Le Tour. There is little for mountain men here. No, in Dunkerque you have to be fast or punchy; preferably both.

The current race format feels like a fabulous mix of six consecutive classics where joy and pain are evenly spread. Challenges include cobblestones and short, very sharp climbs. It's as if Paris–Roubaix just got bigger with the addition of some Flanders flavour. And let's not forget the wind! Echelon racing in big sky country is what you get.

So if you are a spring classics rider then, after a short break, you can return to the scene of your greatest days and badge yourself up for the Tour team selectors who might just have a job for you come July. Equally, if you are a fan of the classics, then come along and fill your boots. I know the Giro is on, but you can always get your Italy top-up come the autumn classics.

If you are going to pick just one day, go to Dunkerque itself. The place has been transformed in recent years and the seafront is a delight. There is even a special series of 'primes' in front of a sponsoring brasserie on the promenade. The stage is run as a kind of criterium with several laps for you to enjoy while you tuck in to travers de porc à la crème and a bottle of appropriately strong

Belgian beer. The wind will blow as it always does, and if the sun shines too you will feel more alive than you can imagine.

And if it all gets a bit too grizzly out there, remember you can always head into one of the smaller cafés while waiting for your heroes to come past, kick back and grab an eau de vie. This water of life is the near industrial strength stuff that pops out of the back of those sugar-beet factories. It is firejuice; the word *evil* forms part of my tasting notes. Locals moderate the caustic taste by adding a large lump of sugar before it is put on top of a café stove to melt and warm. Only then can it be drunk with any joy. It's rough but 'does the trick', you might say. Just like the Quatre Jours de Dunkerque. Give it a go and, like me, you might just love it.

CYCLING LEXICON

Granny Gears: Using the easiest and lowest gear ratio while climbing.

▲ Time to get European racing under way. A few notable distractions in the Southern hemisphere but it's the GP Marseillaise that provides the big blast of springtime optimism for most this side of the equator.

▲ The famous Giro balloon squad strike again! It's a team of enthusiastic media students with the best work experience gig on earth. Their job is to schuss up buildings on the race route where the locals might be a bit busy with hogs to feed, vines to trim and trousers to design.

▲ Before the football World Cup came along to Qatar, the biggest sporting event was the cycling World Championships in 2016. I remember them well. It was like playing billiards in a blast furnace. A flatter and hotter event there will never be. There is no longer a tour of Qatar.

◄ The best trophy in cycling at the Tirreno-Adriatico. No race on earth offers such proximity to your heroes. Hotels are cheap at this time of year and near empty, so you can find yourself in the places the stars stay. 'Morning Tadej. . . three shredded wheat!?'

◄ Milano–Sanremo – a race covering 299km. The sheer joy of catching the first view of the Mediterranean is so intoxicatingly magical the long transition to get here is forgotten in an instant. Monumental.

◄ Heaven or hell? 'Depends on how you go,' said Sean Kelly. Without doubt though the Ronde Van Vlaanderen is heavenly for fans. You will find yourself instantly at home among the most undiluted population of cycling nuts on this planet.

◀ Yorkshire. For six glorious years when God's own county was mentioned people thought about cycling. It had it all. Crowds, 'gorgeous' scenery, great riders, pies and pints.

▶ Bastardo is a lovely place. The town was offered a name change in 1933. They said no thanks we rather like being Bastardos. They are kind, gentle-folk, very unlike the image of the odd-bod here.

▲ *What's Going On?* was a Marvin Gaye song. The answer to which at least locally where the North Sea collides with La Manche is, 'quite a lot, Marvin.' There is no record of him attending the Four Days of Dunkerque. . . but I like to think he popped along. The singer famously exiled himself nearby in Ostend in the early 80s.

▶ If ever a race was defined by a single day then this is perhaps it. Stage 7 Tour of Turkey, 2012. That famous Iljo Keisse finish to the Presidential Tour. Regarded by many, me included, as the greatest finish in cycling history.

Designed by Alison Wragg, @imlachHair

◀ The Last Supper reimagined. This was a birthday tribute to the lovely Gary Imlach. That's me as Judas by the way. I love Alan Partridge. If anyone can tell me the relevance of Phil Collins and Alan Titchmarsh you can win a #CKFC badge.

▶ Things you can win in cycling: Sean Kelly once won a cow, Matt Stephens won a cabbage. The original idea at the Tro Bro Leon was a prize sow. It all got a bit out of hand when the beast got a little frisky on presentation. . . so they opted for a piglet instead.

▲ The magnificent Duomo in Milan. This should be the finalé of every Giro D'Italia to my mind. A race that famously has no defined finish unlike the Tour (Paris) and Vuelta (Madrid).

▲ If you want to get from A to B in Norway there may well be a few Z's along the way. At the Arctic Race of Norway you will find simply the most spectacular roads. Then celebrate your run with a hearty dish of Rakfisk (see page 151). . . or maybe not.

◀ I guess it means 'All eyes on the champs' said the American tourist. Champs-Élysées actually means 'Elysium Fields' a paradise in Greek Philosophy. . . and I guess it is; certainly for cycling fans.

▲ Some say it is too big. Some say they prefer the Giro or La Vuelta. But nobody denies that the Tour de France will never be surpassed. Even the commentary positions have to be double deckers. . .

◄ There is always something to talk about as a cycling commentator. Especially on some of the long transition stages where nothing much is going on so you pick up your inspiration along the race routes. Some tales make it to air. . . some do not. Here is a wall close to the famous balcony in Verona from Shakespeare's *Romeo and Juliet*. Local youngsters show their love for each other by pressing gobs of chewing gum into the archway wall. . . and then write their initials on it. This one didn't make it to air.

◄ You may think Africa is just waking up to cycling. Well our sport has been alive and well on the big continent for decades. The UCI is taking the World Championships to Rwanda in 2025. And if you can't wait then take a trip to the Amissa Bongo or the Tour de Faso.

▲ Once you have experienced a Six Days of Ghent you will want to unpack another. Da-da-da dum. Da-da-da dum. Yep the opening movement to Beethoven's 5th Symphony. . . Sped up this is also the sound derney racers make as they bump over the degrading panel gaps to the giant access door cut into the tight cauldron that is the iconic Kuipke velodrome. Equally as dramatic, yet not something you will ever hear above the riotous atmosphere.

◀ My first day on the job!? No. Here the camera operator is taking tracking shots of The Peace Race, first held in 1948. Cycle racing has been around for a very long time. At its inception in the late 1800s fans would have to wait for news in the morning press. Smaller races might get a mention in dispatches in *Cycling Weekly*. Then came radio coverage followed by Movitone News reports and the first glimpse of action from races you were unable to attend.

◄ Party over. . . or starting? Another great Giro has drawn to a close and thoughts must soon turn to the next. But for one evening there is a chance to let the waters settle. Once the prizes are awarded and the air-fetti flutters to the ground, it's time for me to wander off to a peaceful place and reflect.

Image by Thomas Larabi

◄ Mark Cavendish is one of the planet's great guys. This was us in Oman having a rest from cycling discussing his Buell motorcycle's ram air system – we had a blast!

◄ Podium ceremony Funafuti Atoll Coast to Coast. The winner of The Coconut Cup: Me! Dig the groovy cycling shoes? Three iron postal bikes were involved. I won because the other two, a Finnish Doctor and a Polish Engineer, crashed! Hey: A WIN IS A WIN!!!

NINETEEN

PRESIDENTIAL TOUR OF TURKEY
SLAM DUNK SAUNA

'Brian! . . . You there, Bri?'

'Mate . . . just relaaaax. Go with it . . .'

Now, I know how to relax. It usually involves a pint and a comfy chair by a fire in a pub, somewhere like The Rambler in Edale on a rainy Tuesday afternoon in February. You know, the time of year where you can easily regulate your body temperature by the dextrous use of a jumper.

Right now I was as far from cold as I could be. My body temperature was as high as it had ever been while my other measurable comfort levels were in the strong stubby hands of my masseuse.

I lay on a marble plinth under a cloud-mound of soapy bubbles, wearing only the most rudimentary pair of large-gauge string-net briefs with mesh wide enough to drop a testicle.

The sign on the door read: Cappadocia Steam Room 3 and featured a temperature gauge pointing to 70 and the word *Medium*. We entered a round, foggy, marble-clad room and could barely see the other side through the steam. Inside were four marble plinths, one on each side of a square pool, with small fanned steps in one corner.

I'd been led here, rather touchingly by the hand, by a boulder of a woman called Fatima, who must recently have retired from competitive weightlifting.

She was phenomenal, such was the ease with which she flipped me over onto my belly before more suds and exfoliation grit rained down upon me.

Fatima said not a word as she pummelled, crushed, pressed, needed, chopped, stretched and scraped me towards the colour of mince. The tools of Fatima's trade were flat-gloved, loofah pads and a sponge the size of a cow's head. These, in combination with olive soap, essential oils and two wooden scrapers, were, apparently, something to be savoured.

After about 40 minutes of full-on deep massage, which occasionally involved elbows, I was feeling not a little imperilled. That's when the rapid hand-chops began.

'Thiiis . . . iiis . . . aaa . . . biiit . . .. pai-ai-ai-ainful, Briii. . . . Ah, and . . . sss . . . soo–Oh! . . . HO . . . O . . . O . . . OT.'

At this Fatima stopped. Beyond the suds I could hear her walk round to the outside edge of the plinth.

I don't know to this day whether she had simply had enough of me or whether what followed was just the next part of my Cappadocia Hammam Experience: Level 5.

It was certainly a shock.

I play it over in my mind sometimes in hyper slo-mo. I imagine Fatima bracing for action with a foot on the outside wall before shoving me, in a flash, off the plinth and into the ice-cold pool only a metre below. There wasn't much time to flail as I fell. Flight time? About a quarter of a second. Shock time? Oh, much longer.

I crashed below the surface and was struck by ice lightning. Light bombs went off in my head as I struggled to know what was up or down in this shallow plunge pool. I found the floor and stood up for air.

'WOW! WOW! OOOOOOOOOOOOO . . . AHHHHH . . . HA, HA, HA!'

Shock turned to laughter. I'd survived.

'Get ya sell oot. I'm in next,' said Bri.

Fatima was waiting at the steps. She held the most luxurious robe I have ever had the pleasure of wearing.

She was smiling now as she took my hand and led the enrobed me to another softly lit room with reclining bed-chairs and a barely audible soundtrack of birdsong.

'Please: Drink. You must drink.'

She speaks! I thought, but said nothing in reply. She placed a large jug of water with lemon and mint floating in it next to me and poured a large glass before offering it expectantly.

She waited until I had finished it and then a second one. 'You stay here now.'

I could only nod. I was already collapsing into a post-hammam massage stupor so deep it is known only to those who've taken this path. It was indeed the deepest of deep sleeps.

About an hour later, I was woken by a blinding headache.

'Oooooooooooh shiiiiiit' I uttered softly.

'Ha ha, he lives!' said Brian sitting up chuckling. 'What do ya think?'

'How come you are so bloody chirpy?' I said with one eye closed to the pain.

'Och, you'll be fine. You need to drink. I did this for the first time two days ago. You'll burst into tears a bit later. Don't know why. Then you'll sleep tonight like never before. In the morning you might feel a bit sore on the surface but by tomorrow afternoon you'll feel a million dollars. Trust me.'

He was right. Except for the crying bit. It was bloody amazing. Properly invigorating. Life-enhancing even. Just like it said on the flyer in the hotel lobby.

That got me thinking: Flyers in hotel lobbies often tell fibs. The *Experience of a Lifetime* flyer in a modest Fakenham B & B back in the UK referred to the local Gas Museum that was clearly being oversold. But here in Turkey the flyer titles simply tell the truth.

Walk in the footsteps of Romans, said one. You can do this at Efes, where you stroll down a Roman high street and even visit the library. I'm not joking.

The finest most fragrant dining experience of your life, said another. The food here is indeed amazing. Brazier-flamed meats, fish and vegetables accompanied by falafel, flatbreads and sweet pastries along with simply heavenly salads which bring together fruits, nuts and yoghurts with humus, tzatziki and a host of other miracles laced with fresh herbs and spices. Wow.

Bargains Galore at Sidi's Handbag Bazaar. Yep, Sidi and his like have all the so-called 'genuine fakes' you could wish for – purportedly making their way out of the back door of genuine manufacturers as 'overruns' . . . if you see what I mean. 'Not like your regular "fake fakes".' Well, if you say so, Sidi, my friend.

Each hotel flyer is both accurate and tempting. It's hard to know where to start. You see, Turkey is phenomenal in so many ways: the people, geography, food, history, everything. It's just wonderful. And so is the racing; sometimes unexpectedly so.

———

The day of 28 April, 2012 was bright and sunny in Izmir. Not much wind with temperatures a near perfect 26°C (79°F). It was Stage 7 of that year's Presidential Tour of Turkey and despite the calm weather there was a tempest coming. This was the day when the nicest race that nobody really talked about suddenly hosted one of the greatest finishes in the history of cycling . . . and maybe the world of sport itself. And it was all down to one man: Iljo Keisse.

The penultimate stage of the 48th Presidential Tour of Turkey was not billed as a crucible of excitement. A busy sprint, yes, with the final turn coming at the top of the park and a straight 900m (2952-ft) highway dash to the line. It looked a gift to the sprinters and their lead-out trains. Plenty of time for all the quick men to sort out the pecking order after just 123km (76 miles) of racing towards a beautiful finalé.

But it didn't quite work out that way, did it?

There was a seven-man breakaway up the road with, admittedly, a lack of accord between them. Some believed their chances of victory had vanished, with the peloton closing fast and a modest 49 seconds of advantage and 7km (4 miles) of flat coastal road to go.

Yet one rider wanted to keep going: the Belgian Iljo Keisse. He duly rolled off the front of the septet, and nobody wanted to follow. Belief among the six remaining breakaway men was clearly ebbing; they began weaving over the road and looking back to the peloton. But Keisse pushed on.

A lot of things had to happen if Keisse was to win this day. But a slim chance is still a chance. And he attacked.

One thing in Iljo's favour was that the UCI had not mandated radios for this class of race, so communication was a little sketchy back to the peloton. On-board TVs and live coverage was not really a thing in the team cars in 2012, so they relied on general race radio for timing. Basically the teams could not hear the commentary of Brian Smith and myself as we began to raise the tempo with the finish approaching.

So when the peloton came within sight of the six riders Keisse had left behind, they thought collectively for a crucial few moments that they had caught the break . . . they hadn't. Keisse was up the road, screened by a right/ left chicane that ran across the top of the municipal park towards the water's edge. Then, as these turns unwound, they saw him. And all hell broke loose.

Just after the flamme-rouge marker of 1km (0.6 miles) to go, there was an acute 75° right-hander onto the wide finish straight. Keisse had just 31 seconds on the pack and looked like he was riding for his life – which should've been enough to bring it home. But then it happened: a sequence of events that came together to create one of the finest finishes to a bike race, possibly ever.

Keisse didn't see the stripe of spilled diesel on the ground. We didn't either, but it is clear on the replay. A car had earlier forgotten to put the fuel cap on after filling to the brim. They had then duly taken the sharp right-hand turn and left an arc of danger for riders to discover. Keisse was the first.

As our hero slowed, raising his inside pedal to take the corner, Brian and I thought it was job done.

Brian: 'This looks very much like the day of Omega Pharma and Keisse.'

Me: 'It absolutely does, here is your switchback –'

These were the last calm words I issued for the next two and a half minutes. Keisse hit the stripe of black ice, lost the back wheel and down he went. *BANG!*

'OOOOOH NO!!!! . . . HE'S DOWN . . . COUNT THE SECONDS, QUICKLY REMOUNT, GET YOURSELF SORTED OUT . . . CHAIN'S OFF, HIS CHAIN'S OFF . . . NIGHTMARE SCENARIO, WHAT A SHAME . . . COUNT THE SECONDS BACK . . . OH, THEY ARE GOING TO GET HIM!'

Keisse was now back off the bike at the side of the road, putting his chain back on.

While he fumbled the camera switched to the helicopter tracking the peloton as it charged into the same corner. From the aerial shot there at the side of the road was a man in blue . . . but it wasn't Keisse. It was another rider, Sainz, who, like Keisse, had pushed on from the break and crashed.

The camera then switched to a frantic Keisse . . . head down and going for it . . . The peloton was charging into the gap behind him in the dash for the line. I was shocked and surprised to see him.

'OH!!!! COME ON KEISSE, FOR GOODNESS' SAKE!!!!!!'

It was Sainz at the side of the road Keisse was now 500m (1640ft) out; advantage 80m (260ft).

'IS HE GOING TO CRASH, GET BACK ON BOARD, RESTRING THE CHAIN AND BRING HOME THE VICTORY HERE? YOU'VE GOT TO PRAY FOR THIS. SURELY EVERYBODY –'

– 300m (984ft) to go, advantage 50m (164ft)

'— I THINK IT'S GOING TO BE A HUGE HEARTBREAK HERE . . . THE CHARGERS ARE ONTO HIM WITH 300 TO GO . . . RABOBANK HAVE MUSTERED THEMSELVES, THEY'RE BUSY GETTING THEIR TRAIN SORTED OUT . . . AND PETACCI GOES OVER TO THE OTHER SIDE OF THE ROAD –'

– 100m (328ft), advantage 20m (66ft)

'– OOOOOH HE'S GOING TO GET CAUGHT HERE . . . HE'S GOING TO GET CAUGHT . . . KEISSE'S GOING TO GET WOUND IN . . . AND SO WITH JUST 100M TO GO . . . 50 NOW . . . COUNT HIM HOME, SCREAM HIM ON . . .'

They say you should never hit 100% when commentating because you always need somewhere to go if more drama follows. I was already at 100% the moment Keisse crashed. So, at the line, I almost broke my voice.

'OOOOOOOOOOOOOOH, HE TAKES IT!!!!! JOY FOR CYCLING FANS GLOBALLY: WHAT AN EFFORT THAT WAS!'

I took a moment or two to gather myself, about six seconds or so, before declaring finally: 'I absolutely loved that!'

Brian and I then burst out laughing for sheer joy.

Brian, still chuckling: 'Absolutely amazing! You don't get many finishes like that.'

Me giggling: 'Thank God . . . thank God!!!!'

If ever a moment came to define a race, this was it. The afterglow of Keisse's achievement remains. Going forward, the Tour of Turkey was marked as a beautiful and exciting thing to behold. The fans now make the trip as do the great riders. Mark Cavendish famously found his winning ways again in 2021, leading on to yet more wins at the Tour de France – which meant equalling the great Eddy Merckx and his 34 victories. It's a special place.

At the end of that Keisse-winning year at the SPORZA Awards, they played the finish to the Belgian audience. It was shown with my English commentary. The auditorium duly erupted as I had done.

Yet there remained just one more bit of bizarreness to be attached to this amazing moment. The whole of cycling-mad Belgium must've tuned into the awards, only to hear the host pay tribute – first to Iljo, obviously, and then to the commentator. 'What an amazing ride, coupled with a truly majestic piece of outstanding commentary from the one, the only . . . Phil Liggett.' (Spontaneous applause and whistling.)

'You have got to be kidding me!!!' was my response when my chuckling Belgian colleague showed me the SPORZA clip. Then, just as in the race itself, I burst out laughing.

So, lessons from Turkey: a phenomenally relaxing, beautiful experience. You have to take the rough with the smooth, but you won't regret it. You may shed a tear, find peace and feel both the heat of the action and get snapped back to a chilling reality at any moment. And that's just the massage. The racing, as Iljo showed, can be pretty much the same.

As Brian would say: 'Och . . . give it a go . . .what have you got ta lose?'

CYCLING LEXICON

Half-wheeling: Riding half a wheel ahead of another rider, forcing the pace. Frowned upon.

TWENTY

TRO-BRO LÉON
WATCH THE PIGGY

'What do you reckon?'

Mark had just twisted out a whelk from its spiral home. And it didn't look right.

'Honestly, Mark, you're asking the wrong guy. I'm not a whelk man. I chewed on one for ten whole minutes once and, when I took it out of my mouth again, it didn't have a mark on it. Rubber snails; no thanks. And anyway, it's black. Aren't they supposed to be green?' I went back to my sandwich and watching the Tour de France on the café's TV.

Mark pondered for a moment before he shrugged his shoulders and popped the black whelk into his mouth.

Two hours later we were in hospital. It was a rough start to a tough holiday job.

Mark and I were in La Haye-du-Puits in deepest Normandy. We'd got the job because Mark's dad Ralph was on the management team at Bassett's Liquorice Allsorts in Sheffield. They had bought La Biscuiterie Rouger in Normandy, so we managed to grab ourselves a summer job helping to make gaufrettes in a hot, steamy biscuit factory. It wasn't glam.

On our arrival a big foreman asked wearily what we wanted to do. I said 'casual labour', meaning we would do anything. But the translation didn't really go down too well. His face went a little redder than it already was as he blustered: 'We work hard in this place and you will be expected to do the same.' Apparently in my terrible French I had said we wanted to do 'lazy work'; didn't go down too well.

The foreman did however give me a sitting-down job driving a forklift; a machine I had claimed to be familiar with. I wasn't, of course, but thought *How hard can it be?* Well, I found out that rear-wheel steering takes some mastering. Turn the steering wheel left and the rear turns left, so you face right. Right?

At the end of the first day, I was shown a charge sheet that detailed the total loss. I admit that the 10m/33ft-high stack of Raspberry Specials did come down a bit hard when I hit the base of it. I remember the smell as I panicked and ran over the strewn bales as I charged off, coming up just short of spearing the foreman into another bail of Vanilla Supremes. Sweet. Bizarrely, they let me keep the job.

Mark was a little guy and was given a big stick. He had to stand at the back of a line of rather Victorian waffle presses that opened after going through an oven tunnel. These cast-iron crocodile mouths opened to reveal a cooked waffle about half a metre square, which was then supposed to drop onto a conveyor belt taking it off to be cut into smaller biscuits. Mark's stick was to knock off any biscuits that stuck to the metal jaws before they clamped shut again to be injected with more waffle mix heading back into the oven tunnel.

If he got this wrong – and he did get this wrong – his stick would get caught in the iron jaws and he had to hit the alarm to stop the baking conveyor. If he wasn't quick enough, then the stick would catch fire and the bigger alarms went off. That's when my friend the foreman would show up with an even redder face demanding to know which English prick was responsible. It was bound to be one of us two. On the other hand, the ladies in the factory were very understanding as they went for yet another unscheduled fag break because of our incompetence.

All the talk was of the Paris–Camembert – or 'the cheese race' as Sean Kelly calls it. Sitting at the heart of the French Cup, there are three northern races hemmed in together over seven days at Easter.

It means that if you are to win the Coupe de France you will need to forget about the Ardennes and focus firstly on the Paris–Camembert on Tuesday before swapping Normandy for Brittany over the Easter weekend. The Tour du Finistère, over the hilly interior, comes next on Saturday, followed by the big one, the Tro-Bro Léon, on the Breton gravel roads during what is an enthusiastically celebrated public holiday on Monday.

Connor Swift won it in 2021 and on French TV, in spectacularly Yorkshire-accented French, described the victory as the biggest win of his career since becoming British Champion in 2018. On the start list were Oliver Naesen, John Dagenkolb, Philippe Gilbert, Warren Barguil, Benjamin Thomas, and so on. It was a big deal.

In 1984, Jean-Paul Mellouët's dream had come to fruition. Fed up with predictable racing and perhaps looking longingly eastwards towards Roubaix, he got to thinking: 'Why can't L'Ouest have something similar? After all we have some crap roads too, FFS!' This is a very loose translation of an entirely imagined quote . . . but you get the idea. He wanted something different. It was for a good cause too: raising money for a school in the Breton town of Lannilis, which remains the race hub.

With a distance of usually just over 200km (124 miles), the Tro-Bro Léon covers much of the Breton peninsular. It's the region that juts out into the Atlantic, almost defying the crashing storm-driven waves that have gnawed away at the land of softer regions further south. Brittany is almost like a geographical challenge to the elements. This standing firm character extends to the people.

Lakaat da sentiñ is Breton for 'bring to heal'; to take control; be the boss. They do this rather well.

The most challenging parts of the course are roads they describe as *ribinoù*. Sure, they have highways, but it is these ribbons of farm tracks, gravel and cobbles that offer up the various levels of torture which form the pivotal moments of the Tro-Bro Léon. It is notoriously difficult to master and is regarded as a rite of passage for upcoming riders. Go well here, and you'll go well anywhere. It's a great race to attend because it generates a lot of regional enthusiasm. It's a cycling festival in celebration of a sport Bretons regard as their own. After all, five-time Tour de France winner and local hard nut Bernard Hinault is furiously Breton – in more ways than one.

The view of the founders was that if their new race was to make an impression, it had better be tough from its inception. This was a successful formula and so the race quickly became a badge of honour, not just for amateurs but soon also for the pros. The race was being widely talked about for its huge crowds and great racing, and those lively press reports meant the higher professional ranks wanted in. The race's status changed in 1999 when big pro teams with big names joined the party.

The Bretons are famously passionate rugby players. They are hard men who sustain punishment almost without complaint. Big guys play with the oval ball while those of smaller stature either wrestle or ride their bikes . . . and sometimes both if you are Bernard Hinault, who's known as The Badger, the grumpiest of animals.

In 2019 Bernard was being presented with a huge cake by the A.S.O. on the anniversary of his first yellow jersey worn in Nancy back in 1978. As Eurosport's production truck was close by, I was lucky enough to get a slice. Hinault was smiling for the cameras, so I assumed he might be in a mellow mood. I shuffled up for a chat.

Now it probably didn't help that I accidentally sprayed him with cake crumbs. The conversation was brief:

'Bernard, how would you describe your riding style? Oh, sorry, crumbs . . . heh-heh.'

Big pause as he looked down at his shirt, then back at me. His eyes narrowed. 'I ride like a Breton.'

Like the crumbs on his shirt, I'd just got the brush-off.

There are usually around 25 off-road parts to the course, making up about 40km (25 miles) of the race. So, just as with Roubaix, the 200km (124-mile) run turns into a series of short races within a race, the riders vying to reach those action points in a decent position. If the weather is good, it can run very quickly. It might also be treacherous if it rains, which it does quite often, no matter the season. Rainfall might also be accompanied by wind which, as the Atlantic storms hit the Breton coast, means crosswinds may become a major feature as well. No wonder it is called the Hell of the West.

When the Tro-Bro Léon first began, the prizes were modest. The winner got a pig. Well, it should've been a pig but at the first edition the grumpy sow was having none of it. They just couldn't get her on stage. After a few handlers got knocked over, it was decided a piglet might be the way forward. This generated a good photo opportunity with a smiling champion holding his wriggling prize, and the idea stuck. As was also pointed out to me by a member of the Breton press, the piglet could make a good victory celebration spit-roast for the winner's family that evening. Hard-nosed *and* practical, these Bretons.

Over the years the piglet thing has had a bumpy ride. An escaped piggy once caused a commotion in the truck park, having wriggled free of its new owner. The poor thing legged it with its Breton scarf still around its neck. Sadly, its bid for freedom was all too brief. Moments later, a manoeuvring team bus pressed it into ham.

Despite the mishaps, a piglet remains the feature prize for the Best Breton in the race. Sometimes, of course, this happens to be the overall winner too.

If ham is not your thing, fear not: there is plenty of seafood to be had in the region, and the best way to enjoy it is the fish and potato casserole called Cotriade. These are amazingly hearty dishes built to see off the cold. The ingredients are, it must be said, from the bottom end of the pecking order. All the expensive stuff – sea bream, ray, cod, haddock, lobster, scallops and so on – gets TGV'd to Paris. What is left are the bits and bobs nobody really gets too enthusiastic about – crayfish, muscles, shrimps and, of course, the devil's own creation: whelks.

Every family has its own Cotriade recipe, so you can order the same dish again and again and it will be different each time, but always delicious. With a basket of bread and one of the strong reddy-brown ales they brew in the region, you will be very happy. Just pick out the whelks.

While you are there, be sure to head for the Crozon peninsula and, specifically, the Plage de Veryac'h. At the back of the beach is a humble crêperie, Chez Germaine, with one of the best views on the planet. Brittany has the sort of beaches that in Cornwall would be packed with tourists and ice-cream vans. Here, in Brittany, you might have the entire beach to yourself. So you can watch the sunset with a cold beer in hand at the end of a hot day of racing. Go on, bury your toes in the soft sand and ponder the sparkling ocean hitting the granite stacks at the headland.

The Tro-Bro Léon may well be a hard race, but to a softie like me, in a place like this, it is pure heaven.

CYCLING LEXICON

Yard sale: A crash that leaves numerous riders and equipment scattered on the ground.

JUNE

TWENTY ONE

GIRO D'ITALIA, ETAPPE 9
GIZ A LIFT, MATE!?

'The steel door at the side, the left side of the winding house, and don't be late. It's worth running for, my friend.'

Solid advice, we thought, from Alessandro our pal at RAI Uno. He knows his onions and today was certainly one to make you cry. If you got stuck.

Gran Sasso, the amazing finish to Stage 9 of the 2017 Giro. Simon Yates was imperious, just magnificent, taking the pink jersey and leaving an impressive field in his wake. Chris Froome was over a minute down on the day, coming home 11th. Yates had done it and looked so strong we wondered who could catch him. Such questions were put to the man who, you may know, does not savour interviews. His machine gun delivery rains bullet points on all those assembled in the post-stage press conference.

On the day there must've been five hundred media folk, along with tens of thousands of fans high on excitement and low on oxygen, up here at more than 2900m (9515ft) in the Apennines. It was as busy as you can imagine, being the first major mountain day of the race.

So packed were we, should anyone have fainted, I reckon they wouldn't have fallen to the ground. It was bizarrely relaxing in a weird kind of way. Fresh mountain air with high grey cloud. And a much lower fog of journo'-breath hovering above the horde. I was pondering what would be a collective noun for journalists and came up with a *scribble*. It also summed up the order; there wasn't any.

The public had been told that they must walk down the mountain and that the lift, a large gondola, was for the sole use of media on the day. Lucky for us, we thought. Not so, as it turned out.

There was no way the fans were going to let the media alone have their way. Admittedly, it didn't look hopeful for Giuseppe Public, corralled to the right side of the concrete winding house that was the only mechanical exit from this cold place. And they had a point. There were kids and elderly who would've suffered, possibly severely, in the cold and damp that were now descending in the early evening. Only those with accreditation were allowed to stand in front of the locked doors of the building which was being guarded by the carabinieri. A loudhailer told the crowd that the media had to go down first because they had to continue their journey and work attached to the race. Once the realisation that tomorrow was in fact a rest day got out, though, all those in the holding pen began to . . . ahem . . . scream.

The gondola we were hoping to board, had capacity for only 35 passengers. It looked like a slightly squat vintage coach without wheels. Great big red lumbering thing, it was. A creation of the 1960s: lots of curved glass to enjoy the view through its spider-web framed walls and roof. And there was plenty of time to take in the scenery, for anyone lucky enough to get a ride, because it took around 20 minutes to complete the journey down into the valley some 2km (1.2 miles) below. A lovely ride, but only if you could get on. A big *if* indeed.

We had not been allowed to drive up the mountain. Nobody had. Not even Mauro Vegni, the race organiser. The helicopters were absent too because it was a no-fly zone; you might scare the wildlife. So there was just one way off if you were not walking: 'It's this bloody gondola or nothin',' said Kelly as we raced panting towards the winding house.

At the front of the building, being bayed at by the sectioned-off public, there was already a mass of still-jolly media folk with coveted race accreditation on pink lanyards around their necks. The riders had already departed, having made their way through a narrow tunnel formed by the police. Crowd control was the order of the day.

'There it is, down the side, the steel door.' Sean said this with a skip in his voice just as I stumbled. With cartwheeling arms, I escaped the fall while Kelly chuckled, offering up a panting *eeejutt* for good measure.

We got there. We were not alone.

In front of us stood a mountain of security. She was impressive. Turns out this particular officer was once part of the Italian Olympic judo team. This black-uniformed carabiniere must have stood at around 2m (6.5ft), a height magnified by the doorstep she owned. We became quite close over the next hour or two. It was hard not to get close.

Kelly is a beacon. Wherever Kelly goes, others follow. He's easily recognised, which is nice in certain circumstances like parking control: 'On you go, Mr Kelly.' But today his fame was not a gift. We had company. Lots of it.

Those at the back of the crowd massed at the main entrance had nothing to lose by exploring what Kelly was up to down the side. The others were going nowhere; trapped by the crush of their own making. The swearing had started. No punches yet.

Meanwhile, at the side of the building, things remained quite good-natured for the time being. We stood like disciples in front of our now not-so-secret steel door. It was getting busy with new arrivals all the time. 'What do you know, Sean? Is this a VIP door, Sean?'

'Not any bloody more, it ain't,' said Sean into the belly of our security mistress.

The last remaining riders, including Simon Yates after his press duties, departed from the winding hall. About ten of them only. They emerged from the concrete cave, setting sail down into the gathering valley fog. They had plenty of space to tease us, waving and laughing back at us as they went. Sean looked on with amused envy at their antics. 'Oh, I'd be doin' the same alright, lucky sods.'

Our door remained stubbornly shut. The police had let some in from the front of the building, possibly to avoid a riot. It must've taken about 20 seconds to fill the hall before the batons were drawn to stem the flow and the front door closed again behind them.

'That's bolloxed us then,' said the King. 'What a palaver.'

Three more gondola journeys and an hour went by when suddenly the radio on the belt of our dominatrix crackled to life. 'Control, the principal is arriving. Be ready.' All handily translated by one of our fellow prisoners.

'That'll be Vegni,' I offered. Sean said nothing. His mood was as the sky: darkening.

We didn't see Mauro Vegni for a while, but from the first *Ciao bello* at the back of the pack we knew our potential saviour was arriving.

Sure enough, after a few more minutes he was with us. 'Aaah, Mr Kelly, are you enjoying Giro?'

There was a moment of silence; never a good thing with Sean. 'Well, it would be a lot better without all this bloody mess . . .'

That's all it took to book us another two hours up here.

'Well, if you don't like it, you can always go home.' This was delivered by a grey-faced man who'd had enough of any criticism regarding the day's arrangements.

Sean knew we were in trouble but didn't moderate his words. 'It's just crazy. We have been waiting here for hours all of us . . . and –'

The steel door behind the guard opened just enough to allow a man of modest stature to slide through into an empty winding hall. But just before he disappeared, he let his head linger at an angle for a moment to deliver the most extended sarcastic *ciao* I have ever heard. It was in the form of a hungry cat's long meow, *ciaaaaaaaao* – and he was gone.

'Bloody hell, Sean, we're bolloxed.'

'Yes, well. It had to be said. Bloody mayhem. I had to say something.'

We watched the cables tighten to announce the departure of the race director. It was hilarious. He was alone. Standing in the dead centre of a gondola capable of taking 35 was Mauro Vegni, his back to us as he went. A lone charioteer speeding away.

'That, Sean, is the biggest F-you I've ever seen.'

Sean just nodded.

It took another hour and a half before we got off that blessed mountain. A day remembered by everyone but not necessarily for the amazing racing.

———

All grand tours have a tough climax ahead of each rest day and before the final day parade stage.

The format may well be predictably familiar, but that does not make it any easier to bear. There is a pattern to the Grand Tours; a fashion, you might even say. Over time the formula varies, but it is evolution not revolution. First, an opening nine days of progressively harder stages with climactic weekend tests, the toughest coming on the second Sunday just ahead of the first rest day. There is never a longer run of days than these opening nine stages. After that come two runs of six days, the first sequence towards the second rest day, and then six more punishing final tests before the Jerseys are awarded.

The 9-6-6 format is long established. Sure, there are variations – starting the race 'out of country', for example, will mean an additional rest day might be needed for transfer logistics – but 9-6-6 is the norm.

Organisers love a tough Stage 9. They can't help themselves. Chucking in something brutal at the end of the long Grand Tour intro is apparently irresistible.

Yet woe betide any race director who makes life too tough. A peloton has been known to protest if life on the race is regarded as overly punishing. They might even down tools or call for a ride-through, effectively neutralising the stage.

Unjustifiably tough racing cost Giro race director Angelo Zomegnan his job back in 2011, and the Monte Crostis stage was cancelled by the UCI. Too tough going up and too dangerous coming down. The riders complained; the UCI listened and agreed. *We are not circus beasts* was the refrain. Riders do have opinions and indeed collective power, so do not provoke them with your course design.

The trick is to create a race that offers mountain drama for the spectators with the temptation to do battle for the very best climbers. Yet at the same time the course must remain human enough to allow the survival of other riders whose chances of stage glory might lay elsewhere in the hills, valleys and open planes of the race. Simply put: if you are going to go brutal, keep it sensible. . . . don't take the piss!

Yet everyone knows there must be pivotal points within all Grand Tours where the big questions are asked of those going for the overall title. And if you are going to ask big questions, it is probably wise to do this on the day before a rest day so at least the riders can comfort themselves in the knowledge that some pain relief is at hand by the stage end . . . be that either a rest day or the 'parade day' race finalé.

Thus you can almost guarantee that the toughest of Grand Tour days will come on Stages 9, 15 and 20. For me the hardest of these three crucial days is on the ninth consecutive day of racing. It's not just the physical challenge, either; it's the psychological burden. At the end of this traumatic challenge, riders will be not even halfway through the race. It may be cruel, but it's also fascinating.

Mauro Vegni chose to go to the top of the Gran Sasso on Stage 9 of the 2018 Giro d'Italia. Tough to get off, as you now know. Tough to get up too; just ask Chris Froome.

Froome came into 2018 hoping to do the Triple. The Giro d'Italia offered the great man the chance to hold all three Grand Tour titles at the same time. Having won the 2017 Tour de France and Vuelta at the end of that summer, he came into 2018 believing in the treble. The idea was to do a Grand Tour Grand Slam by winning all three in the same season. Time to start things rolling in the fight for pink.

We all know that Froome produced a miracle ride on Bardonecchia towards the end of the race to achieve true greatness by winning Giro 2018. But on Stage 9 to Grand Sasso, it looked like being a very different story. This was the day that everyone thought Froome had cracked on the big rock of the Appenines. Froome lost over a minute to the leader Simon Yates.

Sure, it may have been the fact that Chris came to the Giro hoping to ride into form during the race. He needed to moderate his performance if he was to achieve the treble. But after all the efforts of surviving Etna a few days earlier, he came to the dreaded Stage 9 – and went pop.

It looked like the Giro curse that had done for Bradley Wiggins and Geraint Thomas had come to haunt the team once more. But it wasn't rain or a badly parked police bike that did for Froome . . . it was a beastly Stage 9 monster day that saw our deliberately undercooked hero get fried.

This was a perfect example of a race director getting the dreaded Stage 9 right. A hugely dramatic day in so many ways. Mauro Vegni played a blinder in terms of the race planning. As for the mountaintop evacuation at the end? Well, let's just say he beat Sean Kelly and soloed to victory on the descent.

CARLTON COMMENTARY

'Ah, the Luxor Obelisk: Eye, Lamp, Hawk, Dog, King . . .
and we all know what that means!'
Luxor Obelisk TV close-up, featured at every Tour finalé

TWENTY TWO

GIRO D'ITALIA ... FINAL DAY
MUSSO AND THE MIRRORS

I'd been in a hurling mood since about 11 p.m. For the past few hours, the noise from the restaurant below my Milanese studio apartment had been far too lively for my liking. I lay awake resigned to their ignorance. It was around 1.30 a.m. when the last-straw guffaw echoed around the quad six stories below . . . and my mind started rummaging for a missile to send back some of the angst.

My pencil-lipped mood suddenly lightened as I remembered an overripe beef tomato I had plopped into a pedal bin earlier. It was a short weary stroll from bed to my kitchenette bin whose lid slapped against the wall as I pushed the foot pedal to reveal the bruised, juicy weapon.

Using my handy cyclists multitool, I undid the safety tether of the giant mirrored window – modern buildings in Milan's business district are all skinned in mirrored glass – and swung it inwards flush with the wall. I had a clear view of the target below through the now unglazed yawning hole. The tomato sat plump and heavy in my hand. From the feel of it, I instinctively knew that I'd be accurate. I could pick my spot.

The art of a sniper is calm calculation and I spent a long minute or so wondering who of the office nobs burbling below was the most objectionable prime target. But my clear mind started to be clouded by consequences. The tomato was bigger than the average-sized cricket ball and from this height would hurt. Also, if it were to shatter a glass or two, there might be nasty consequences for them and for me. In the end I opted for a spot on the pavement close to the end of their long table. That way: message delivered and nothing more than a few dry cleaning bills for revenge. Perfect.

Holding on tightly I hung out of the gaping hole in the mirror-building wall, resting my belly on the frame with my left arm limp but fully fruited up. There was not much backswing to the shot; and the release, when it came, was fully finessed like that of a well-practised pensioner on a bowling green. Gravity was my friend.

I had all too little time to admire the near perfect parabola, but so beautiful was it that I spent most of the following hours, eyebrows up, in a smiling light snooze simply recalling it. What an arc it was!

The explosion was spectacular. 'Air soup' is the only way to describe it. A vent of lava has never been more impressive, though quite probably equal in terms of perceived threat. At ground level everyone jumped up as one, glasses and chairs flying. Each had their own expletive for the moment; there was the odd shriek for good measure.

Then . . . silence.

They knew.

And they did indeed shut the eff up. They also looked up to see that one of their crappily designed mirror walls had an eye missing. The open window meant they could quite easily have found me had they come looking for laundry compensation. But they didn't. Party over. It was time to go. They picked up their mottled jackets and left . . . all 20,000 of them (according to the reflections bouncing off their dreadful creations).

Milan is not a pretty place. The industrial heart of the Italian nation has always been a functional city proud of the fact that it pays the bills of the other more frou-frou cities putting this place in the shade in terms of Renaissance architecture and ancient monuments. You see, Milan makes stuff. Has always made stuff. High volume manufacture needs effective infrastructure and straight-line planning, without too much appetite or time for sculpture and decoration. From Victorian times it was brick-built and smokey-black busy. Then came the 1960s when suddenly square box, clean line, concrete construction became all the rage – and Milan was suddenly cool.

That's when the cherry-coloured chinos and purple safari suits moved in. 'Yeah, white patent-leather sandals, baby, with orange sponge sole . . . and pea green socks . . . *Ciao bello!*'

Fifty years later another fashion change in this heartland of 'style': mirrored buildings replaced the concrete. Along with titanium grey suits, shirts and ties. The treble-grey cool business look, to be checked out in the reflection of any building in the business district. This is a place that is very confident of itself.

Oh dear.

I was once asked by the organisers of the Giro d'Italia what they could do to move the event closer, in terms of stature, to the Tour de France. I suggested a couple of things but primarily I said they should stop moving the finish around. Keep it in Milan, the home of the daily newspaper *Gazetta dello Sport* whose pink pages are reflected in the Maglia Rosa worn by the leader of the race. I suggested they help the fans visualise the end of the race with a familiar climax. The Tour has this in the Champs-Élysées and La Vuelta with its circuit in Madrid. They should do the same, I said.

And it's true that any finish in Milan is always spectacular, not least because there is one exception that proves the rule about Milan being architecturally ugly: the Piazza del Duomo and its surrounding galleries in the centre of town. This place is just about the most beautiful backdrop that any race could possibly wish for or imagine. It is stunning. So much so that Mussolini placed his private offices right here, overlooking the magnificent square and cathedral. Indeed, rather significantly, he chose to spend much of his time in this Milanese beauty spot instead of Rome.

In 2018 I was invited onto the veranda overlooking the finish line, above the exit to the magnificent grand arcade, the Galleria Vittorio Emanuele II. It connects the piazza to La Scala, the centre of world opera. In these magnificent halls roofed with leaded glass, extraordinarily expensive things can be bought – like an espresso from the exceptionally well waitered tables of the busy cafés. Anyone can sit at these tables, but the less showy-offy can also choose a far more affordable option outside.

Above all this on the first floor sits a secret place: Musso's office. I know of its existence only because I was invited up to the nearby veranda for a very welcome spritz by a high-up chap who managed a drinks brand. My pal Marti and I were enjoying the view of the finish line from our cloistered vantage point when suddenly the hostess went out to get more ice. We were alone.

Marti lent across the table to issue a conspiratorial whisper. 'Eh, do you want to sit in Mussolini's chair? It's here in this place! Come!'

He beckoned me to a door off to the side. We crossed a mosaic hallway on near comedic tiptoes, opened some double doors – and we were in. What a weird and spooky place it was.

An impeccable 1930s' leather chair sat behind an equally stylish mahogany table of the same era. Beautiful Venetian glass chandeliers and wall lamps illuminated paintings and frescos featuring all the right flags and scenes. You know the stuff: all very early 1940s-friendly, shall we say.

This was a hushed tour of evil by two blokes who were behaving like school kids: a bit wide-eyed and slightly giddy on naughtiness.

Marti was kind of whisper-shouting: 'This is the very desk where he signed his orders . . . This is his private drinks cabinet with his favourite glass . . . Here is his very pen' and so on. We were having a (spooky) ball.

In a way it came as a relief when the double doors we had quietly used to gain access were slammed open by security.

A rather diminutive woman marched in ahead of a wall of man-meat wearing earpieces and dark glasses. She wasn't happy:

'WHO THE HELL GAVE YOU PERMISSION TO ENTER HERE?'

It turns out you can only visit this place under strict government control. The authorities are determined to keep this historically significant room for scholars only. The danger, of course, is that it might become some kind of shrine to be feted by the right. Its existence is kept very quiet. Until now, that is.

We were clearly not learned folk. She could tell that because I was caught sitting in Musso's chair with my feet on his desk for a photo.

Before being thrown out, we had to stand in front of the headmistress and delete all photos of the room from our phones. We then had to say we were very sorry. And then we had to say sorry again . . . 'but this time like you mean it.'

We had been very naughty boys.

———

Most Grand Tours end on Stage 21 with a sprint stage. Sure, there is the usual parade of the heroes, usually on the first of a multi-lap circuit course before the racing begins. It's all set up for one last dash that gives the quick men, who've suffered in the mountains more than most, a last hurrah to bring the show to a close. The standings overall are not designed to change too much on this final party day. A couple of minor places might get shuffled a bit, but order is usually maintained for what is a celebration of all that is great about the event.

But sometimes, just sometimes, the last day is the decider. And such final days are far more common at the Giro d'Italia than either Le Tour or La Vuelta. And that is because of the fashion, in this most fashion-conscious place, to have a time trial decider at the very last. It makes for a great show.

Several times in recent years the Giro title has been won and lost in a climactic solo 'race of truth' against the clock.

The Giro has suffered for many years by being regarded as the little brother to the Tour de France. This is for a variety of reasons. The big one is funding. The Italian race does not get the same level of state support as its French neighbour. Where Le Tour is regarded as a national Grand Projet, in Italy the Giro suffers from being regarded as a bit of a Milanese event. Rome is not given to closing the city too often to accommodate a race whose history lies in a rival city. Odd I know, but it is the attitude. National funding does not come easily to the Giro.

Its place in the calendar also has an impact. If Grand Tours are a meal, then the main course would be Le Tour de France. The sweet end to proceedings is La Vuelta. So the entrée or starter is the Giro d'Italia. No bad thing to start the Grand Tour season, you may think, but the field reflects that early start. The roster of riders who choose Italy is often not one that will race in France. And that means the best riders can be absent from the race for pink.

So, in order to keep us hooked on what is truly a great race, organiser Mauro Vegni, and before him Michele Acquarone, have sought ways to make the Giro different. For the past ten years or so, the Tour de France has moved away from long time trials and very long mountain stages. The Grand Tour fashion has been for shorter punchy time trials and dramatic mountain stages with the peaks compressed into shorter days. The natural reaction of the Giro was a move to be different and go the other way: big and long dramatic days of climbing and time trials aplenty. In so doing the Giro has gone fishing for riders who might prefer the kind of challenges that the Tour and Vuelta no longer provide. It's been a very successful strategy that has also provided some amazing race finishes. It means you can get late surprises that are fantastically entertaining. And if the event ends with a time trial, those surprises can make for a very spectacular finish to a race. No parade here . . . just solid battling to the very end. Gladiatorial, you might say.

In 2012 Canada's Ryder Hesjedal beat Joachim Rodrigues to the title in front of the Duomo. Five years later, the same piazza saw Jos van Emden win the 2017 finalé ahead of champion Tom Dumoulin, who denied 2014 winner Nairo Quintana. And then, of course, in 2020 Filippo Ganna took his fourth stage win as Tao Geoghegan Hart tore the pink jersey off the shoulders of Jai Hindley.

So both a tasty and costly finish in equal measure. A bit like those espressos under Mussolini's office.

Why, then, is the Giro final stage not always there? Well, it all comes down to money. The Giro has a lower level of central government funding compared with the Tour or Vuelta, and needs to find cash. It does this very well, selling the start and finish of every stage, and building in paid-for highlights along the route each day: the location of intermediate sprints, for example. Everything has a price, even if sometimes this might be modest; like support covering crowd control and security in a busy town centre en route.

The Grand Départ, as well as the finish venue, generates significant funds. It's the same with most other races. And it is the start venue that generates the most. This is because there is a build-up party to any Grand Tour, which can last days or even weeks. Some starts turn into festivals. Having attended several Giro starts, I can tell you they are wonderful.

This funding model is also one of the reasons the Giro is so well travelled. No other grand tour has started further from home than the great race for pink. At the 2022 route announcement of the Tour de France, the organisers made a big fuss about Denmark featuring as the furthest ever starting point for the Yellow jersey. Well, the Giro's Pink Jersey was there in 2012 for a three-day festival in Herning and Horsens. That year the UCI gave permission for an extra rest day to help with the transfer back to the sunshine of Verona. This extra-recovery day initiative set the template for future extreme remote starts. In 2018, the Giro started from Israel. It was amazing.

Such is the ambition of the Giro organisers, they have even mooted the possibility of starting the great Italian race in the United States. Four days of racing on the East Coast to end with a short stage early finish so everyone can catch the afternoon plane to Italy; then a rest day, and the following night a Team Time Trial.

This hasn't happened yet, but the planning template exists. If it does come to pass, not only would it be magnificent, it would also generate significant funds. Success would also mean you will see such things again and again.

Anyway, back to the finalé. All the money chasing does not alter the fact that for me, and many others, Milan should be the race finish every year, but can Milano afford it? Oh, and before you ask: Rome don't want it.

In both 2013 and 2014 the Giro organisers, RCS, revived the magnificent Roma Maxima. Previously known as the Giro del Lazio, it had been absent for five years after the financial crisis of 2008. Now the city seemed to treat its return as a bit of a nuisance.

But what a race it was! Out from Rome before coming off the hills to finish close to the Colosseum – amazing. But the feeling from the city authorities was lukewarm. In the VIP guest tent in Rome, one councillor quietly said to me: 'Cycling in Italy is a Milanese affair. It's not ours. And we as a city are just too busy to keep closing for this . . .' He gestured with a sweeping hand that held a plate of egg pasta sprinkled with shavings of white truffles towards the throng of fans who appeared perfectly delighted to be there. 'I mean this . . . these . . . them . . . huh!!!' He struggled to find the words and those that did pop out of his mouth were accompanied by spittle tracer bullets. The words that popped into my mind, I kept to myself.

So, let's dig into our Milan Plan, then. 2012 was brilliant. Canada's Ryder Hesjedal went into the lead on the first real mountain day – helped, I might add, by the new commentator on the block, Daniel Lloyd, a former Garmin–Cervélo rider (he tells everyone) who was now out of contract. If only he'd pinched one of those British Championships he finished second in twice, eh!? Well, lucky for me and Garmin, he was a free agent. Kind of. Still playing the role of Loyal Lloydie each morning before he joined me for commentary, he dutifully rode a big part of the course and reported back to his old team. I think they paid him in socks.

One day Dan came across a fast descent off a plateau that led to a sharp right turn over a very narrow bridge. This was not detailed on the road book and was commentary gold. It was also vital information for Garmin and their chosen son, Ryder Hesjedal of Canada. All this was detailed by Alan Peiper in an article for *Cycle Sport* magazine called 'How We Won the Giro'. It all hinged on that amazing moment when other teams were wondering what the hell was going on; 40km (25 miles) to go and they were attacking the pack. No wind to speak of on the plateau. What was afoot? Other commentators were flummoxed in their commentary positions. But we knew exactly what was going on. Garmin bossed the descent and shot over a bridge wide enough only for two abreast at most. Behind them at the pinch point was a huge traffic jam. On Garmin sped to take the jersey that day. Ryder lent it to others after three days before taking it back and sealing victory in, yes, you've guessed it, the final time trial ending in front of the Duomo in Milan. Dan never got a mention in Peiper's valedictory article . . . but he liked the socks. Knowing Lloydie, he turned them into coffee pods via eBay. Cheers, Alan.

I'll never forget the look of sheer joy and shock on Hesjedal's face as the air-fetti machines did their job blasting into the sky above him gold, silver and pink foil ribbons that tumbled around him in that magnificent setting. His wonderment was nothing to do with the place itself, but it is so beautiful it could have been. Next time you are in town looking for tangerine Versace socks, give it a try, why don't ya . . . You can catch them in the reflections of your ugly glazed hotel later. Just don't ask to see Mussolini's office. It's out of bounds.

CYCLING LEXICON

Dive Bomb: A dangerous cut inside a group of riders turning into a corner.

TWENTY THREE

TOUR OF NORWAY
'OPEN WITH GREAT CARE!'

'So, what do you think?'

'Erm . . . it . . . oh, dear! Wow! It tastes of . . . death.'

It's hard to put into words just how challenging the smell of rakfisk is. If you are talking to a Swede, you could simply say it's a bit like surströmming and they would understand. As for the rest of the world . . . how anyone actually gets to taste this fermented fish is beyond me because you must first get past the most intense putrefying odour I have ever encountered. Apparently the first to break though such a test was a Viking. Must have been hungry.

Even the most die-hard cycling nomad is unlikely to have spent much time in Norway. It's not at the top of many cycling bucket lists. This is an injustice. The place is truly stunning.

It's a land known for its amazing fjord vistas, the beautiful Northern Lights, gorgeous Setesdal jumpers – and, of course, rakfisk, which you should brace yourself for . . . or better still avoid. But cycling? Other destinations vie for a rider's attention. Well may I suggest you give it a go. Cycling, I mean; not rakfisk.

Norway is a country of contrasts. People generally tend to be very quiet, contemplative even. Yet they can get rather agitated too. Explosive even. There are Viking genes in there. So take care.

The Norwegian psyche was once explained to me by one of our engineers after he had got over his reticence and finally talked to me on the last day of the Arctic Race of Norway. He told me that if a Norwegian goes on a 'short', two-day walk into the wilderness, the experience will be entirely ruined if he should meet another person out there.

'What, even if you just said hello and moved on?'

'Oh, being able to say hello would be a disaster. I mean, even if you should catch a glimpse of someone maybe five kilometres from you walking in the opposite direction, that would be upsetting. Completely ruin the experience. It would take me hours to get over that and re-find my *ensomhet*.'

He explained that the closest word in English is 'solitude', but that *ensomhet* means so much more than that. It is a deep solitary bonding with nature. A spiritual endeavour. A withdrawal. A release.

'And how often do you seek this *ensomhet*?' I asked.

'Oh, I'm no hermit. Twice a month perhaps.'

So every couple of weeks my mate Magnus just disappears on an adventure he likes to share with nobody. Yet this very same man, that very evening, almost had to be torn from the ceiling at the after-race party. He went as wild as everyone else that night; no inhibitions on display. Joyous mayhem, it was.

The next morning I was about to knock on his door, but a small Post-it note stopped me. *Ensomhet*, it said. I understood.

The Norwegians are amazingly hard to pin down. They like their own company. They like to party. They love their country and they like to share it. A little bit.

Norway does not shout too loudly about itself. It gets on with it. With everything. Norwegians are quietly industrious people working either alone or collectively. But when they party. Hold on to your hats . . . or horned helmets . . . this will be wild.

Norway is also one of the richest nations on the planet thanks to the huge gas and oil reserves that sit within their territorial waters. Waters they have crossed historically to relieve the coastline of Britain and Ireland of many things. Gold, silver, tools, clothing – and women.

Historically this race of phenomenal seafarers was feared and revered in equal measure. If they came calling, they pretty much got what they wanted. The last word ever uttered by anyone stupid enough to wander over to a parked-up longboat was *hello*. You can never put those two halves of yourself back together after such a mistake.

But it wasn't just banditry. They began to trade, establish settlements and influence culture. Villages in Scotland, Ireland and north-western England were founded and flourished. Liverpool and Dublin have a deep Viking heritage. They went much further too, accidentally discovering Iceland while looking for Shetland. From there they reached the shores of Canada.

When Vikings come along, everything changes. Even in the world of sport. And they do like to mix things up a bit. Biathlon and Nordic Combined are sports Norwegians were made for. One combines cross-country skiing with shooting in an endurance competition that mimics hunting. The other mixes cross-country with ski jumping in a kind of *nothing gets in our way*, point-to-point. All very Viking. Cycling, on the other hand, was always a bit more marginal to Norwegians. It was viewed as a way of keeping fit during the short summer. The sport needed a hero. And it got one when along came King Knut. He turned the tide.

Knut Knudsen was virtually the founding father of Norwegian cycling. From 1972 he practically owned the 4000m Individual Pursuit. This World and Olympic Champion then went riding on the roads of Italy, where he won a total of six stages of the Giro d'Italia, wearing the Maglia Rosa twice during the races while going on to finish runner-up overall three times. Knudsen won the Tirreno–Adriatrico in 1979.

Eight years later, on Bastille Day in 1987, Dag Otto Lauritzen became the first Norwegian to win a stage of the Tour de France.

A decade later, Kurt Asle Arvesen began shaking things up, winning stages in all three Grand Tours.

And then came the great wave of sprinting hard men: Thor Hushovd, Alexander Kristoff and Edvald Boasson Hagen.

The Mighty Thor became Word Champion in 2010, the first Scandinavian to do this, and the first Norwegian to lead the Tour de France. He's widely regarded as the greatest Norwegian cyclist of all time – but he had company.

Alexander the Great started tearing up the classics. Milan–Sanremo and the Tour of Flanders as well as many other victories, with four stages of the Tour de France including the iconic Tour finalé up the Champs-Élysées in 2018.

In all types of terrain, Eddy Boss was making a noise even as a youngster. Ranked third in the world at 22 years old, he went kicking over hornets' nests on his TT bike. Ten times a National Champion and also three times National Road Race Champion; five stages of the Dauphiné; runner-up in the World Championships. Remarkable.

Such was the popularity of these three riders that cycling grew hugely in the national psyche. You will have seen the Norwegian Corner, the party zone on Stage 21 of the Tour. A little bit of Norway right there on the exit of the tunnel onto the Rue de Rivoli in Paris. There are so many Norwegian flags being waved, I'm surprised they can see the race go by. Lars Petter Nordhaug, Odd Christian Eiking, Vegard Stake Laengen or Kristoffer Halvorsen are their new heroes.

The kids of today would describe this success as totally sick. Which is ironic. I first tasted rakfisk about five years ago. I still have the aftertaste.

If you fancy trying rakfisk and joining a Viking party, there are a couple of choices: Tour of Norway or the Arctic Race. Of these two, the Arctic Race is the youngest and, to my mind, the best because of where it sits in the calendar.

The Tour of Norway ran seven times between 1983 and 1992 before taking a break. It was back on in 2011, usually running in May, and has been with us ever since. We've had the Tour of the Fjords, the Hammer Series and many other one-day races, all attesting to the exponential rise of cycling in Norway.

The World Championships even came calling in 2017. Bergen provided a fabulous backdrop to some amazing racing, where Peter Sagan made it three Elite Road Race world titles in a row.

But it is the the Arctic Race that does the business in every sense. It takes place at a key time in August for those targeting La Vuelta, the final Grand Tour of the season. With the backing of the Tour de France organisers A.S.O., it is phenomenally well run and has grown into a key event in the most spectacular surroundings. The field of riders is always a treat and there is something to test all types.

There has never been racing so close to the North Pole, and the geography enchants and surprises. Climbs like Storeheia or Korgfjellet may not be familiar to you, but this remarkable part of the world deserves your attention. There are rouleur stages passing along the edge of stunning, mirror-like fjords, sprinter stages into picturesque towns and villages, and full-on classic stages where the terrain begs for aggressive riding that is hard to control. Even sprinters get a look-in. It's got it all.

For me, Norway sells itself by its sheer beauty. But adding that Viking spirit to the mix makes for a very special kind of venue that the world of cycling ignored for far too long. Well, we are here now, and I strongly suggest you make time to visit this amazing part of the planet.

Just a couple of things you should know before you set off for the Arctic Race: never upset a Norwegian. Unless you are a lot bigger than them. And that is not likely. I came home from Norway with neck ache. Looking up for conversation is a rarity for me but even at 6' 3" (1.87m) I was 'the little guy' amongst most of the TV crew. My sound engineer friend Magnus was 6' 7" (1.97m) and considered himself 'average'.

Secondly if your rakfisk lunch comes in a tin, open it immersed in a bucket of water. The fermentation process produces pressure, and it will spurt everywhere. A colleague of mine foolishly opened one in his car. From that moment on, it smelt like a hearse.

So, if you are a team wanting a fine preparation race for La Vuelta, ask a Viking for help. If you just want to test your legs in the most stunning scenery you can possibly imagine on good roads without the punishing heat of the Mediterranean summer, give Norway a try.

And if you are hungry, stick to ham sandwiches. You'll thank me.

CYCLING LEXICON

The washing machine: The churning action of moving position within a fast-moving group.

TWENTY FOUR

CRITÉRIUM DU DAUPHINÉ
ACCORDION TO HIM

'Et voilà!' said the barman as he gently slid over a small dish of peanuts to go with my beer. 'You are 'ere for the festival?'

'Oui, certainement,' I replied. 'C'est enorme, non!?'

'It certainly is! We have been waiting for years, and finally it is here.'

I've always wondered at this polite duel between those who speak different languages but want to make a conversation more convivial by attempting to speak the other's tongue. On we went with our little linguistic dance, the barman speaking English and me French. It was all very nice with no irony to it. Just two middle-aged duffers trying to make the other feel comfortable. Now, to be honest, I'm usually the first to give up on this game, but on we went a little longer.

The Tour de France had just wheeled into town, taking over much of this rather strange but beautiful place, Puy-en-Velay, part of the pilgrim trail and heavy with religious iconography. To be honest I was a bit thrown by his talk of waiting for years – just two, I thought – but I parked this and we danced on.

'Who do you think will win?'

This was easy: 'Michael Matthews, l'Australien. Il est vite. Fort. Le favori pour moi.'

'Matthews? Australien? Which division? . . . aaaaaah, Les Étrangers. Of course. How is his button work?'

'Pardon???' This was me back in English, not French. I thought I must have missed something. 'He's pretty quick,' I offered.

But my answer clearly had a tiny hole in it for my friend. He began wiping down the zinc bar while looking at me with a wary air about him. He paused and stared at me. The mood had changed. All I could hear now was the mumble of conversations at the outside street tables and the intermittent squeak of a slow-turning ceiling fan. He looked me straight in the eyes and lent in to offer a slow statement laced with amused suspicion – as if he'd discovered the answer to a little secret.

'For me, the winner is a . . . Belgian.'

I nodded in mild quandary as a selection of Flemish riders raced through my head.

'He is "on the button" as we say.'

I was nodding in a sagely *I know what you mean* kind of way, as if we were sharing deep wisdom now. I took a moment for a gulp of beer, leaving a foam moustache behind; less than cool. I caught sight of it in the mirrored wall behind the bottles in front of me and slurped the lip clean as I lent in conspiratorially: 'Go on,' I said.

We were both smiling now. Our faces came a little closer together as he said softly: 'Patrice Balmond. He is the one.'

I sat up: 'Qui? I mean who? Is he with Cofidis?'

My friend exploded: Laughter, loud and long, and all the way to wheezing empty. Then a huge breath and a second wave – and on it went. He was struggling for breath. I had absolutely no clue what was happening.

Before he could gather himself to speak, still laughing but coming off peak, he slung the wet bar towel over his shoulder and slid over a flyer.

It read: *World Accordion Championships.*

In these parts it's not just about the Tour.

———

Cycling fans the world over know all too well that the Tour de France is in serious mode when it visits the Rhône-Alpes encompassing the Drôme, Ardèche, Haute-Loire, Puy de Dôme, Cantal, Rhône, Isère, Haute Savoie, and the Hautes-Alpes.

Sure, there are other amazing regions famed for cycling combat, but there is something special about this area of South Central Eastern France. Otherwise known, by my old pal David Duffield, as 'the lumpy stuff bordering Italy, up a bit from the Med, towards the middle.' I do miss Duffers.

The Rhône-Alpes is a spectacularly beautiful region and at the same time brutally challenging. Rivers like the Rhône, Loire, Isère and more are fed by the snowmelt from the mighty peaks that stand guard over the hardy folk who live here and the tough folk who race here. An area thought of as France profonde . . . deep France, real France. And also home to real racing.

For many this is where you find the beating heart of the Tour de France. Alright, yes, if you are Pyrenean, we are taking a huge liberty here, but we'll make up for that later.

In 1945 *Le Dauphiné Libéré* newspaper group was formed to bring local news to the folk of the Dauphiné. It was a way of binding the disparate areas of the great region together. Not by printing a region-wide paper, no. They decided what it really needed was no less than 24 different editions to be printed. Every day. Making local news really local, I guess.

This project was going to cost a lot and it was indeed a difficult start. They had to think of something to get the business moving. Headlines like 'Frédérick Étoile Mangé Mon Hamster' were not going to cut it. More was needed to fire up the readers.

Knowing the region was a favoured part of the mighty Tour de France, the newspaper proprietors decided to sponsor their own race with 'just the best bits of the Tour' as they saw it. And thus in 1947 the Critérium du Dauphiné Libéré was born. Suddenly they were shifting around 270,000 papers every day with front and back pages featuring their 'home race' and the bits in-between detailing the other news from your local version of the 24 daily editions. Remarkable.

And the race has been with us ever since. With only a short break in 1968 during the student riots, and also the year after; just in case it all kicked off again.

Visiting the race, you will discover many marvellous things in this part of France profonde. It is a spectacular mix of all things Gallic. The mighty Rhône and Loire rivers cut through the hills and mountains where boar hunting remains popular. The unlucky beasts form the essential ingredient of a wholesome casserole so rich and fragrant it should only be served in winter months, which tend to be short but harsh in the Dauphiné.

2023 saw the 75th edition of the Critérium de Dauphiné. We are talking proper history here. Its longevity is in no small part due to its place on the calendar, making the race the near perfect tune-up for the Tour de France itself.

Riders take on this mini-Tour which contains elements deliberately designed to mirror some of the tests to come in la Grande Boucle a few weeks later. You see, some of the very same roads used in July are run here. It could not be more convenient for teams with big summer plans to test legs and strategy over eight days of quality racing in the hills and alps of the Dauphiné.

Go well here, the theory goes, and you will thrive at the Tour de France. And since 2012 the Brits have made quite a habit of turning Dauphiné success into victory at the Tour. Indeed 7 out of 11 editions fell to those Brits who went on to lift The Big One on the Champs-Élysées. Happy days for Brad, Chris and Geraint, all built on a foundation of eight days of Dauphiné racing.

It makes for a spectacular roster of talent every season. Yes, there may be some exceptions to this rule. Old Black Socks himself, Lance Armstrong, preferred to do his thing in Switzerland, which has for some time overlapped the Dauphiné, thus functioning as a perhaps quieter alternative for those wanting to operate out of the spotlight – or in Lance's case, in the shadows.

The Tour de Suisse is, of course, a great race in its own right; but the kudos of the Dauphiné is placed just that little bit higher. And it's not just the roster of stars or the parcours that make it special; it is the public response as well. You see, there is great regional pride attached to an event which, like so many others, came about in a commercial deal to sell newspapers. The *Dauphiné Liberé* daily was the original sponsor, though the inevitable decline of the press led ultimately to the transfer of race husbandry to the Tour de France organisers, the A.S.O. It is in their capable hands that the renamed Critérium du Dauphiné has gone from strength to strength.

The crowds are impressive too. Always have been. The *Dauphiné Liberé* was the paper of choice for those whose doors the race passed by. And a big region it is too. Bigger than the map suggests . . . if you were to flatten it out, because what we are all here for are, of course, the Alps.

My, what a test it has always been. 2022 saw the final weekend feature the Col du Galibier, Croix de Fer, Grand Bournand, Colombière, Plateau de Solaison. The lead-up to that final weekend featured five days of 'barroudeur' stages and an individual time trial. The only riders not really catered for were pure sprinters. Frankly, the organisers had to work hard to find 39km (24 miles) of flat road to run the time trial. So the quick men were busy elsewhere in a host of one-day races designed to keep their engines running smoothly. The Dauphiné is for Grand Tour hopefuls wanting to measure themselves before the big one.

If you fancy dropping in to the event, I can spend hours recommending so many things about the region, but let me just say that Côte du Rhône is one of them. Please know that at any price point you care to explore Côte du Rhône will always be the best pick. Trust me, I have tried all the alternatives. It is so very good: reliable in the extreme, always satisfying, fruity-spicey, quick to please with a long finish . . . a metaphor for the race itself. The Critérium du Dauphiné.

———

Back at the bar it was getting late.

'Right now, the CIA control everything here in Puy-en-Velay,' said the barman.

'You are kidding me!' I said.

'No, it's true. They want to make sure there is no trouble. Sans polemic dans le competition.'

'Ah . . . Are we talking accordéons again?' I ventured.

'OF COURSE!' said my new best buddy.

'Le Confédération Internationale des Accordéonistes . . . what do you think I am talking about?'

'Oh nothing, my friend . . . give me another glass of Côte du Rhône, would you? Juste un petit boule before bed, I'm up early. There's a race on, you know!'

CYCLING LEXICON

Fishtail: Rear wheel locking and slewing sideways when using rear brake over aggressively.

JULY

TWENTY FIVE

TOUR, FINALÉ
CHAMPS FOR CHAMPS ON THE CHAMPS

'Rob, I've got a terrible feeling they are going to win this!'

'Naaaah, Brazil are just too strong. Mind you, Ronaldo looks a bit peaky.'

Just then the camera gave my Dutch pal and I a brief look at the man who struck fear into all of France – and he wasn't well at all. A good or bad omen depending on your loyalty.

We had planted ourselves in yet another Irish pub clone to watch the World Cup final. This was a big deal in France. Honestly, the fuss they made when the Handball Team won the 1995 World Championship was extraordinary. 'The first time a French team had won a World title . . . in any sport,' explained a Eurosport producer candidly. 'We are not really team players here in France. We like to do things on our own, in our own way, like Hinault.'

Still basking in the reflected glory of the 1985 Tour and the Badger's fifth win . . .

As this was 1998, the pain of the long drought of French winners of Le Tour was, at this point, just a dull ache. It had only been 13 years. Little did they know the discomfort of watching other nations take the yellow jersey abroad was set to smoulder and intensify over the coming decades.

So here we were, watching the 1998 World Cup Final. France was ready to let rip and indeed Brazil, the tournament favourites, were being bamboozled early on by a French side that simply ran riot. It took 20 minutes for Brazil to have a shot on target . . . while 'Dinner's in de Oven' as I was childishly calling the France captain Zinedine Zidane, was simply majestic; teeing up chance after chance . . . this looked ominous.

'I reckon this is going to get a bit tiresome if they score, Rob. We should have an exit plan.'

Naturally being slightly boorish, and not a little drunk, we had been busy supporting Brazil. As chances started to come for the men in gold and blue, France keeper Fabian Barthez was being forced to make some great saves and we were getting animated. We were not rooting for France. To be fair, our slightly too loud *ooos* and *aahs* were being tolerated. But as every French chance went awry and Brazil looked more threatening, the pub was getting restive. More than the occasional frosty glance came our way. Our tipsy jollity was clearly starting to irk.

Truth be told, I didn't give a damn who won the game – I'm a cycling nut for goodness' sake – but I began to realise that we might be in a bit of trouble should Brazil go on to win this World Cup Final.

'Rob, I think we had better dial it down a bit. If France score, we should . . . cheer, maybe?'

'No fuckin' way,' said Rob in that deeply Dutch cantankerous way.

Then the roof blew off.

A corner from Petit was met by 'Dinner's in de Oven' . . . who apparently never scored with his head. BOOOOOM!!!!

France 1–0 Brazil.

As the place exploded and I cheered – just in time to acceptably join the mayhem – Rob took my cue, punching the air in cod ecstasy. Insurance. Our safety now a little more certain.

France were now rampant but were not adding to their tally. They hit the side netting, squandered chances in front of goal. '*Plus tard!!*' was the group refrain. We tried to appear sympathetic.

'Imagine if they could actually finish off any of these moves,' said Rob, about to dip his top lip into the creamy head of a freshly poured Beamish. He never got to take the drink.

No sooner were the words out of Rob's mouth than another corner swings in, to be met by the man who never scores with his head. Zinedine Z'again, as I was now calling him. Half time: 2–0.

'Let's go, Rob. This is not our party.'

We climbed on board his Vespa, as unlike a scene from *Roman Holiday* as you could imagine.

We weaved about the deserted streets with me hugging Rob like a hibernating bear: eyes closed, goofy smile. Absolutely no eyes were upon us as we wobbled drunkenly along empty Bois de Boulogne avenues back to our hotel.

Just as we pulled up there was another city-wide roar . . . a strange thing to hear. The entire country had just risen to its feet in rapture.

'Let's go to the Champs-Élysées,' I said. 'It'll be mega.'

'OK, CK . . . hold on!'

I remember that ride fondly. We were on the quai following the route the Tour takes on its way to 'le circuit' that draws the great race to a climax. And as France was a bit busy elsewhere at that moment we enjoyed the full loop with absolutely nothing to disturb us.

We buzzed past Eurosport offices over Pont d'Issy onto the North Bank. Mid bridge you get a phenomenal view of the Eiffel Tower in the near distance. Flood lit against a black sky like a vast amber tree. No time to ponder . . . big pinch point coming up with a right-hander onto the famed Quai itself – Baron

Hausseman's wonderful expressway into town. He was given carte blanche to redesign the city by Napoleon III. He swept a lot of the original buildings and their higgledy-piggledy medieval streets away to create the grand avenues and the spectacular signature buildings we know so well today. It was radical and modern back then. Who'd've thought of building multilane highways into town in the nineteenth century? Well, he hadn't imagined the arrival of the car; the idea was to move armies around. They still do on 14 July in celebration of the République. Of course, Hitler found it handy too, but we won't dwell on that.

The City of Light is just that, even at night, particularly this night: there is just so much space. It makes many other European capitals feel hemmed in.

The Quai itself is genius, dipping down to the water's edge, bobbing under tunnels as it passes by the Grand and then Petit Palais. Then, still hugging the Seine, the road lifted us up to Pont Neuf as we speared between the Trocadéro and the Eiffel Tower, each designed to look at each other. We did too and burst out laughing as we sprang into ironic song. It was fantastic.

For weeks our French colleagues had been singing a hugely annoying ditty into our faces: 'Allez en final . . . allez en final . . .allez, allez, allez en final.'

After they made the final, this conveniently adaptable refrain became:

'Champions du monde, champions du monde, champions, champions, champions du monde.'

Naturally, as we were both cycling nuts and foreigners, our song was a little different but it also fitted the template.

'We don't give a fuck, we don't give a fuck, we don't, we don't, we don't give a fuck.' Magic!

We went on to sing this all night, smiling into the faces of rapture as they sang their version back at us, assuming we were joining in . . . but all the while we were keeping something back for ourselves.

At that moment, though, we were the only people in this beautiful and amazing city who were not watching Le Match. It was dream-like.

Onwards to the quai side of the Louvre, we took the big left into the tunnel which emerges in front of the gilded statue of Jeanne d'Arc. Another 90° left at Norwegian Corner onto the Rue de Rivoli. This is the crucial point of the final stage of La Grande Boucle. Past WH Smith on our right, we sped onto the Place de la Concorde with its majestic green and gold fountains. It's here you hit cobbles for the first time. They were once covered in asphalt on the orders of Général de Gaulle, who didn't like students digging cobbles up and chucking them at the National Guard during the riots. Over the years this rude surface has worn down to reveal, once more, the beautiful fan shapes of the original cobbles won so painfully by those serving hard labour who cut them from granite as part of their punishment for goodness knows what.

Gentle high-speed left, cutting diagonally to the Tour's final corner – a quite benign right-hander but so, so important to get right on the day. In 2012 Bradley Wiggins in his yellow skinsuit shot around this corner at the head of a magnificent Sky leadout train for Mark Cavendish . . . or Lord Élysées as we called him. He practically owned the place. Boss that last corner if you can and your rivals are trapped behind your line . . . Perfection would see faster and faster teammates peeling off before Cav' got released. Fast twitch muscles at full revs.

Up on the hill, staring back at us, the Arc de Triomphe. Rob hunched into a sprinting position with me acting as air brake, taking in the view along with the breeze. I just burst out laughing. This was it . . . the finish line!

I threw my arms in the air as I crossed what became Cav's line. Bloody marvellous.

We sped on up the rise . . . around the Arc and l'Étoile, returning down the other side of the boulevard until we passed the metro at Franklin D, near the gardens where the team busses and television trucks would station themselves for Stage 21.

Just as all of France was watching the trophy being lifted, we parked up outside the Hôtel Plaza Athénée and walked back down Avenue Montaigne towards the fountains at the centre of the Champs-Élysées.

We sat down on a marble bench looking up at the Arc de Triomphe . . . it's a magnet in times of celebration, and the hordes were now being drawn to it. There was no great dash to get there. It was more like a slowly filling bath. But France wasn't running any more; they were ambling in bemused, numb wonderment. It was quite something to behold. They simply couldn't believe what had just happened to them. A team, the French team, had won 'Ze Fooking War-ld Coup!', beating multiple world champions Brazil 3–0 in the process.

'Hey, Cyrile!' I called out to a Eurosport colleague I spotted draped in the Tricolour. He looked a little bashful but was beaming. He shouted over: 'You will allow me this night, I hope!?' We gave him the thumbs up as he was swallowed by the throng.

We stayed perhaps another 20 minutes. Just watching the vast boulevard fill to the brim. There must've been a million or more people there, I'd never seen anything like it.

Around this time, the first windows shattered. 'Bedtime, CK!' We made our way back against the tide of those mobbing the boulevard that a short time ago had been deserted. The doorman at the Athénée was concerned. He gave us a nod as if to approve our departure while clearly wishing he could do the same.

Turned out we had done the right thing. The next day the Champs-Élysées looked like a war zone. Luxury shop windows were smashed by looters along the full reach of the boulevard. Many people were injured too. And not a mention of any of this in the press the following day. The World Cup was too big to dent.

'Bloody football fans wrecking our boulevard,' said the cycling producer. 'Pas de respect.'

And he was right. Paris belongs to cycling, and vice versa. Ask anyone with a passing knowledge of the sport, and they will conjure up in their mind that final wondrous day in celebration of the sport we love as it bobbles its way to a majestic finalé upon its finest cobbled boulevard.

We lent it to another sport that day. They bruised it . . . but three weeks later we got it back.

———

Welcome to the Sprinters' World Cup!

The final day of the Tour de France is amazing. It is a very big deal, as you know, but particularly for the quick men. It's the one stage of all races that the fastest riders on the planet regard as their very own. You see, the game is over for those going for the Yellow Jersey. For the skinny guys their battles are behind them: Stage 21 is their parade.

It's always a convivial atmosphere as we start with the rollout, usually somewhere impressive beyond the Paris Ring Road, the Périphérique. It's a familiar format: somewhere a bit Chateau-y, you know: nice backdrop for cycling royalty and all that. A starting point for Le smacking de la gob . . . as they don't say. But you get the idea.

So, as we depart one of the houses of one of the Napoleons, coverage is filled with skinny blokes with champagne in plastic flutes being handed out of team cars containing grinning Sports Directors and the occasional VIP Herbert who's not sure how to smile.

This festival atmosphere goes on for over an hour or so with a series of on-the-move photo opportunities making up what struggles to substitute for action.

If this were a wedding, then Camera Bike 01 would be the equivalent of Colin from Synergy Photographic in Stevenage whose flyer claims they *Make Magic Happen* (while also making a bloody nuisance of themselves with flapping arms and pointy fingers). The mildly compliant yet vaguely distracted subjects need to be corralled into a series of set-ups. It finds such camera operators verbally bouncing from Sergeant Major to Support Councillor in a trice.

'Right, can I have the groom's family now . . . GROOM'S FAMILY! PLEASE!!' Then dropping aggressive just long enough to offer: 'Lovely, that's lovely . . . eyes on me now . . . wonderful . . . I SAID EYES ON ME!!!!! Aaaaaand, there we go! Beautiful. RIGHT, EVERYONE . . . I NEED THE GROOM AND THE BEST MAN . . . WHERE'S THE BEST MAN, PLEASE???'

Geraint Thomas is missing; he's gone for a piss. And Chris Froome couldn't care less because he's now having a chat with Dan Martin.

The cameraman heads over to the parents of the groom. 'Monsieur Brailsford, s'il vous plaît!!!! OÙ EST MONSIEUR G?'

They say never work with animals or children. Well, cyclists are a combination of both. A bit juvenile and not given to following instruction from anyone but their real masters.

So good luck with that, Colin . . . . Or rather Maurice from Euromedia who is trying to complete the same task. It's chaos.

But do not despair. Within the happy ranks of party guests, you will always find those for whom such a big day of celebration will only be truly memorable if it ends with a mighty punch-up. They are the ones with the poker face in the group shots. The ones with thick necks and shirts buttoned up too tightly . . . or indeed skin suits and aero helmets. Do not mess around with the hard men. They have war in mind.

'THANK YOU, EVERYONE . . . WE WILL DO THE GREEN JERSEY LATER.'

———

Yes, I know there have been final stages of La Grande Boucle that have decided Yellow. Time trials usually, the most famous being Greg LeMond's victory over Laurent Fignon in 1989. The margin? Just 8 seconds. I can still hear the France Television commentator's plaintive call . . . 'C'EST PERDU!!' Well, it was lost for France. But it was also won for America.

Despite such outliers, it's safe to say the final stage of the Tour de France is for the sprinters. And where do you start? In my time calling them home, it has always produced drama.

2005 – When the pure sprinters got their timing wrong and Alexander Vinokourov miraculously held on for the win as the sprinting hounds' jaws closed on his tail.

2006 and 2007 – Wins for Thor Hushovd sent Norway into rapture. He had so many fans camping at the tunnel exit turn in front of Jeanne d'Arc that the Norwegian corner was duly named.

2008 – All the stars aligned and so did the lead-out train for Geert Steegmans. The Belgian Tramcar proving that an endurance sprinter, on rails and up to pace from distance, cannot be caught. A win memorable not least because I roared with laughter on-air that day . . . having backed him!

2009 – Mark Cavendish's first 'Sprint World Cup' win, one of four consecutive Tour finalé stage wins for the great man. A run that made us consider renaming the famous arch 'Le Mark de Triomphe'. It felt like he owned the place.

2013 – The return of another occupation force from Germany, Kittel edging André Greipel. The pair of them then dominating Stage 21 for four years with two wins apiece.

Then came Dylan Groenewegen, Alexander Kristoff, Caleb Ewan, Sam Bennett, Wout van Aert – a truly international roster of the very quickest on the planet. Wonderful.

It takes a career's worth of hard graft to pull off a win on the Champs-Élysées. Any sprinter is going to struggle in the mountains, so just getting to Paris is a phenomenal achievement in itself. And then, when they do arrive, they come up against a field of rivals like no other.

Time to perform on the biggest stage of the sprinting year. After the hard work there comes the demand for bravery, power and timing, mixed with a little madness. Then, and only then, if all these things come together . . .

sprinting magic happens. It's a day like no other and one that simply must be experienced.

'CAN WE GET ONE WITH ALL THE JERSEYS TOGETHER NOW, PLEASE!!!??

'Oh piss off, Colin. It's over . . . We're having a drink!'

CARLTON COMMENTARY

'Mouth agape like a basking shark.'
To describe any rider gasping for breath

AUGUST

TWENTY SIX

TOUR VTT (MBK)
SKINNY DIP DANGER

'Can't . . . stand . . . it . . . any . . . more!' I murmured into the pitch darkness of my baking prison cell.

It wasn't just the intense heat; the air hung heavy and deathly still. I was cooking and gradually beginning to simmer. I sat hunched over my crossed legs upon a drenched sleeping bag. Then two salty beads of sweat teamed up, with torture in mind. Into my left eye they sped. I was livid. Time to escape.

The Lac de Verney sits high in the French Alps approximately 7600km (4720 miles) from Calcutta, but here I was in a black hole of my own making. I'd pitched my tent on a limestone gravel spit at the lake's middle shore while performing what must've looked like a Ninja shadow-boxing exercise.

You see, I have a pathological fear of the mosquito . . . and he was here, along with his Savoyard family freshly emerged from the mirror-flat mountain reservoir just 20m (66ft) from my spot. Since sunset my tiny friends had been doing their level best to latch on for dinner. Well, I wasn't having any of that bollocks.

When I say I don't get on with mosquitoes, I mean I have a real problem with their anti-coagulant; the stuff the little bastards pump into you to help the blood flow more easily into their bellies. I have a *very* bad reaction to this. One man's mosquito bite is this man's swollen, half cricket ball, blister-mound – which will scar. And then become a permanent aide-memoire to yet another shit night and itchy nights thereafter.

So, to avoid waking the next day looking like I'd been beaten with spanners, I pitched my tent in a flurry of Keystone Cops' style activity, often breaking away on looping runs off and then back to my humble accommodation. Upon each return, panting heavily, I would fix another pole to its keep, then hare off again as the flying teeth started whining.

I had performed about six of these circuits before the tent was ready. Zip undone, I didn't want any nibbling guests inside, so I set off for the final time just as one of my thousand new friends bumped into my right eye. It was felled by a meaty blink but was now trapped under my top eyelid. As I jogged, yelping and fumbling for its corpse, all I did was push it deeper around to the back of my eye socket. What the hell use are these bastards anyway?

My last loop was the climax for anyone who might've been watching the show. Running with one finger in my eye and the free arm hay-baling an invisible insect cloud, I sprinted the last circuit like a madman, then dived home and zipped shut the fly screen.

'Ha-hah,' I shouted at the rapidly forming mozzie posse on the fine netting.

'TA GUEULE!!' screamed another grumpy camper. Now this, directly translated, is rudely overfamiliar French and means 'Your hole!' – a very abusive way of telling someone to shut up. I did.

But first, feeling triumphant, I eased up close to the flysheet for a chat, whispering softly: 'Starve, you bastards!!!!'

The Tour VTT, Mountain Biking's blue riband event, had come to town. Its modest caravan was now settling down for the night. Unlike its older, far more famous and far better funded illustrious cousin, Le Tour de France, this younger Tour was exclusively for those with knobbly tyres and had only the most rudimentary accommodation: tents. At least I was alone in mine. Some teams shared eight to a teepee. Cosy.

The Tour VTT ran for four years in the mid 1990s and was all set for a return in 2020 before it got COVID cropped – like so many other great, long planned for events.

———

Over the years, the Tour VTT may have lacked some continuity on the calendar, but that in no way diminishes its importance to mountain bikers. They often reflect on the amazing quality of the rosters that attended this rare gem. It's the stuff of Mountain Biking folklore. In 1996 the start list included a very young Australian teenager, Cadel Evans, who later won the Tour de France and the World Championship on the road. Swiss Superstar Thomas Frischknecht was competing, widely regarded as the father of the Mountain Biking scene. And also a very young Miguel Martinez, who that year won Bronze at the inaugural Mountain Bike event at the Atlanta Olympics, turning that to Gold at the Sydney Games four years later. Martinez, the man who is, remarkably, still competing at the age of 46 at Continental level with Amore & Vita–Prodir.

Though it came directly after the Tour de France had been completed, the A.S.O. somehow persuaded everyone involved in the production of the great race to stay on for another ten days of fun for this Mountain Bike fiesta. It was sold to the broadcast crew as a kind of Tour after-party . . . and the organisers did their best to make it fun for everyone involved. Each night was party-time. All dining bills were covered, wine and beer included. 'Order what you want and the tab will be taken care of,' said the race plan. Well, we didn't need asking twice. The natural response was to dive right in . . . deep. Every night! It was exhausting.

Now, I've always marvelled at the apparent 'right to revolt' that is so widely maintained in France. On so many occasions I have witnessed perfectly genial and sensible colleagues simply lose it, usually when full of grape juice in its myriad forms. And, being a bit of a stiff Brit, this can be quite an experience. In France what they regard simply as 'emotional freedom of expression' is what we on the north side of the Channel might call 'a rowdy piss-up'.

Earlier this steaming night, we had gathered at a mountaintop village and taken over the modest square. The locals had been out bought. Smartly dressed grumpy farmers and their wives were turned away from the only gig in town: a small brasserie with every one of its tables for two sweatily occupied to bursting point by at least four hot and hungry VTT Tour badge holders.

Entrée: Paté (take it or leave it).

Plat: Poulet frîtes, Steak frîtes, Soupe de Poisson.

Fromage.

Pichet de Vin: Rouge.

Pain.

Job done.

As well as the bread, the other thing on the menu that was à volonté was the wine. Oooops!

The mood throughout the meal was jovial, save for a minor scuffle between two of the race security motorcyclists who'd each been making a fool of themselves over the previous two days in pursuit of a rather pretty young VT editor. As the wine flowed and the imbalance of hydration took hold, one of the barrier boys stumbled over to the beautiful war memorial drinking fountain in the centre of the square and buried his head in the water. He drank as heartily as any caveman would. Suddenly this looked like a fabulous idea. Within minutes the fountain was accommodating a dozen drinkers. With bums in the air. This aquatic frenzy looked like puppy feeding time at the rescue centre. There was jostling.

Gazing over their bobbing arses, I noticed the old lead sign asking for respectful use of the fountain in memory of those who had fallen in the war . . . Napoleonic.

Just then someone lent over the drinking crew with a bucket and perhaps the innocent intent of serving those without a place at the trough. But as he returned to the tables he began to smile . . . Everyone knew what this meant.

Now, despite the fact that on this hot night a dousing of water would surely have been most welcome, we scattered. It was the first act in 40 minutes of absolute mayhem. Any and every conceivable vessel was filled and hurled empty with enthusiastic abandon.

It is probably still remembered in hushed terms of disdain at that pretty place. *La nuit du l'eau*, it might be called. They will recount much. And maybe in particular an Englishman spotted by one of the producers who called out: 'REGARDEZ CARLTON!! . . . IL EST SEC!!! IL EST SEC!!!!' At which point the still dry Englishman realised his time was up. He dutifully put his treasured Minox half-frame camera in a plant pot and, rather theatrically, marched, cod-military style, up to the fountain. There he came to attention and saluted the fallen while singing 'God Save the Queen'.

I think I managed to get half of the first stanza away before a full fire-bucket of cold mountain water exploded on me. It was wonderful fun.

Four hours later I was wet once more, but not in such a nice way. Now desperately hot and with a pounding hangover headache just beginning to chime in; it was time to make a break for it – the lake, that is – after first fumbling for my underpants. I'm not French, ya know!

From the viewpoint of any alpinist who might've been up high contemplating the valley far below, it may have looked like a firefly in action. My bluey-white Irish skin, fairly dayglo by night, was zigzagging water-ward as I deftly placed my feet between stones and the odd cowpat.

I was so hot that when I did eventually dive in I'm sure there was a sizzling sound like a blacksmith dousing a horseshoe.

What I didn't expect was the cold.

Oh . . . my . . . God!

You can go glacier skiing throughout the summer in the French Alps. So the mountains which feed this reservoir are high and the water is snowmelt. I was being brought back down to chilled rather quickly. It was, in the purest sense, breathtaking; I couldn't really speak. All I could do was make noises of sheer relief. 'Oooh . . . ayyyyy . . . ooo. . . pff . . .'

Gradually I calmed into silence and just floated there, occasionally looking back at VTT Tent City while wondering why nobody else was doing the same. 'Too pissed,' I murmured to myself.

The next sound I made was 'uh-oh!'

Some way off to my right a dog had launched itself into the water. I heard the splash and looked over. It was heading my way!

I didn't worry too much at first, but as it got to within about 50m (164 ft) or so, I could see its teeth. It was growling!

Then the barking and shouting began. There were three of us involved: one dog barking and two humans shouting . . . me and the bloke on the bankside. It was quite muted at first, almost half-hearted:

ME: Just piss off, will ya . . .
DOG: *Woof!*
BLOKE: Oh verdomde hel!

But as the dog got closer, all parties got a bit more animated . . .

ME: AAAAH!!!
DOG: Woof, *woof,* WOOF!!! (translation: I'M GOING TO RIP YOUR BOLLOCKS OFF!!!)
BLOKE: AAAAH!!!

I was in full panic mode, thrashing about, trying to splash the dog away . . . I know: splashing . . . it's all I had.

And then, all of a sudden, silence. At least, from me and the dog.

Up he swam and had a really good look at me. I couldn't speak.

He sniffed and snuffled; sneezed a bit of water in my face; gave a sort of disappointed whine . . . maybe a doggy apology; turned and swam back to shore. Where his owner was now trying to sound encouraging: 'Goede hond, Zephyr . . . goede hond!

I regained my faculties. 'WHAT THE HELL WAS THAT, MY FRIEND?'

'So sorry. Jongere . . . come over!'

As I approached the shore the dog was on a leash by the man's side and wagged as I emerged from the water . . . weed-stained Y-fronts doing their best to stay sartorial.

'He thought you were a seal, sir! Apologies to you.'

Turns out my mate here was a fish farmer on the Dutch coast. His dog's job was to protect his nets from seals who wanted an easy meal of the sea trout he reared.

'He vos joost do-ink his job, you see? I walk him at night when there are no swimmers in the lake. Except tonight of course!'

He gave a kind of apologetic nervous chuckle. I guess for all he knew I might have been dangerous. I was certainly dressed like Superman . . . undies on display and all.

I wasn't angry I was just knackered. 'Good night' was all I contributed to the exchange as I turned for my tent.

And it was a good night. I lay down with a core temperature now low enough to take me soundly off to sleep. Others didn't fare so well.

In the morning the riders awoke covered in mosquito bites. Two actually made the news section of the highlights show because they could not ride. Both had been bitten so badly on the face they needed vast doses of antihistamines that made them too dopey to race. One of the poor guys couldn't open his eyes properly anyway, his badly bitten eyelids were so swollen. I think I got off lightly.

When I did open up my tent in the morning, there was a loosely wrapped package at the door. It was a Dutch sausage. A note on the paper said simply: 'Sorry' and was signed: 'Kees & Zephyr' with an x-kiss and a paw drawing, which I took for a doggy high five.

———

The Tour VTT does not exist any more. They have tried to reincarnate it several times – but it just won't stick financially, I guess. Running such a race directly after the Tour de France was always going to be a bit optimistic. Three weeks of La Grande Boucle is enough to fatigue not just the viewer, no matter how committed a cycling nut, but also the camera guys and support staff. Asking some of them to stay on for what amounted to another fortnight, what with set-up schedules and all, was a bit much. Effectively five or six weeks away from home. There was also the fact that every two years the event would be smothered by either the football World Cup or the Olympics. Basically, mountain biking is often bullied by other sports and cycling disciplines that steal the limelight. The Tour VTT, however great, was no exception.

You could say mountain biking has been around since the late 1800s. You could argue that even before then the bone shaker was adapted to rough ground with leaf springs brought in to help preserve the undercarriage of those messengers using them. But it was the US Army that recognised the potential of adapting bikes for rough ground found in a war situation. The 25th Infantry Bicycle Corps was formed in 1896.

Cycle-cross became its own sport around the 1940s, whereby machines designed to maintain winter fitness were then put to the test in formalised races. So it was only natural that as the bikes got more specialised, some might think of exploring even rougher terrain.

The first real mountain bike adaptations took place in the United States. Fire roads in the heavily forested areas of California and Colorado were the playgrounds. These rough tracks were there to give fire crews a chance during occasional wildfires, some of which might have been started by early mountain bikers themelves!

The first rudimentary designs were based on Schwinn cruisers with drum hub brakes. So heavy was the breaking on these downhill mountain tracks that the oil within them would sometimes catch fire and the riders would have to repack the drum with new bearings and oil. Soon, of course, there was real racing, the events themselves called Repack races.

It wasn't until 1978 that Joe Breeze produced what is regarded as the first purpose-built mountain bike. Tom Ritchey then took it to the next level with a company called, naturally enough, MountainBikes. A formalised design and a growing movement meant big manufacturers were quick to get involved. Trek, who liked Richey's products so much that they bought the company, began mass production.

It was now mountain bike boomtime: so much so that in 1988, 15 years after I modified my own road bike, I got involved and bought myself a scarlet red Diamond Back Topanga. Nobody in Norwich knew what the hell it was. And yes, I know, there are not too many mountains in Norfolk, leave me alone. I still blast around Richmond Park on my trusty steed – and yes, I know there are not too many mountains there either.

The Tour VTT may be dead, but mountain biking is alive and well in the Alps and, of course, globally. You can still find stage races for the discipline, but there are also amazing stand-alone events to be enjoyed worldwide. If you want to have a go, then may I make a suggestion?

The Sella Ronda Hero event at Val Gardena is amazing.

It's a festival that draws in tens of thousands of mountain bikers to a race that is simply a riotous, joyous mix of mayhem and elite sport. At the start, what feels like a thousand riders go off in waves with the elite stars off first. The field is wide in terms of ability, so you will find a place to start. Just pay your money and have a go. You won't see much of those upfront battling for the win, but you'll have a blast with like-minded riders prepared to test themselves on a course designed for the best.

Mountain biking. It's not just a sport, it's a community. You will find friends wherever there are mountains on this planet. And sometimes, like me and my pal Zephyr, where there are lakes too.

CYCLING LEXICON

Wheel sucking: Sitting in a rider's draft while refusing to take a turn.

SEPTEMBER

TWENTY SEVEN

TOUR OF BRITAIN
SHEEP BENDING

ONE THOUSAND AND ONE . . . ONE THOUSAND AND TWO . . . ONE THOUSA – BOOF!

Never has a sight been more welcome than that bloody parachute opening . . . I burst out laughing at the sheer relief. It was the most beautiful thing in my life at that moment . . . but only for a moment you understand, before something far more stunning captured me: the sun under a blanket of cloud lighting up the sea off Morecambe Bay towards Northern Ireland. Never did Great Britain's western coastline look so beautiful . . . Hanging there facing into the light, I was coming down vertically and able to enjoy the view running all the way down towards the Welsh borders and up to Furness at the foot of the Lake District and the borders of Scotland. A truly national vision. It was quite a moment.

I hung there half-cupped in my seat straps with bent arms holding the steering toggles. Almost dreamily I watched my fellow novices falling out of the gently buzzing Cessna above me, their static lines doing the job of opening their creamy shoots just like mine. In that surreal moment we looked like jellyfish, I thought to myself, as the faint sound of the aircraft served only to emphasise the quiet. This . . . was lovely.

The only thing stopping me melting into the moment was the hammered-home mantra of Alan, our jump instructor, his nasally, nerd-with-power, spotlight-moment message ringing loud:

'The forward descending rate of a parachute of the type you are using will be around 7 miles an hour – which is jogging quickly. Like when you are running – quite fast. Do you understand?'

All together: 'Yes, Alan, we understand.'

'And the wind speed is added to this velocity. Do you understand?'

Slightly more uncertain: 'Yes, Alan, we . . . understand.'

'So if the wind is blowing at 8 miles an hour and you are running *with* the wind, how fast are you moving forward?'

I put my hand up. 'Fifteen miles an hour?'

'Yes indeedy!'

I was now top of Alan's class. The other jump students were each giving me a *don't encourage him, FFS* kind of look. I put my hand down quickly.

'Yes, FIFTEEN miles an hour . . . and that is at best today . . . and this can get a bit tricky when you are landing!'

'Your parachutes are designed to save lives, not to Charlie about in the sky showing off. They are emergency bail-out chutes from the US Airforce. They are guaranteed to open. You can steer them, but they are not designed to mess about with. No, their design is simply to get you to the ground safely and quickly. So you will land hard and you will land fast. And . . . you will land *too fast* if you are running with the wind . . . WHAT DO WE NOT WANT TO DO WHEN WE LAND?'

All together: 'We do not want to run with the wind, Alan . . .'

'CORRECT!'

So there I was with a forward motion of 7 miles per hour being mitigated by a wind blowing around the same speed. I was coming down vertically. Job done.

Not quite. The idea was that after the chute had opened we were to get our bearings and, using the left and right toggles, steer ourselves until we were over the airfield. At this point we would then turn to face into the wind for a safe landing. But, as usual with me, I had a problem. Because I had been so busy admiring the scenery, I was now too low to make the trip back to our base. I was way off course. And so, as is also usual with me, I duly panicked. I knew I had no chance of making it all the way back, but I still decided to give it a go. I turned for home and ran with the wind. Sorry, Alan!

Travelling at between 15 and 20 miles an hour (24–32 km/h) in the forlorn hope of making it back to the muddy airstrip, I was losing altitude quickly.

Nearby I spotted a speeding Land Rover pick-up on the country lanes. Alan was bobbling about, hanging out of the passenger window and screaming into a megaphone: 'TURN INTO THE WIND!! RIGHT NOW!! . . . NOOOOOOOOOOOW!!!!'

Ground rush is a weird thing. You have absolutely no natural concept of the pace of your descent until the very last moment. The world seems a long way away. From the start of the jump until perhaps the last 150ft (45m), you see the earth as a distant unthreatening thing; off, over there, out of harm's way. Then at the last moment it suddenly races towards you at an ungodly pace. It's freakish.

THE GROUND WAS COMING TO GET ME!!! I yanked the left toggle too hard and went into a dramatic half spiral just before I slammed into Planet Earth.

It felt like a crash.

There are two kinds of cyclist: those who have been down hard, and those who are going to go down hard. Those who have already made that short trip know all about having the wind knocked out of you. The body involuntarily empties itself of wind on impact. Being heavily winded in a crash results in a strange phenomenon as the air is expelled. You moo like a cow with the forced exhalation. This can go on for quite a while before you inhale again.

My moos were now being matched by frantic bleating from the flock of sheep I had just speared through, knocking several over in the process.

Mooooooooooooooo – Baaaaaaaaaa went our exchange.

I knelt with fists in the mud, trying to give my diaphragm a chance to pump air back into my lungs. And as urgent panting stabilised into breathing once again, I became aware of Alan's wellies about six feet away. His hands were on his hips and he was not happy.

'Heh!' was all I could muster.

He just pointed to my chute before trudging back to the pick-up. I collected my silken bundle and sloped over.

'Get in the back,' said Alan.

'Can't I get inside, please? I'm freezing!'

That dreadful voice again: 'You are shivering due to mild shock, it's not cold. And you are also covered in shit . . . so in the back.'

I was no longer Alan's top student.

I slumped, stinking, upon my balled-up parachute as we jiggled home. Despite my thumping return to it, Britain's countryside is amazing. The sky remained stunning; the hills were as green as any you might ever imagine; and I wore the dreamy uncertain smile of an incident survivor.

The Tour of Britain is a wonderful race. It threads its way around this great island and, in an attempt to live up to its name, has made a good job, over the years of visiting most corners of the nation. The race shares its wares evenly and is all the more wonderful for it.

The history of the Tour of Britain has occasionally been as bumpy as Wales and occasionally as flat as Lincolnshire. But it is has become, under the stewardship of Mick Bennett, truly Great. To many casual observers, the UK is now a hotbed of cycling fanatics who have produced a string of superstars dominating the sport for the past decade. But the history of the sport on Crazy Island, as my pals in France call it, goes back a long way.

The Tour of Britain has now found itself with a place in the calendar that makes it perhaps the ultimate preparation event for the World Championships. Its stock has risen exponentially in the pro ranks over the past decade or so, reflected in start lists heavy with diamonds.

But this international sparkle was not always there. Planning for a Tour of Britain began while the Blitz was raging. Two years after the Battle of Britain, the British League of Racing Cyclists was created in 1942: and just two years later, as the Battle of the Bulge was raging in Belgium, the Southern Grand Prix took place in Kent . . . under the overhead whirring of doodlebugs.

That all went rather nicely and so, in 1945, just as things on the Continent were drawing to a close, optimism was sweeping the nation and a race from Brighton to Glasgow was run.

Then, mercifully, the war ended. A strained nation duly went back to football, rugby, welly chucking and conkers. Britain was skint. City mayors were too busy rebuilding infrastructure to be bothered with a cycling event coming to town. Sport is easy if all you need is a ball, a welly or a conker. Bikes were not cheap, and so dreams of a full Tour of Britain withered on the vine under the post-war gloom.

All looked lost until 1958 when some bright spark at the Milk Marketing Board came up with a sponsorship package in support of a national cycling race. The name was a bit different, however: The Milk Race.

Now, it's not the sexiest title. The race wasn't either. Indeed from 1960 to 1984 it was entirely confined to the amateur ranks. Nothing wrong with that. A great many elite sports were the same: Rugby Union, Tennis, Track and Field. But cycling didn't really capture the imagination of the nation until 1985 when it went . . . professional! Sponsors, money, PRIZES!!!!

Suddenly, with the arrival of elite athletes, press interest spiked. So much so that a rival event sprang up in 1987: keeping it at the breakfast table, the first Kellogg's Tour.

For seven years there were effectively two Tours of Britain. This was so British – and so British Cycling. If someone has an idea, instead of people uniting behind it, there is a battle to be the one true Ark of the Cycling Covenant where all power shall be centred. *Boom!* Blown to bits. Split sponsorship and a dilution of purpose did for the events: the Kellogg's Tour went snap, crackle and pop after Maurizio Fondriest won in 1994 – having outlived the Milk Race by one edition after the Milk Marketing Board folded.

Four fallow years passed before the PruTour came in 1998 . . . and went in 1999.

And then came . . . MICK!

In 2004 – not that long ago – the all new and shiny Tour of Britain was created. It had legs right from the start. Teams like T-Mobile, U.S. Postal, Quick-Step–Davitamon. Tom Boonen won that day into Nottingham. It was fantastic.

Since then, Race Director Mick Bennett has overseen a national race that has matched the rise of the superstar British cyclist . . . lots of them. Hitting the wave perfectly, the Tour of Britain has surfed up the UCI classification system – 2.1, 2.HC on the Europe Tour, 2.Pro W and any minute now, 2.UWT. If you don't know your UCI codes, then please head to a more boring book for the detail. Anyway, it is a bloody good race and recognised as such.

Now, Britain has very few mountains in the Alpine class. None in fact. Great Dun Fell in the North Pennines is the highest pass in the UK. It stands a mighty 835m (2740ft) above sea level. Mont Ventoux sits at 1909m (6265ft).

So yes, Mick and the gang have to play at a smaller altitude, but the race is far from easy or uninspiring. We get to play with part of the planet that many believe is God's own back garden. Indeed, so undiscovered have the roads of Britain been for so long that many pro riders had no idea there was anything that looked much different to London on the island. What hit them were the many landscape treasures that they didn't know existed and which we Brits take for granted. It's said that when the Bardiani team were given a nice hotel in Sidmouth in 2016 they liked it so much that three of the party booked to come back on family holidays. Hope the weather held up for them!

Then there are the fans. Millions of them over the eight days. Whether the race passes through Devon, Wales, Scotland, the Borders, the Midlands, East Anglia, it matters not. The welcome is warm and enthusiastic. And, of course, we must add the biggest of draws to any visitors to these shores: Pubs. For me, it's got to be The Rambler at Edale, if you are asking.

So what we get is a cycling festival with eight days of proper racing warfare over varying hilly terrain across Great Britain, designed to test the spirit and resolve of those planning an assault on the World Championships that follow closely behind. So good is Mick Bennett's proving ground that many opt to miss La Vuelta to take it on.

The list of winners since 2004 testifies to its magnetism. In no particular order, the podium has featured Primož Roglič, Mathieu van der Poel, Julian Alaphilippe, Dylan van Baarle, Bradley Wiggins, Edvald Boasson Hagen, Rohan Dennis, Simon Yates, Michal Kwiatkowski, Steve Cummings, Lars Boom, Matteo Trentin, Tom Dumoulin . . . you get the idea.

Thanks, Mick.

CARLTON COMMENTARY

'Nothing worse than a lazy monk.'
When passing religious institutions with doors closed . . .
normal on busy cycling days

TWENTY EIGHT

WORLD CHAMPS
THE KING AND THE FOOL

It was a well-known group ride venue we found ourselves at one Sunday morning on the outskirts of Paris. There was a bunch of about 40 riders gathered together around the Trotting track, about to head off towards Bois de Boulogne. It was a lovely bright crisp morning with nothing to spoil the day . . . save for one prized branleur who decided to make an announcement to the group before we set off.

Some of the other riders clearly knew what was coming. 'Oh, mon Dieu, c'est Fabrice!' murmured one. The rest just mumbled groans.

Setting himself up to address us was a little stocky guy who looked a bit handy for a 50-something. He was trying to make himself look bigger than he was. Hands on hips, straddling his bike's top-tube, he began what I was later to find out was his regular challenge to the group.

'It is I, Fabrice Duchêne, and as some of you may already know, had I not been tied to the family tringle à rideau business I could have been a star. If you know me, you know I am the best.'

'What's he talking about, Sean? Do you know him?'

'Nope, never heard of him. He's talking bollocks. He's a curtain-pole maker.'

'He should pull himself together,' I said with a self-congratulatory chuckle. 'You know, like curtains.'

Sean scowled as he moved the joke to a darker place. 'Well, I'm going to pull him apart.'

You rarely see Sean angry. When he is, he's ice-cold impressive. Sean rolled up to our hero through the group as we moved off. 'OK, my friend, if you're that good, show us what you've got.'

'With pleasure, loser! ALLEZ!!!!' shouted Fabrice and he attacked.

To be fair, his best shot wasn't bad. Off he launched, out of the saddle, quickly gaining about 20 bike lengths on everyone, except for Sean.

A grinning yet panting Fabrice glanced behind, expecting to celebrate a huge gap. All he saw was Kelly right on his wheel; still planted in the saddle; mouth closed and smirking.

'Salop!' screamed the now gasping *could have been* and went again. Kelly simply changed his tempo and gently moved up alongside the still attacking Fabrice.

Kelly was loving this. Without any visible sign of physical toil, he said: 'Is that all you've got? I thought you said you could've been a World Champion.'

'Aaaaaaaaah!' screamed Duchêne as he stamped on the pedals in a last-ditch attempt to drop Kelly who was simply cruising.

There was about another minute featuring maximum effort from the idiot and minimum stress from Sean, before Fabrice pulled to the side of the road, fell off the bike and threw up. He was completely crushed. Between gasps for air, he managed to ask: 'Who – are – you?'

'Ça, c'est Sean Kelly. Monsieur Paris–Nice. Le Roi,' I explained as Sean rolled off up the road.

A dawning of recognition washed over Fabrice's face. And then he called after the now departed Sean: 'THEN WE ARE THE SAME . . . YOU WERE NEVER A WORLD CHAMPION EITHER!'

Sean arced around in the road and headed back. He looked like an assassin.

Fear now replaced arrogance. 'Excusez-moi, Roi!' he called towards Sean.

The apology came just in time. Sean turned his bike around, eased out of the saddle and with a few smooth-as-silk strokes on the pedals launched himself away from the group and was gone.

'Did you see that!?' said one. 'That is a real thoroughbred.'

'Who the hell invited him along anyway?' said Fabrice. Nobody answered.

———

Sean Kelly finished third into Chambéry at the World Championships of 1989. It had been the same result in Goodwood seven years earlier. But this one result really stung. Greg LeMond won the World title for the second time ahead of Russian Dimitri Konyshev. Kelly had raced more events than anyone that season, which was his way of things back then.

'I just raced where I was told to,' said Sean once, 'and sometimes a rest might have been more valuable. You never know until the day.'

The year before, Sean had won his seventh consecutive Paris–Nice and taken his Grand Tour title at La Vuelta, leaving him a little depleted for the 1988 Worlds at Ronse in Belgium. He finished 25th. A year later, though, the stars were aligned. Chambéry beckoned on a course that suited Sean if he could survive the climb that came around 21 times on the lumpy circuit.

That season, Sean had contested the notoriously challenging Tirreno–Adriatico instead of Paris–Nice, which he'd owned for the previous seven years. It meant the rhythm of the season was different. The Worlds were the target, but not just for Sean. That year, Greg LeMond won the Tour de France by the narrowest ever margin of just eight seconds over Laurent Fignon. Sean Kelly won the Green Jersey. But their paths then diverged, Greg taking on just two one-day races before the World Championship. Sean had sustained a far heavier programme.

In Chambéry the rain came down late in the day as Sean was clawing his way over the final climb to bridge to LeMond and Fignon, who had been attacking. There were now six upfront coming into town.

After a long and busy season, that pesky climb had chipped away at Sean, yet he was confident this day would be his. 'I was busy thinking about being World Champion, I backed myself to win.' So did everyone else. It didn't happen.

After such a long layoff after the Tour, it took Greg LeMond some time on the day of the Worlds just to feel OK. He later told Sean he'd even considered withdrawing earlier on the course. But such a long race – 259.35km (161.1 miles) – meant there was time to get back into the rhythm. By the end, Greg was flying and duly took his second world title.

There is no way Sean Kelly should have lost in Chambéry, but the Worlds are a strange beast. As you know, Sean finished 3rd. The race for those rainbow stripes is a notoriously difficult puzzle to solve.

The World Championships have been run in one form or another since the inaugural track worlds at Chicago back in 1892. After that, there were various associations that attempted to bring the cycling world together until the UCI finally took full control around a hundred years ago. Alfredo Binda of Italy was crowned the first road race World Champion at the Nürburgring in 1927.

Since then, provided there is not a war on, the coveted rainbow jersey has been one of sport's oldest and most recognised winner's emblems. The right to wear these coveted stripes for an entire year is the honour. No matter your team, the World Champion's stripes will not be diminished by advertising. It means so much to all cycling fans to see. And for a commentator, being able to say: '. . . and here comes the World Champion' has a wonderful ring to it.

The race for titles covers a week of events, which is a magnet for all cycling enthusiasts. Going to a World Championship is a unique experience in so many ways. The festival is a gift to both riders and fans alike. It has history, drama and entertainment in abundance. You'll see your heroes and rising stars in a series of single-day challenges across the age ranges. It's the future, right now, with the Juniors. Then the best of the Under-23 white jersey brigade who've already made a name for themselves but now need to prove it. And, of course, the Elite superstars duking it out for ultimate kudos.

This huge, end-of-season gathering has a near rock-festival nature to it. The amount of good will and bonhomie surrounding the host city simply has to be experienced to be understood. There is nothing bigger.

There is also business to be done. All the major teams and players turn up . . . with managers and agents busy as hell signing up riders who have run well and ditching those who have been hanging on. So, both beautiful and brutal, on and off the bike.

I reckon the level of interest and entertainment often exceeds a Grand Tour. There is so much going on. As a fan you can simply immerse yourself in it – if you can find a hotel room, that is.

It's true that the busiest versions of the World Championships are usually when the host venue is in Europe. But from the fans' perspective I reckon the most exciting editions are those that leave the traditional homelands of cycling and explore the globe.

Glasgow has taken great pride in being the first Super Worlds, meaning a whole range of races, which often feature in their own stand-alone World Championships, coming together for one *HUGE* festival.

But if you are intending to keep your funds for something extra special, hold off until Rwanda in 2025. I can't possibly describe how special this will be. Africa gets a turn, and a cycling-mad nation will host its biggest ever international event of any kind. It will be a Championship like nothing before. Trust me.

If you are a fan, be like the riders and take your chance to go for it. This is how the World Championship love is being shared over the next few years:

2023 Glasgow seeing all disciplines, including BMX and Cyclocross, will be run as part of the biggest ever Worlds in the history of the sport.

2024 Zurich, Switzerland. Close to the UCI headquarters. Sure to impress.

2025 Rwanda. Like nothing ever seen before. The whole country and much of the continent will stop for this.

2026 Montreal, Canada. A guaranteed festival of entertainment in a beautiful city.

2027 Haute-Savoie, France. Where we get all Alpine once again.

Delightfully, no matter what the terrain, on any particular year, nobody can be sure who will become a World Champion. What is certain is that if a rider hits form at exactly the right time, even within the race itself, they will have reached the top of the world. Miss your chance, and you may never get another. That's why Sean Kelly was so pissed off with a curtain-rail maker from the Paris suburbs. Because however much of a prick the guy was, he had a point. A sore one to be sure.

CYCLING LEXICON

Flick: The act of dispatching a rival, either by prowess or cunning.

JUNE, JULY & SEPTEMBER

TWENTY NINE

GRAND TOUR REST DAYS
A SNIP TOO FAR

So there I was, gently snoozing on a rickety Z-bed under the shade of a fig tree by the pool. Resting like a pro. The previous two weeks of racing had shaken up the oil and water in the old brain, and now I was letting the foam clear. The final rest day of the Tour had to be taken seriously. Coming up were the Pyrenees and then the run back to Paris. So, time to relax. And it was going very well: for about 40 minutes.

'Get up, we're driving to Montpellier!' Sean commanded as he kicked my sun-lounger.

'Eh? What?' I was struggling to come around and focus; but something was clearly amiss. 'What the hell's happened to your hair?'

'We are going into town to fix it.'

'What do you mean "we"? It's your hair problem.'

'Yes, but I could do with you driving. I'm a bit upset. I look like a fuckin' peach melba.'

The previous evening we had arrived for our rest day at a lovely pension up in the hills north of Béziers. Sean had decided to have his hair touched up and asked the lady owner if there was a local hairdresser who might pop over. 'Not too expensive, you understand. Not complicated,' he explained. She knew just the person.

Mid-morning saw Jeanette, a young mobile coiffeuse, arrive by tractor with a plastic bin of equipment. This looked like the kind of price bracket Sean was after, and soon he was sitting on a wooden dining chair in the courtyard with a plastic cape being attached.

'So, what colour would you like, monsieur?'

'Strawberry blonde or maybe Ash blonde,' Sean declared.

'Excusez-moi?' she asked, mildly perplexed.

Sean was clearly going to struggle explaining Ash blonde, so went for the former: 'Fraise Blonde, s'il vous plaît.'

'Vous êtes certain, monsieur?'

'Absolutement,' declared Sean softly as his eyes closed and he settled into the pampering zen.

———

It's hard to drive when you are trying to stifle a laugh. I wasn't helping myself either. 'Were you a fan of Kajagoogoo, Sean?'

'Quiet! Just drive.'

We managed to fix Sean's hair in Béziers – for far more than he'd hoped to spend.

———

Welcome to a break in the races. You have made it this far. Still the final push to come, but it's time for some respite to help get yourself in the mood before we go again with the final chapters. So let's make like the pros and rest – except that they don't. Not really.

Rest days are often rather busy. You never actually get to rest much at all. There is always something to do, like laundry, research, resolving minor family issues back home and, of course, the thing everyone dreads: Team press conferences. Oh FFS.

For some unfathomable reason Press Relations officers feel duty-bound to arrange a get-together so reluctant team managers can meet tired and grumpy journalists who are invited to ask questions that will not be answered.

Nobody who attends these is remotely interested in being there. It's all so bloody obvious and staged. The only people happy with it are the guys who have arranged it.

PR is a subgroup of journalists who have sold their souls. Sure, there are press releases to write, which accounts for the journalism bit; but there is then the commercial duty to promote an employer, which is where the path of truth diverts down a cul de sac. Gloss and fluff are the tools of this trade: spin!

It is the job of the press, now sitting in the secondary school gym hall next to the team hotel, to get past the smoke and mirrors and find out what's really happening in the team – after, for example, the verbal abuse and punch-up everyone heard coming out of the team bus on Sunday.

Of course, there is absolutely no chance of finding out anything regarding such incidents. Yet our editors have told us to go 'just in case'.

Nothing doing. All we get is men in T-shirts congratulating men in T-shirts, with, if you are lucky, a reasonably well-known rider who has drawn a short straw and knows he must reveal precisely zilch to those who want to know the real story.

'So, Josselin, what happened on the coach on Sunday?'

'We are a team. We 'av passion for our journey. Zats it.'

This is then followed by some verbal sports-mulch otherwise known as . . . the bleeding obvious:

1 There are six days to go. Nothing is decided.

2 We will be strong and now target stage wins.

3 Everyone is looking forward to Paris.

4 The team can take many positives from our performance.

5 We would like to thank our sponsors, *blah blah blah*.

'So does anyone have any further questions?' asks Trent Cardboard, a member of the Chartered Institute of Public Relations. Or Chipper, for short . . . which he most annoyingly was.

'Is it true Peter is leaving at the end of the season?' ventures a hopeful hack.

'As you know our contract negotiations will not be allowed into the public domain until the end of September. Any more questions?'

Silence.

'Well, thank you all for coming and giving my life some meaning. I realise none of you want to be here, but I have done my job, so fuck you.' Would be honest.

For fans, getting close to Tour rest days can be a joy. Plan your itinerary well, and you will reap great rewards. You will more than likely bump into stars like Sean Kelly, Chris Boardman or Bradley Wiggins off duty, usually at what will the next day become the *finish* town of Stages 10 or 16.

We will be resting the day prior at these cities, where we will wait for the race to come to us at the resumption.

If you hope to bump into riders like Peter Sagan having a pizza or Vingegaard a salad, then you will find them on rest days at what will be the *start* towns of Stages 10 and 16. So remember, journos at the finish and riders at the start. Easy.

Be sure to study the race plan when it comes out, then simply book your B & B as above and, when the time comes, just wander about until you find us. It's alway nice to meet like-minded folk, so do come and say hello.

The riders themselves never rest entirely. They head out on training rides to keep the legs spinning. Some do more rest-day Ks than others. And some riders simply do not like rest days at all because it breaks the rhythm of the racing and therefore affects peak fitness predictability and planning.

Meanwhile, for those who have been trapped in TV production trucks, it is time to emerge mole-like into the light and get aboard hire-bikes to pretend.

Sean himself is given to going for a spin . . . often as a VIP guest surrounded by enthusiasts. This can end with a Meet Sean Kelly dinner, which he enjoys. Hence the need to smarten up. It's good business too; he's earned it.

As for me, if I have time, I take a chance to go hunting wine with my old pal the German commentator Karsten Migels. Over the years we have made it our mission to follow the shittiest handwritten signs that simply say *Vin*, usually accompanied by an arrow. We follow these into the depths of France profonde and have, on many occasions, discovered some beauties bought direct from the producer at a fraction of the table cost in a restaurant.

Once in the Rhône region we ended up in a barn where the farmer's wife was labelling up bottles of red destined for Maxims in Paris. We were given a glass to try. Honestly, I had never tasted anything like it before or since. It was just gorgeous. I ended up buying a case of the stuff – minus labels of course. I paid €9 a bottle. Cash. I'll drink to that.

The best thing to do on rest days is simply to catch up with colleagues. This might sound odd, but on a Grand Tour life is so frantic that we are usually either travelling, working or sleeping. So a rest day is the one time we all get to go out to dinner. This, of course, has to be planned well in advance and usually involves us taking over a place. One of the most memorable was a brasserie you should try – not expensive at all but weirdly wonderful, if a bit spooky too.

Once Sean had fixed his hair, we met up with our French Eurosport colleagues at the Bar des Amis in Béziers. Inside we were immediately struck by an apparent shrine to Rugby. Shirts in cases adorned the walls along with photos of one man in particular: Armand Vaquerin.

The Times newspaper once listed him along with Bernard Hinault as one of the Top 10 Frightening Frenchmen. Vaquerin was a phenomenon. He won the French Championship with AS Béziers a record 10 times and represented France at International level between 1971 and 1980. He was without doubt one of the most intimidating hardmen ever to play the game. Balding, bearded, short neck, big shoulders. Immensely powerful. Scary. He was a loosehead prop, but sadly lost his playing a game of Russian Roulette in this very restaurant. The bullet hole is in the wall apparently; discreetly hidden behind a picture. The night we were there, I had seared brochettes of ducks' hearts with sauté potatoes and salad, there were ten hearts on the skewers. They tasted like mini fillet steaks; delicious. We were joined by some fans who had spotted us. They of course telephoned their mates and we had quite the get-together. It was lovely. Everyone reminiscing about Tours past and present. It went on rather late.

So, a Grand Tour Rest Day is the biggest misnomer in sport: nobody actually rests. If the race has begun abroad, the opening rest day will be a long transfer, often involving a flight. It's spent simply getting to the host nation and setting back up again. Examples include the Israel start to the Giro d'Italia in 2018 and then Hungary in 2022, or the Tour de France beginning in Denmark the same season.

So ignore opening rest days on such flyaway tours. Instead make your plans for the aforementioned 'regular' rest days where everyone is gathered together, and you will not be disappointed. But please, if you should notice Sean's hair has changed colour slightly since the start of the race, play safe. Say nothing.

CYCLING LEXICON

Hurt Box: A place of suffering. Not pleasant to be in.

OCTOBER

THIRTY

IL LOMBARDIA
FLIGHT OF THE BUMBLER

'LLOYDIE CALLING,' said my iPhone while displaying a particularly goofy picture of the beardy god of cycling, which I'd snapped one drunken night at some bar, somewhere.

He was chipper as you like. 'Hi, mate, I'm towards the back, row 28, where are ya?'

'I'm at the gate; they won't let me on.'

'Yeah right, where are ya?'

'I'm looking at the bloody plane and can't get past "Rosa Klebb" who's on the phone.'

'You're kidding me!'

'Not kidding. Are the doors locked yet?'

'No, they're still open. Still haven't slammed the luggage lockers.'

Drizzle was gathering into rivulets on the plate glass terminal window animating my view of the flight crew who would soon pilot 'my' flight to

Milan. I can't have been more than 40ft from them as they merrily chatted away dealing with bits of paperwork.

Time to interrupt Rosa.

'My friend says the doors are still open.'

She muffled the phone to her shoulder: 'I'm sorry, the flight is closed . . . No, wait! Did you check any bags into the hold?'

This was a loaded question and in my panic I didn't realise that they would either have to let me on, or unload my bags from the plane.

As I said the words, I immediately knew it was a bad answer: 'No, I just have hand luggage . . . D'OH!'

At this she got back on the phone. 'No more passengers,' she informed the plane.

At this moment Rosa put down the phone, then very slowly folded her arms and turned to me. She was now staring deep into my apparently worthless soul. A smile so thin it was dead across her face.

'There is another Milan flight in two hours. Would you like me to book you onto that . . . , sir?'

I watched as the plane was pushed back. Towards the tail there was another face to ponder. It was pressed up against a round window with hands cupped either side to improve the view. Through the rain I couldn't tell for sure, but I knew in the middle of Dan's goofy mush there was a massive grin.

Lloydie, or The Eel, as I christened him that damp October evening, was as happy as you can imagine, having slithered his way on board; made all the more amusing of course because I had failed. Such low-peril contests can be immensely satisfying . . . for the winner. And, to be fair, if it had been the other way around I would have been laughing myself.

About five minutes earlier, the music in Wetherspoons faded between tracks just enough for us to hear: 'PASSENGERS LLOYD AND KIRBY . . . YOUR FLIGHT IS NOW CLOSING.'

Before my glass hit the table, Dan was already running. He knew the airport layout forensically after so many filming trips for GCN over the years, and so it was that his route past Perfume and a kiosk selling London Bus money boxes and Beefeater Teddies was the shortest.

I bustled past Drinks & Fags – it had a more chi-chi name, but you get the idea – steering my aluminium flight bag as best I could around idle shoppers and arriving at the gate no more than 30 seconds after Dan, leaving a hundred 'sorries' in my wake.

Let's take a moment here for a question: Is it easier to be nasty to a bald, panting, rather flustered, middle-aged, tubby bloke than to a sinuous near-athlete with a bright smile, healthy quiff and a twinkle in his eye?

Dan got the pass, I pulled out my credit card and waited for the next plane.

After landing in Milan, I got a text telling me which restaurant everyone was in. They included a picture of a beautifully cooked sirloin that had been sliced finely with a rock salt and fresh rosemary seasoning along with pepper-speckled roast potatoes to the side. This was my very dish, awaiting my arrival.

Of course, the taxi took an age and my phone ran out of battery. Apparently they all assumed I had binned the night and gone to bed in a grump. To be fair, I had thought of doing just that. I wasn't happy. So my lovely meal was picked at by a bored highlights producer who never knows when he's full. Massi Adamo is a great friendly bear of a man, but that night he was the hungry version of himself.

Soaked, I backed my case through the door of the restaurant to slightly drunken cheers from the team. The welcome could not have been warmer save for the slightly apologetic look on Massi's face.

On my plate sat the last three thin slivers of beef, and no spuds. Still, it was hard to be pissed off when everyone was so upbeat and tipsy. So I got on with it. 'Pass me that bread, would you, Massi.'

'Sorry, Carltoni, I thought you wouldn't make it, soooooo . . . ya know. Sorry.'

I made a beef sandwich and ordered a beer.

They'd all had a great time . . . partly at my expense of course. And the cost was about to increase.

As is the custom, they divided the total bill equally between the party, except for one person. And that person was *not me*, FFS! There was a guest from Canada who was not expected to pay anything. So I duly paid my share of everything . . . including my part of Kid Canada's bill. Added to the cost of a taxi from the airport . . . and the extra plane ticket . . . I made no money that weekend.

Lake Como is one of the planet's most beautiful places. Created by snowmelt from the Alps, it sits like a vast dancing Mercedes star with the mountains gently giving way to lower ground towards the two southern limbs. At the end of the westerly leg you find Como town, which Il Lombardia, the last of the season's monuments, calls home.

The Race of the Falling Leaves helps to bookend the classics season perfectly with Milan–Sanremo, La Prima Verde having done its job in the spring. Lombardia comes as a beautiful celebration of all things that have passed so far, and in this most Catholic of countries it gives classics riders who can climb a chance of redemption or celebration, depending on how good they have been on the bike the past year. Of course, these days there are other races that have snuck onto the late calendar, but Lombardia feels like cycling's way of saying farewell – and a more glorious finalé you will be hard pushed to find.

Over the years the finish has bounced around northern Italy, ending in Milan, Bergamo and Lecco, but since 1961 its most common home has been Como.

The race was founded upon revenge. *Gazetta dello Sport*, the Milan-based national sports daily responsible for the Giro d'Italia itself, was outraged that Milanese superstar Pierino Albini had been beaten in the 1905 King's Cup by Giovanni Cuniolo, a rider from the upstart city of Tortona 75km (47 miles) to the south. There had to be a rematch.

The hype was so significant that tens of thousands of fans turned out to call them home. Except the pair didn't finish. Only 12 riders came home inside the 2 hours 40 minutes cut-off, after which the course was closed; it was time for an aperitivo, after all. One of the early cycling greats, Giovanni Gerbi (pronounced Kirby in my house), triumphed. Of course he did.

A template had been set and the Race of the Falling Leaves had been created. Two years later, in 1907, Giro di Lombardia became the official name, and cycling's most consistent feature was now thriving. It raced on through the First World War and only missed 1943 and 1944 because there was a lot going on at the time with Italy deciding who to fight for.

As you can gather, the race itself was a huge success – and remains so. Always drawing the very best from the very best. From the interwar years into the 1950s this was The Big One, with the likes of Alfredo Binda, Fausto Coppi and Gino Bartali sharing the honours. Coppi won five times and finished solo for each of those occasions. Indeed, it was the same battle plan again and again. Hiding in full view, you might say. Everyone knew Coppi would attack on Madonna del Ghisallo, and could do absolutely nothing to stop him.

Standing upon the mount, facing the southern banks of the central lake and the bustling bars and lakeside palaces of Bellagio, is a chapel to La Madonna del Ghisallo. She was declared the patroness of cyclists by Pope Pius XII. Inside is a cycling museum featuring historic jerseys of the greats, and there burns an eternal flame to all cyclists no longer with us. It's lovely.

My favourite story from those mid-century days dates back to 1956, when Fausto Coppi was up among the breakaway with an arch-rival from that year, Fiorenzo Magni, behind in the pack. The race director was asked by a police motorcyclist if a car containing Giulia Occhini might be allowed to pass the peloton so she could be at the finish to celebrate with Coppi when he won. Giulia Occhini was known as The White Lady after she was first identified as a 'friend' of the great man while skiiing in San Moritz. Her extramarital affair with Coppi had scandalised society at a time when divorce was not allowed without a papal decree and adultery was still a crime.

The race director allowed her to come forward, and as she passed the bunch is said to have asked her driver to slow alongside Magni so that she might sneer. Incensed, Fiorenzo set off on a suicidal solo pursuit of the break. Such was his anger he made it into the front group and immediately set about hurling insults at Coppi. A huge argument began and while they quarrelled André Darrigade attacked. It's fair to say that the podium that day was a little tetchy – a Frenchman on top, and Coppi and Magni silently seething on each side of him.

Considered a climbers' classic, it does not stop quick strong men from winning. My long-time partner in commentary crime Sean Kelly won this most arduous of races three times. Only Binda with four and Coppi with five won more.

It's so tough. In terms of both distance and terrain, there are few more demanding tests. An average of five major climbs running over 250km (155 miles) with a downhill run to the finish . . . you had better have a lot of tools in the kitbag to win. Yet, after all the torture, you will most likely be sprinting. No wonder they call Kelly The King.

There are, of course, different ways to win and from different kinds of rider too. Tony Rominger used his time-trial skills to win twice in the '90s. In 2015 a winning solo attack came on the penultimate climb from Tour de France winner Vincenzo Nibali – a result that finally cemented his place in the hearts of Italian fans who had long referred to him less than favourably as The Sicilian.

Being so long and tough, there are plenty of chances to get it wrong – and both riders and the general public have faltered over the years. The 2020 edition was infamous for two major crashes. Firstly Remco Evenopoel, who misjudged a corner leading to a narrow bridge, hit an unguarded sidewall and flipped over it into the ravine. Later the same day German cyclist Max Schachmann was hit by an unofficial car in the final Ks of the race. Both riders suffered multiple injuries but thankfully recovered.

Luckily the thing we remember most about this amazing race is the sheer spectacle. If you are going, do visit Bellagio. Walk out of town up the hills heading south towards the chapel. When you are at the top of the cobbled streets, find one of the cheaper streetside cafés and order the simplest pasta dish you can find. Never go fancy in Italy. Everyone who knows, keeps it modest. Even a humble tomato sauce will be delightful. So don't go mad. You will be needing all your energy for the race itself.

Sean Kelly says that commentating on Lombardia can prove as exhilarating and emotionally shredding as riding it. And he should know. What I know is that there are few places on the planet more beautiful and enjoyable. Once you've had lunch, take one of the lake boats to Como. They are not expensive. Go up on deck and breathe in that mineral air. When you dock, grab a seat at a shoreline bar and watch the race live on GCN+ on your mobile. You can, of course, let your gaze drift in the quieter moments to marvel at the geography, architecture and sheer beauty of everything set before you as the low warm sunlight of October adds an intoxicant to the mix. It is heaven on earth.

Unless, of course, it's pissing down and Massi has eaten your steak dinner.

CYCLING COMMENTARY

'It's all very well taking a big chunk, but you've got to swallow it.'
Rider attacks the pack and finds himself solo with 80km to go

THIRTY ONE

CRO RACE
LIP SMACKING

The local DJ was having a hard time diverting people from sunning themselves at café tables or sitting with their backs towards him while dangling their legs off the harbour wall. The nation's Tour was coming to town . . . in about three hours. He had a job on.

Thankfully he wasn't shattering the peace. The bars and restaurants of Split were full of people picking at impeccably steamed cod loin in capers, which arrived in little foil pyramids surrounded by discs of herbed potatoes. Simple but perfect.

Split, on the eastern shore of the Adriatic, is one of many gems stretching all the way north-west to my personal favourite spot Crikvenica, which has also hosted the race. This region is where Dalmatians come from. Yet, unlike the coat of these lovely dogs, it is spotless. A piece of heaven . . . before Zagreb.

Let's be as clear as the gin-bright waters lapping the shoreline: Split is a stunning place, as is much of Croatia. But, as you may know, the race, and the place, has had its troubles.

Stage 2 of the 2016 event was part of a race still called the Tour of Croatia. That was before things fell apart. Back then, all was going swimmingly. Mark Cavendish came into town. He won the day and went into the leader's jersey. This was cycling royalty blessing a race that had only been revived the previous year following a long gap that began with the financial crisis of 2008.

As the 2015 Classics season drew to a close, everyone began to ready themselves for the start of the Grand Tour season with the Giro d'Italia. The calendar was more than a little bit crowded. Teams were spoilt for choice, with a host of short preparation stage races available.

The Presidential Tour of Turkey vied with Giro del Trentino and the Tour of Romandie for attention. It was quite the selection. Then came the Tour of Croatia. And not a single World Tour team came along.

Then the race was broadcast on Eurosport – and got everyone talking. The place was stunning.

Cycling is basically a long-running tourist advert for a nation. It's a moving caravan that can be guided almost anywhere you wish to promote. Do this well, and tourists will come. The pictures of the event were simply sumptuous. Suddenly everyone was thinking about Croatia for a holiday. The 2015 race was deemed a commercial triumph.

The Tour of Croatia organisers had cleverly seen the template set by Turkey and simply copied it. A stage race for sprinters, with a mountain thrown in for good measure to keep the GC alive for the rest. And all set within spectacular coastal vistas and ancient monuments, mountains and beautiful cities en route. It had it all.

Cycling teams love a clear hit of a race and so the 2016 edition was another rip-roaring success with star riders aplenty.

The World Tour teams flooded in with Astana, Dimension Data, Tinkoff, IAM and Trek making the trip. With the likes of Andrea Guardini, Mark Cavendish, Erik Baška, Matteo Pelucchi and Giacomo Nizzolo, it was a sprinter's paradise. Meanwhile, in Turkey, just one World Tour team came to play. Game over? No.

The Tour of Croatia love affair continued for another year: Vincenzo Nibali sprinkled yet more stardust about the place. It was on track to become a huge draw in the April sunshine. And then the arguments began.

As Turkey fought back, with its World Tour status, the Tour of Croatia did itself no favours at all. I'll spare you the whys and wherefores, but basically the event turned in on itself. Civil war broke out. An alternative race was offered and invites sent out. Two Tours of Croatia? Crazy.

To cut a long story short, the race had to be rebranded because two sets of organisers were at each others' throats. They had something stunning and they tore it apart.

Finally sense prevailed. The flag of surrender was waved regarding April, and the race swapped springtime for autumn. A new, younger and more focused operation emerged and the CRO Race was born . . . in October. And the big teams are indeed coming back with named riders swapping spring sunshine for the warm glow of autumn. Thank heaven for that.

Croatia is a passionate place. But like the country, the race and the generations can be divided. You will find the kindest, most open hospitable people in this wonderful country. And yet the older generation in particular are rather mistrustful and aloof. Rude even.

Away from the tourist traps of the coastline you may encounter the kind of disdain kept for an old enemy, because you may well be regarded as such. The war that tore apart the Balkans in the 1990s was brutal and the United Nations was called on to try and keep the warring factions apart. As a result these peacekeepers were regarded as protecting everyone's rivals. Working for the other side. The soldiers of the UN didn't cover themselves in glory either. *Srebrenica* is the only word you need issue to darken any mood.

In the long ago days before the break-up of Yugoslavia, the Western nations were of course the rivals beyond the Iron Curtain. Yugoslavia's ally was Russia. And the ingrained disdain for perceived Western arrogance and cultural frivolity remains part of the psyche for some of those who grew up in such a time. There was a lot of propaganda about, and the West did not get talked about favourably at all. Largely dismissed as a failed, ignorant and corrupt system.

So when you find yourself off the beaten track a bit, frosty might sometimes be the welcome.

The hotel in Zagreb was very grey, or was it beige? No, that was the food. Penitentiary grey – apart from, that is, two magnificent beacons of kitsch redemption. Clearly someone had thought long and hard about the lights in the reception of our Zagreb Business Hotel. *The Business Matters*, said the clunky legend.

'Comrade, this place needs to get with the groove,' the conversation must've gone in the early 1970s. After all, Brezhnev was visiting Zagreb – time to 'get with it'. A local wiring expert was drafted in and handed a free rein and a bottle of gold paint. More engineer than artist, he did his best with the brief.

He took a ball of cable that had been ripped out of a vegetable-irradiating factory and stuck lily-type shades made of coned sheet metal on the end of each strand. He then painted the whole thing gold and called it Groovy-Max 2. A more modest title than Groovy-Max 1, which would have sounded far too Western-decadent.

Sadly our designer/engineer/fantasist had got the scale all wrong. It belonged in the vast ceiling void of a conference hall. So there I was, standing under God's Spaghetti, having my head gently cooked while I waited for the grump behind the desk to acknowledge me. The beeps coming from her creaking box-monitor suggested she was finishing a game of *Donkey Kong*.

It was then I realised Brian Smith had disappeared. He emerged from round the corner with a smirk. 'You're not gonna believe what's back there. Check out the lips!'

'Do you mean lifts, Bri?'

'Noooo. Next to them. Lips!'

Brian held my place in the one-person queue just in case old granite-chops reset to 'interested', and off I went, following a red glow.

There next to the lifts was a doorway, to the frame of which someone had nailed one of those flashing rainbow light-cables a vicar might use at a Scout disco. Above the entrance was a scarlet neon sign, just as Brian said, in the shape of a pair of enormous lips. The sort of thing that would trouble the copyright lawyers for the Rolling Stones, but without the tongue.

Back at reception, Brian had our room keys. They were actual metal keys; not pass cards. I liked that.

Standing arms folded with her back to the wall staring straight ahead was the receptionist.

'Did she say anything?'

'No, just handed the keys over and pointed to the lifts. And Lips. Can you believe that?'

'Do you think it's a nightclub?'

'No, I don't,' he said darkly.

The next day we went to breakfast.

'Peas?' I said to nobody as I inspected the grey-green rehydrated pulses. I hadn't seen them since my infant school lunches back in the '60s. I was remembering the dreadful taste. Clearly dwelling too long, I upset a 'server'.

'You want peas?' came the gruff voice from behind. 'How much you want?'

'Oh, I'll stick to toast, thank you.'

'Peas on toast?'

'Do you have any beans?' I said softly.

'No,' she said with more volume.

Thankfully, later that day was just the best finish to a race you could hope for. High on a hill is the old town of Zagreb. At the top of a cobbled road, you leave the drab concrete creations of the business district and climb heavenward onto cobbled streets and beautiful houses. The road gets steeper towards the top. Enough to challenge any but the best puncheurs. Survive the climb, and you are free to push for the line. It's very selective.

Over this crest in 2019 came Alessandro Fedeli, who gave Delko–Marseille a huge late season boost. He'd beaten Bahrain Merida's Jan Tratnik on the killer slope. Three other riders crossed the line before Adam Yates in a rapidly closing group of eight which did enough to give Mitchelton Scott the title. It was a firecracker finalé to another wonderful race.

After the ceremony we were told to head down the other side of the hill for a drink. And thank heaven we did. Wow . . . what a street. It was an explosion of hospitality and joy. You know those old Elvis movies where there is a snare-drum strike before the music bursts to life and everyone dances on cue? It was like that.

I just couldn't believe it. Brian and I found the quietest bar for grown-ups we could and settled in. Lounging in spectacularly comfy armchairs on an open terrace with heat lamps to toast us. The waiter brought leg blankets.

'These are for later when it gets cold . . . in about three hours.'

He was clearly expecting us to stay. And we did.

I have never seen Brian so happy as we ambled our way through a spectacular roast pork dinner accompanied by some amazing Croatian red wine as rich and fruity as Brian is not.

The next day we were still full of the afterglow of an amazing experience. Croatia is truly wonderful. It may have its contrasts, but take them in your stride and you will love the place. You will make friends, but as in life you will come across some niggles. Don't let that put you off.

After our plane came to a halt in London Gatwick, everyone began grabbing their belongings when a rather senior Croatian lady got a bit animated. I have no idea what had upset her but as everyone stood up she made a general announcement:

'You Western idiots! You have no culture, you have no history, you have no manners!!!!'

There was a one-second snare-drum-beat before the entire plane burst out laughing.

CYCLING LEXICON

Endo: Short for End Over End crash.

THIRTY TWO

NATIONAL HILL CLIMB
STAIRWAY TO HELL

'Well, that's bolloxed that little arrangement, hasn't it!?'

Mr Seel, the newsagent, was not a happy bunny. I had just resigned from the most tortuous paper round in the United Kingdom. Which meant he now had to drive the round himself.

Sure, I only had seven papers in my meagre sack. Something which drew jealous disdain from those paperboys and girls working more concentrated street rounds with heavier loads of 50 or more evening newspapers. But I'd had enough. Or, should I say, my bike had had enough. The Hercules Jeep in gold and ruby metallic paint had been a handsome beast. But skittery country roads under heavy weather were not my friends and the repair bills to my once lovely bike were not covered by the money I got from Mr Seel. My dad told me to tell him to stick his job up his arse. I was far more polite.

The press and cycling have long been paired together. For a century or more, the Tour de France has bonded with *L'Équipe*. In Italy the Giro and *La Gazetta dello Sport* are as one. Races like the Dauphiné Libéré and the Herald Sun Tour took their name's directly from the press.

And you could say my old hill farm paper round was also sponsored, indirectly, by the *Sheffield Star*. I was paid the princely sum of £4 a week to deliver those seven papers in a loop that took me over two hours along the

Derbyshire borders. I suffered this course six nights a week for two sleet-filled, darkening months into winter before both my bike and I had had enough.

'What the hell is wrong with ya? Where's your gumption? It's only a few bloody hills. Get out!' This was the printable version of the tirade as I picked up my final pay packet.

The hills and dales of Derbyshire are gently rolling for the most part. They sit at the foot of the Pennine Way, the 'backbone of England'. It's a range that extends all the way up to the Scottish Borders, but its southernmost tip was on my doorstep in Edale. The official start of the 430km/268 mile-long trail over the peaks begins in a modest carpark at the back of the Old Nags Head, whose welcome notice kindly offers: *Dogs and Muddy Boots Welcome*. No mention of bikes.

When the rains clear, Edale is a spectacularly beautiful place, set in a vast geological bowl on the north side of the great crumbling mountain of Mam Tor. To the south of this huge gravel mound is Castleton, home of a unique feldspar semi-precious stone called Blue John and famed for its caverns where this purple and amber-coloured stone is mined.

So Edale has the starting point of the Pennine Way and Castleton has its mines. You'd think they'd get together and promote each other's merits. But no. They remain steadfastly suspicious and possibly a little jealous of one another.

Despite their proximity as the crow flies, the two places are not at peace. Finding signs from one ancient settlement to the other is simply impossible because they do not exist. Yet signage to places much further afield are clearly displayed. What's going on?

'Oh we don't 'av much to do wi thems that live ova t'ill,' said the bar lady at the Old Nags Head, 'I reckon since Jarvis Cocker moved in t'Edale they've bin right jealous of us.'

I'd heard much the same disdain at the Castle Inn on the other side in Castleton: 'Tourists!? They dorn't 'av tourists. All they've got is walkers, who buy nowt, carryin' their own sarnies n'suchlike. Oh and that Jarvis Bloody Cocker. Well they can keep 'im!'

Yet despite the antipathy there is a road link between them. Not that you'd know it. A route so ancient it had pre-Roman significance. It escapes the steep edges of one vast bowl and leads to the lip of the other. It also happens to be one of the steepest, open road slopes in all of England. Rising over 125m (410ft) in altitude over a distance of just 900m (2950ft) is Winnats Pass. Stunning. And if you ride it – *if* – then you will find it to be pure torture. Which is why it is the most revered venue for the National Hill Climb of Great Britian.

1966 was a vintage year. England won the World Cup. The Beatles performed their last gig as a live touring band in San Francisco. LSD was made illegal. Jaguar decided to ruin the world's most beautiful car by making a four-seater version of the E-type. NASA completed the first space link-up and of course Peter Greenhalgh set the Winnats Pass course record at the British National Hill Climb: 3 minutes, 11.2 seconds to be precise. A mark that stood unbeaten until 2021!

I love the National Hill Climb. I was there in 1966, by accident. My dad Bill had decided to take me and my young brother Paul to Castleton for the day and we happened on this amazing festival. Back then the weather was lovely, which probably accounted for Peter's amazing time.

The National returned the following year in more grizzly conditions and so Greenhalgh's time remained unbeaten. Same again in 1972 and in 1977. It was then the organisers called time on Winnats Pass and decided to share the love with other challenging roads in the UK. And they didn't come back . . . *for 44 years!*

Despite this huge gap Winnats Pass remains the most frequent host of the National Hill Climb since it started at the height of the war back in 1944. Originally it was a contest for those hardy souls who rode their heavy iron bikes into the hills during the war to plant hundreds of miners' lamps on the outskirts of Sheffield so that, with the city blacked out, the Luftwaffe would bomb the curious sheep instead of the steel factories in the valleys below.

So it was that in October 2021 the event came home . . . and the big temptation for the 230 or so riders taking it on was that the course record, which had stood since 1966, was there to be beaten. Surely comparing a rider on an iron rig in 1966 with the carbon boys of 2021 was never going to be a contest!?

Naturally, the weather had something to say on the matter. Would the rain and cold that kept Greenhalgh's time from being beaten through the 1970s affect the challenge once more?

It was a very close-run thing!

They timed them out from under an open awning to the cheers of the hordes clinging to the side of the mountain pass. There were possibly 2000 hardy souls under brollies all cagouled up against the chill. The riders set off at minute intervals onto a course just 900m (2950ft) long. A race between two cattle grids with an average incline of 12.9% but a maximum gradient of over 20% towards the top. It offered a 125m (410ft) altitude gain over the short run. That is as close to a road going straight up as is possible to navigate.

Andy Nichols went off as rider 228 and the timekeepers must've loved the power of their moment when he stopped the clock. The crackling loud hailer announced with faux sympathy.

'Sorry, Andy, you've missed t'course record. By 0.4 of a second. Un-luckeh!'

Andy's time: 3 minutes, 11.6 seconds.

But just two riders later came Tom Bell. The rain throughout the day had been constant but light. Visibility was fine but the surface was not. The issue wasn't gullying water, which can happen on Winnats, but the muddy boots of the multitudinous fans who kept encroaching onto the road to offer boisterous encouragement to the riders, adding to an already unstable surface that saw riders' back wheels bouncing and slewing as they struggled for grip and drive. It was mayhem.

As Bell neared the line, it was clear the mood of the timekeepers had changed. If the old mark was to be broken, let's make the difference a big one.

'Three minutes, Zero One Point Six. *A NEW COURSE RECORD!!!!*'

The crowd exploded and started dancing all over the asphalt ribbon. Pandemonium.

I don't know if Andy Feather was distracted, but on he rode through the mayhem.

Suddenly everyone realised. 'RESPECT THE RIDERS . . . RESPECT THE RIDERS . . . CLEAR THE COURSE . . . GIVE 'EM ROOOOM . . .' called the Steward before, with the loudhailer still open: 'For fuck's sake . . .'

Andrew Feather also beat the old mark, but was destined to finish his wet and cold trial in 3 minutes 08.5 seconds.

It was all over. A new benchmark for Winnats Pass after 55 long years in the hands of Peter Greenhalgh . . .

So, after a gap of 44 years hill-climbing returned to its old home that October day. Glory for Tom Bell, but for most of the rest their dreams lay, just like my old Hercules Jeep, broken.

2021 – Tom Bell 3.01.6

1977 – John Parker 3.22

1972 – Granville Sydney 3.23

1967 – Paul Wildsmith 3.43

1966 – Peter Greenhalgh 3.11.2

1963 – Granville Sydney 3.18

1959 – Gordon Rhodes 3.49

1957 – Eric Wilson 3.56

1953 – R Keighley 3.43

1949 – Bob Maitland 3.50

1947 – Vic Clark 3.28

CYCLING LEXICON

Bonk: The sudden loss of energy common when riders fail to feed properly during a race.

NOVEMBER

THIRTY THREE

TOUR DU FASO
GOLDEN TEETH

The ceiling fans were a worry. The one above me spun with just two of its three blades, making a poor job of creating a breeze. The third vane was broken and almost off duty. It hung down limply from a few wooden sinews while describing a small circle above our head. Clearly the victim of some minor violence. The open-sided restaurant was vast and packed; 200 covers at least. Everything was big about this place, especially the noise. Dinner time in Bobo-Dioulasso was clearly coming to a close. It was just approaching 10 p.m. and the after-dinner rakki was being passed around as we placed our order.

'Eh pour vous, Monsieur?'

'Fish please!' I half shouted. 'Un, poisson. Grand et piquante. Merci.'

'Aaah, ze spicy feeesh. Very nice,' exclaimed the waiter in English with a slight tilt of the head. The gesture worried me. I'm sensitive to these things. Was it *nice choice* or *uh-oh*? I couldn't tell. I let the question fade to the back of my mind because I wanted to get back to Gilbert's story of his recently divorced grandparents who'd split after 60 years of marriage.

The waiter, clearly a character, scribbled the order on the rudimentary newspaper tablecloth and left singing a song, ostensibly to himself, yet one clearly designed for others, and particularly us, to hear: 'Poisson poisson, pour les très grands garçons . . . très grands garçons demandent poisson . . .' As he sang, many faces turned our way, grinning at a shared tease. We smiled back and nodded toward any eyes we met.

It wasn't much of a tune and my hope was that this was the waiter's way of remembering our order on the way to the kitchen rather than anything darker regarding my order. I say *kitchen*; it was an open grill in the far corner where goat seemed to be the dish of choice. After all, I noted, it arrived very fresh, courtesy of the poor creatures tethered in the pens. You could see them bleating occasionally across a dirt floor yard full of dented oil cans. So they would be fresh . . . 'but what about the fucking fish? Oh shit.'

'Calme, calme,' said Gilbert, my Franco-Italian friend. He was A.S.O.'s man on the ground for outside projects. He wasn't worried. He didn't have to be. He'd ordered goat curry, so he was fine.

'Look, we are approximately 700km (435 miles) from the sea, Gilbert, and refrigeration is not something I can imagine being all that reliable around here.' My companion started blowing smoke rings stage left. My troubles were clearly my own.

I began to lose it. I lent in with a rasping spitting whisper: 'That fish is going to kill me! Then who'll voice the highlights for ya?' Gilbert just smirked and shrugged as he tapped a tail of cigarette ash into a cut-off Coke can. Debate over.

As I slumped back into my seat, the lights failed. The instant darkness was met with roundly mumbled cheers of the unsurprised before everyone simply got on with candlelight until the generator was fired back up.

Just as the useless fans started their gentle waltz above us once again, the waiter headed back with our beers. As he opened them, I started to ask: 'Monsieur, le poisson –'

'Oui, oui, monsieur, patience s'il vous plaît,' and he was gone. Bollocks.

The music, which had been playing constantly, was suddenly turned up for a tune everyone seemed to know. All customers, bar us, were on their feet dancing rhythmically to the beat. It was fabulous. Gilbert and I had given up battling the noise with any conversation and settled back drinking in the atmosphere and sipping our beers.

Two minutes later the fish arrived . . . almost by parachute. Our waiter made his way through a bouncing throng with our order on a tray held high above his head. He set it down with a relieved bump in front of us. 'Poisson Hrissa?' he said panting. I held up a finger of acknowledgement and before me was placed a still smoking aquatic beast. It was huge and lay on its side on a bed of sizzling vegetables. As I pondered it, a burnt eye popped, the bubbling fluid seeping across its charred head.

'Excusez-moi, monsieur, une question!'

The waiter stopped half turned in his retreat. 'Oui!?'

Now, when under pressure, my French can sometimes get a little mangled. This was such a moment.

'You did ask for fish?' he enquired while pointing to his scribble in the paper tablecloth.

'Oui.' It was now I wanted to ask how fresh the fish was, but instead I scrambled the question into: 'How *old* is this fish?' Oh dear.

The waiter stiffened. He then smiled and picked up the enormous serving spoon that came with the feast. Theatrically he raised it and then, with some gusto, began to beat the hell out of the table.

WHACK, WHACK, WHACK, WHACK . . . WHACK . . . WHACK . . . WHACK!

The entire restaurant was now completely silent, everyone staring at us.

'LE MONSIEUR ICI –' (pointing at me) '– ME DEMANDE UNE QUESTION.' A few titters began to break out. 'IL ME DEMANDE: QUEL *AGE* EST LE POISSON?' The odd giggle came from within the jolly mob.

He went on in French: 'ALL I CAN TELL YOU IS THAT THIS FISH –' He picked up the fish and looked into its gaping mouth theatrically. '– THIS FISH . . . DOES NOT HAVE ANY GOLD TEETH!'

The place exploded with laughter. 'Il n'y on ne pas des dents d'or,' they yelled repeatedly as if it were the best punchline they'd ever heard. It was mayhem.

In the cacophony the fish was returned to me. I was by now busily trying to pretend I was enjoying the joke too . . . Taking it on the chin in a very Englishman abroad *ho, ho . . .yes indeedy* kind of way. Embarrassment now far exceeded any fears about food poisoning. I tucked in.

Gilbert, his mouth full of curry and rice, was chuckling away. 'It's a river fish, you idiot. They probably caught it around the corner. Couldn't be fresher.'

It was indeed absolutely delicious.

The next morning it was time to leave for Ouagadougou, our ultimate destination. A mix of metalled roads and dusty tracks beckoned as usual in a race that, for many, captures the original spirit of the Tour de France itself. When Henri Desgrange planned the inaugural route to La Grande Boucle it too had beaten earth roads, a sense of adventure instilled by a near total lack of support for most unsponsored riders and a thrilling sense of the sheer immensity of the task melded together in a long-distance stage race. A celebration of cycling, which also sold a few newspapers!

The Tour de Faso remains true to many of those original ideas. There is the elite-ish race, which often features national teams. Along for the ride, though, comes a festival event that shadows it. And this really is the heart of what matters here. This wonderful race is about as far away from the current incarnations of Grand Tours as you can get. Competitors largely sleep in tents and the high temperatures are constantly punishing. It may not be like any Grand Tour you have experienced, but in truth it is possibly far closer to the original idea of an endurance event conceived by Henri Desgrange all those years ago. The collective pioneering spirit can be tasted in every mouthful of dust you will certainly collect along the way.

This is a race that simply oozes fun. The amateurs taking part are its heart. They come from all over the great continent and beyond to test themselves personally in the biggest race Africa has to offer. Sure, the Amissa Bongo in Gabon, which starts the season in January, would probably argue the fact. The Gabonese race has a much more impressive professional rider roster attending, but the sheer volume and diversity of the participants here at Le Tour de Faso is mind-blowing and truly sets it apart. It's like a riotous exercise of sweaty, dusty fun in temperatures nudging 40°C (104°F): very hot, but joyous.

The party at the start and finish areas lasts the entire day. The morning of each stage has acrobats, comedians, singers and, of course, dancing. Lots of dancing. It's impossible not to get swept up in it all.

The nation of Burkina Faso is at its heart Animist. The belief that the Earth and everything we encounter on it and beyond must be cared for and respected, be that a pebble, a fly or a human being, the wind, the rain or the universe itself. It's quite a view. Modern in some senses.

Having worked and travelled around much of West Africa, I can tell you that Burkina Faso may look poor by Western standards but it is so rich in so many ways, particularly compared to the desert nations that lie further north. The far stricter religious cultures of Mali and Mauritania, for example, are perhaps born of places where human existence is far more precarious.

In Burkina there is agriculture . . . hard-won from the savanna's edge where rivers flow. So they grow stuff. That means they have markets and money. Not much, but some. This modest wealth buys clothes, building materials and food. What's left can be spent on fun. So you have the African Film Festival centred here, in open-air cinemas largely. Which are amazing. You have music, lots of music. And booze! And that's a huge bonus when you come down from the desert countries and their religious police, who don't just frown on a bottle of beer, they beat it, and you, with long sticks (at best).

When you come to Burkina it is such a welcome relief. It's a very human place. The veils of your Western European cycle racing experience also begin to fall away. You see things that surely reflect the early days of cycling.

The race has come a long way since the inaugural tour back in 1987. It took 18 years before the UCI finally took it under its wing, adding it to the Africa Tour calendar.

At each start zone you'll find the best riders in printed Lycra team kit, straddling freshly washed bikes. They've made an effort. Lining up behind them are other amateur teams with slightly lesser grade bikes, also freshly washed, but with a simple bib showing the squad name. Then come the privateers with no kit to speak of; just a number pinned to a T-shirt, their iron bikes largely dirty. Who cares!? What everyone shares at the start, apart from a handful with a race face on, is an enormous grin.

The single official car, which was both race caravan and race direction, had a man with a megaphone leaning uncomfortably out of a side window to call the start. No sunroofs either needed or wanted here. He sped off screaming something enthusiastic but unintelligible – and it was time to go racing!

The entire field then kicked up an enormous dust cloud and duly disappeared, before it had even left!

Absolutely everyone was cheering and partying. And, just like my fish supper: It . . . was . . . fan . . . tastic!

CARLTON COMMENTARY

'It's not pretty, but like a lucky drunk in a minefield . . . he makes it.'
Djamolidine Abduzhaparov's sprinting style

THIRTY FOUR

SIX DAY RACING
THE BIG LOCK-IN

'OK, everyone you can say "he is dead" . . . and then we leave the transmission.' The director's call in my ear had kind of a *hey ho, there you go* tone. I was flabbergasted.

Imagine this: You take a regular 250m (820ft) UCI Velodrome track and you chop about 85m (280ft) out of it. This tightens the banking and shortens the front and back straights into mere high-speed transition runs to the next bend. Add 24 riders hand-slinging in the Madison or bunched together for an Elimination race, and you have mayhem. What could be more crazy than that? Well, I'll tell you.

Whoever thought of mixing several motorbikes pacing riders all together on such a short track!? Oh my dear Lord . . . if it goes wrong you might just get to meet Him sooner than you'd hoped. It's as if Six Day Racing wasn't mad enough, so somebody just had to invent the Derny Race.

It's 22 October, 2014 and the Amsterdam Six Derny Race is about to get under way. There's the 'grumbling biscuit tin' sound of six motorcycles designed in the 1930s with soft brakes and a push-lever accelerator, filling the velodrome with high revving engine noise and the smell of two stroke oil. Each derny is set to pace a rider, making it a 12-vehicle contest whose outcome will depend on the fine balance between power and effort.

The best derny men have usually been great riders themselves. Later in life they moved forward onto the motorcycle – swapping Lycra for leather, you might say. Or indeed pedalling for petrol.

One of the all-time great six-day men was Cees Stam. Multiple World and European pacer and derny racer. He'd done it all on a Six Day scene that fills the winter months between cycling road seasons like nothing else. And here he was about to pace a modern Six Day hero, his grandson Yoeri Havik.

Gently at first the dernys set off, circulating in line while giving riders time to get up to pace at the top of the track before dropping in to be collected by the motorcycle.

The riders adopt their standard racing position as they pair up behind the motorcycles. The ideal gap is around 6cm (2¼ inches) from the front wheel of the bike to the rear fender of the derny. This gives maximum aero effect, allowing speeds usually around 80km/h (50mph) and maxing out at around 90km/h (56mph), something entirely impossible for a rider without the motor-pace assist.

The speed slowly rose to a cruise of about 75km/h (47mph) when the gun went to start the 100-lap run. Immediately the sound of the engines changed and the 2000 spectators inside the compact velodrome roared with expectation.

When you first see it, you will be struck by how 'un-cool' the derny man's position looks. Knees are flared out, while sitting bolt upright like a butcher's delivery boy. It may look funny but it has a serious effect. The derny man punches a huge aero tunnel into the wind that the rider slots into behind. It makes for extreme speeds and dramatic racing.

The Stam–Havik pairing was a dream team. Both knew each other like no other – instinctive, you might say.

The best derny men know just when to ask the rider for more pace. It can never be flat-out from the start. It's a real balancing act. Lose your rider by asking too much, and it's race over. Equally, not being demanding enough will let others take the victory.

If the rider should disengage from the back fender even for a moment, he drops out of the aero tunnel and is hit by the wind – as if he has slammed on the non-existent brakes of his track bike. If this happens, there is a real danger of a rider being hit from behind by a following team.

Coming off turn four onto the miniature home straight, they were running in third place with 20 laps to go when Yoeri called 'Hoi, hoi, hoi' from behind. This means 'Go, go, go', so grandpa Stam upped the pace to around 85km/h (53mph). Unfortunately this pace was not matched by the pair running second. As they exited turn four, the slingshot effect of the banking saw Cees Stam run into the back wheel of the slower running Nick Stöpler, who was thrown, miraculously, to safety towards track centre. It was the start of an horrific chain reaction . . . Stöplers' bike was eaten by Stam's motorcycle, which crashed heavily, bringing down Havick behind him him. The next derny in line, travelling equally fast, had nowhere to go and slammed so hard into Stam's chest it got airborne before also crashing and bringing down more traffic. The scene was horrific.

Stam came to rest by the inside hoardings over which the medics vaulted and got to work. CPR was clearly being administered, so we cut to a replay. Not nice and certainly not sensitive but better than watching the stricken derny man. A rudimentary screen was set up around Stam . . . Unfortunately this simple act of discretion was then taken to mean the end by the man calling the shots.

I knew declaring his death was a very bad idea, so I kept it neutral. Firstly there was nothing official. Secondly, even if we knew he was a goner, then surely the family should be told first, before the rest of the world . . . and definitely not via a TV commentary team.

Thankfully my instincts were entirely correct. The next day from his hospital bed Cees Stam's family wished us all a happy resumption of the event. A wonderful *show must go on* message from a Six Day great. His nephew Yoeri eventually won the Amsterdam Six, partnered by Niki Terpstra. He dedicated it to his grandpa, who retired after the incident but is thankfully still with us today.

———

Six-day racing is amazing. Yes, there are plenty of crashes to worry about, but this is almost a function of the spectacle. A qualified risk. It is high-paced, high-octane entertainment that helps fans bridge the quiet time between road seasons. And it could not be louder.

If you are going to try one, then let it be Ghent. It's so intense and thrilling I have described it as 'a dogfight between F16s . . . in your kitchen.' Yet it is so much more than just racing. It is a festival.

The Ghent Six manages to position itself as a unique sporting experience. And I can tell you that the best way to introduce anyone to track racing would be to take them along. They will have their mind blown by Madison, Keirin, Sprints, Flying 100s, Elimination, Derny racing, Scratch, Points and on and on.

This stuff has been going on since the 1890s when it was formalised with a six-day endurance festival in Madisson Square Garden. The venue then gave its name to the most famous hand-slinging event on the schedule. Back then the racing was 24 hours a day with cabins for the resting riders whose teammate was busy racing solo events. These days it is a bit less punishing, with afternoon and evening sessions the norm. The cabins remain, however, for rider rests between events.

Velodromes, and particularly the short form of them, have always been cauldrons of sensory assault. The crowd noise, the music, the beer, the sheer madness of it all mixed with phenomenally exciting racing, originally designed to generate income from gambling. The races are relatively short but they just keep coming. One after the other with the essential ingredient: entertainment.

But no velodrome roar has ever been quite so consistently intense as the noises that come out of the Kuipke. Built in 1927, it burned down in 1962, and the 'new' velodrome opened in 1965. I don't think they have painted it since. And let's not talk about the toilets!

That said, if you get a chance to buy a ticket, then do not miss out. They go on sale for the following year the very day after the Sunday finalé. It's clever marketing because the fans are still fizzing from the action they have just enjoyed. So be quick, they usually sell out within a day or so. It is simply a pilgrimage nobody should miss.

What will strike you on arrival is just how small the place is. *Kuipke* means 'Little Tub' – an apt description of the compressed size. And it is a very good job that the racing is amazing, because the facilities are rough. Even the track itself is compromised by the 'Ghent bumps'. So tight is the 167m (548ft) tack that in order to get all the equipment into the centre they had to cut the boards to create a large upward opening hatch. Over the years the edges of this doorway have degraded so much that every lap each rider experiences the da-dum . . . da-dum, as front and back wheels get a reminder of how rough and ready things are here. Don't go expecting luxury.

What you can expect is fun and an extraordinarily warm welcome. You will instantly be made to feel very much part of the six-day family. It's like the least exclusive club on earth – and for that we should be grateful.

Before Cees Stam took his tumble in Amsterdam, I had the unexpected privilege of sharing a meal with all the derny men. I was with my commentary partner, the double Pursuit World Champion Tony Doyle, MBE. We were first to arrive in the modest deserted canteen. While Tony was collecting our stamppot, I took a seat on one of four large empty tables, each set to host a dozen hungry competitors. As soon as I sat down, in came the derny men, in full leathers and helmets after a pre-session warm-up. Despite plenty of vacant tables they immediately joined me. No airs or graces, no ignoring the stranger. Basically their view was: If you are here, you are good enough. I got a nod and a 'Hey jongen!' greeting from Stam and the well known Beast of the Boards, Walter Huybrechts, planted himself right next to me. I was immediately both flattered and at ease.

Tony arrived with two mounds of mashed potato with veggie bits in it and a knackwurst to the side on our paper plates. Just right for a cold damp November evening. There was of course no menu, everyone had the same. Vegetarian? Don't eat the sausage. Simple.

The next night when I saw Stam crash, I felt like someone I really cared for had been hurt. I was never happier to hear the good news of his condition. My happiness doubled when Yoeri and Niki Terpstra won it for Grandpa. Magic.

CARLTON COMMENTARY

'Aru has no luck at all . . . probably down to all those mirrors he's cracked.'
(tbf he was quite handsome off the bike)

DECEMBER

THIRTY FIVE

TUVALU COAST TO COAST
COCO NUTS!

The flagman's arm must've been aching. The afternoon heat was punishing and the worst of it, around 40°C (104°F), was in the middle of the rough airstrip that cut through the main body of Funafuti Atoll like the spine of the island.

Colin, the sewage engineer form Gateshead, was beginning to wobble. It could well have been the heat haze as the air shimmered like a desert mirage; but I think it was just Colin wobbling. It was so hot that as I blew a bug from my forearm the air caught in the slipstream of my breath burned my skin. As we assumed our in-line starting position, you couldn't hear much save for the constant shush of waves crashing onto the ocean-side rock of the lagoon. The heat that blanketed us muffled other sounds and so, even if Colin had counted us in, we wouldn't have heard him. We just hunched over our bars and looked through sweat-stinging eyes, waiting for his red flag to drop.

There were three of us in this race. Aari Leppeniemi, the surgeon from Helsinki, buck-toothed, ginger tash, wishing he was taller, very competitive.

Tom Krafczyk, the electrical engineer from Krakow, bearded and bronzed, as jolly as they come, except when racing. And me, a sun-blocked up, bluey-white bloke from the Derbyshire borders on the edge of Sheffield, running Radio Tuvalu as a UN volunteer, and determined to win.

The Coconut Cup was a trophy widely swapped between various sports. It featured a coconut sitting on a wooden plinth between two brass pillars sawn from a curtain rail, supporting a plaque whose title was spelt out in mini cowrie shells. It was a prize applied to any competitive challenge thrown up between the island's expat community who found themselves forced together in the middle of the Pacific Ocean on a speck of an island some three days' sail from Fiji. This trophy afforded the winner the very modest satisfaction of being Top Polanghi (foreigner) until the next sporting challenge dreamt up the following week. It also brought with it a gift from our sponsor, the Vaiaku Langi Hotel: a most welcome Tropical Cocktail Special served up at the modest two-rooms-and-a-bar establishment that sat about 50m (164ft) off the airstrip we were about to hurtle over.

Between us we had commandeered the entire island stock of delivery bikes. They had been left on the sidewall of the post office while sensible folk napped away the punishingly hot part of the day. These heavy iron beasts were a gift from the Commonwealth Office. Sturdy, you might say. Designed never to break down, with solid rubber tyres and a large flat delivery cage welded to the front. They were never intended to be race bikes . . . until now!

With the lagoon behind us, our destination was the ocean-side of the island next to the diesel power plant. A full race distance of no less than 580m (1902ft).

We tensed as Colin gave us a one-finger warning. The flag fell in slow motion just like our start. We all snapped to action, but the bikes were not so willing. As one we stood up on the pedals, pulling the bars like the very weightlifters we were at this moment.

Humphing and hawing off the line, we strained to gain any momentum. Through gritted teeth I spit-counted the pedal strokes of my launch: 'One . . . two . . . three . . . four . . . five . . . six . . . seven . . .'

It took a long time before any of us sat down again. Aari was the first into the tuck and was looking good half a bike ahead of Tom and two bike lengths clear of me. I reckon I was carrying 20kg (44lb) more than the Finnish midget but hoped power would count in the end.

Bridging the airstrip, we hit rougher ground and I began to gain on Tom's wheel. The Polski Rocket was into his second stage cruise, but I was still out of the saddle, gaining. All was going very nicely as we came together into the last 200m (656ft) before a sequence of events, lasting no more than a couple of seconds, defined my spectacular and unexpected victory.

Later, as we sat under a pandanus leaf awning overlooking the aqua marine lagoon, I played the crash scene over in my head in slow motion. The barman had just presented me with what must have been the world's biggest cocktail glass: a drinking coconut in full green husk with the top flamboyantly hacked off. Into this was poured a very healthy dash of Gordon's Gin followed by a straw. I hugged it like a cushion as I drank, taking full advantage of the chilled flesh.

Tom stared at me with a tissue pressed against the open wound on his chin. 'Enjoy it,' he said. 'Next week we are sailing and you know I'll win.'

I stopped drinking for a moment and stirred my prize with the straw. 'How bad do you think Aari is?' I enquired smugly before returning to the trough.

'Ask him yourself,' said Tom, guiding me with his eyes to the bar door. Aari had been bandaged by his wife who was a nurse in the hospital.

'Mummy!!' I shouted.

'What??' said Aari.

'You know: Egyptian mummy!' I replied.

Tom fell about laughing. Aari managed a thin smile.

Not 20 minutes had passed since the Big One . . .

Tropical atolls are low-lying tops of coral reefs or volcano lips. Sometimes both. The exposed ground is rough and gravelly; pale in colour, not unlike dried bone. It is a crumbly and uneven surface that is not forgiving at all. Potholes, some with sharp edges, are everywhere. To win this race, you had to avoid the biggest holes; so there was a certain amount of zigzagging in this combative sprint of ours. Let's get back to the action . . .

My face was a vision of purple due to a combination of sunburn and effort. My cheeks were billowing like a trumpeter as I pulled up alongside Tom. His face was equally hilarious: tongue hanging out to one side like a happy spaniel leaning out of a car window. Aari's teeth were biting into his top lip. We had about 150m (490ft) to go.

The first expression to change was Tom's. Suddenly his eyes went wide as saucers with his mouth like a cat's arse as he veered right to avoid a deep hole. He did break, but just failed to avoid Aari's back wheel, which sent the feisty Finn into a big wobble matched by his jangling cheeks and a *loooong* word that sounded a bit like DUUUUUUCK! . . . but wasn't.

Aari experienced what is sometimes called a high-sider. His back wheel slipped around behind him before suddenly coming to a jarring halt as the tyre bit-in sideways, the effect being to spit Aari into the air.

I got a full view of him from underneath. He was still in one piece at that moment.

Down he came with a hard crumpled landing onto the edge of another hole. Ouch!

As he landed, Tom crashed into him. Double ouch!

We were only a short distance from the finish, so I thought it only right to amble on. I touched the wall of the generator station to claim victory before riding back to the pile of man meat displaying a variety of quality cuts.

'You alright, guys?'

I don't speak Finnish or Polish . . . but I got the drift of what they were saying.

If you intend to visit what is often described as the world's least visited country, the 'easiest' way is to fly via Fiji. Your destination is an airstrip built by the Americans during the Pacific War and now, thankfully, asphalt-covered. I guess that smoother surface means that the winning times have shortened in the coast-to-coast battle . . . but I'm sure you can claim it as your own if you fancy.

Funafuti Atoll itself is a joy. A huge dazzling sapphire lagoon sits in the middle and there are so many locals with boats that it will take very little to enjoy a trip and create for yourself one of those classic photos: a Single Palm Tree + you in a deck chair reading *The Times* + a bottle of something in an ice bucket. Get the angle right, and you will appear to be sitting apparently marooned in the middle of the ocean, on your very own cartoon islet, looking smug.

I would say it is well worth the trip. But to be honest, there are perhaps too many other very beautiful places, far closer to home, that you would have to fly over to get there. But if you do make it, ask for coconut crab at one of the few restaurants you'll find there. These creatures do not travel well and tend to be hyper-expensive in one of Sydney or Auckland's top restaurants. The crabs tear apart and eat coconuts using giant mandibles. These claws exceed the size of their bodies. Think cricket ball-sized callipers. Their flesh has a hint of coconut about it and is absolutely delicious. They are also extremely common in Tuvalu, so fill your tummy like you would not be able to afford to do anywhere else on the planet. Then go racing, coast to coast. I never wrote my name on the power station wall at the finish. But you could!

CARLTON COMMENTARY

'He threw everything at the day . . . but sadly it was toys
out of the cot at the end.'
Nacer Bouhanni, not happy being beaten

THIRTY SIX

ZWIFT
'DEAR SANTA . . .'

Welcome to San Francisco, said the sign. 'Give me your documents and wait for me to speak,' said the blank look and outstretched hand of the United States Border Force official for whom I had already given an hour of my life before finally we met.

'What is the nature of your visit, sir?'

I knew not to say anything about the work I was supposed to be doing . . . such an admission would have opened me up to a whole world of poo. Taking work off Americans is not overtly encouraged.

'I'm visiting a friend.'

'What friend, where does he live and what is the nature of his business?'

'He's invited me to the opening of his café.'

'You working at this café?'

'No. I – I'm there for the grand opening.'

'What's the name of this café?'

'Oh . . . it's a pop-up venture . . . a cycling theme.'

'Red lane . . . move on.'

Five steps along the slightly sticky red vinyl flooring, I pushed through a pair of heavy rubber warehouse-style doors into a zone of mild anxiety. Red lane had seats. This was not good. I had just waited an hour in line to meet my first grumpy friend. I assumed this new zone was going to take a good bit longer. I mean . . . seats!

Red lane was an interesting place to be for theology students. Was it purgatory or limbo? I couldn't decide. The area was filled with a mix of the desperate, the bored, the grumpy and the nervous. In time I would pass through all these states.

Finally I was taken to a room with a high table where my luggage was already open.

'You own this computer, sir?'

'Yes, I do.'

'Please switch it on.'

I did this and it blinked into life.

'Thank you, sir, that will be all. Enjoy your stay.'

'*What? That was it? After two and a half hours?*' is what I thought. 'Thank you, sir,' is what I said, and left via the green lane.

My taxi driver was a lovely Iraqi chap 'from the first war', he explained, 'before the rush.'

'Don't worry about it too much, my friend. They just like to make clear that you are entering a country where authority has to be respected. It's a kind of welcome warning. They do it to everyone. Where to, sir?'

What I didn't tell imigration was that I was in town to help out with the launch of an amazing global gift to cyclists: ZWIFT.

Now unless you have been in a coma since 2014, you will know precisely what I am talking about. Back then the entire project was something of a mystery. It had been explained to me by the impressive Eric Minn over a coffee in London's Soho. I liked him immediately. Eric explained his vision for global domination, and it seemed at once both highly ambitious yet entirely deliverable. If you ever meet Eric, you will be impressed. He misses nothing. 'You need a new shirt,' he said as we crossed the road to the Rapha café, the upcoming venue for the London leg of the big launch.

I just about poured myself into a Rapha shirt size XL. It looked like a wrap.

He explained that I would fly to San Francisco for the West Coast launch to be linked simultaneously with both New York on the East Coast as well as London over the pond. Nighttime London, afternoon New York and late morning San Francisco.

Two weeks later I was in California with a couple of days to go until the big launch.

My hotel was a modest affair just on the blanket border. This was a demarcation zone where daily support of soup, a clean blanket and $15 are given to the homeless. They got this provided they did not wander out of the zone. Otherwise, no goodies. Believe it or not, this package of assistance exceeded levels offered by many other states. As a result, there are a *lot* of homeless here in town. It was apparently far worse when I visited, but even at the last count in February 2022 there were officially 7,800 homeless people in San Francisco, of which 4,400 were without shelter. That's a lot of people. And most of them seemed to be my neighbours where I was staying.

Apparently rather foolishly, I had decided to walk to the Bay Area and get myself something to eat. 'How far to the bridge?' I asked at the modest reception.

'About a mile. I'll call you a cab.'

'No, it's OK, I'll walk.'

'I would not advise that at this time, sir. It can get a little challenging on the streets.'

'What, four in the afternoon?'

'I would not advise walking in this neighbourhood at any time, sir.'

WARNING: Objects may be closer than they appear is a phrase etched onto the mirrors of Harley-Davidsons. *WARNING: Hot surface* is written on blowtorch nozzles. *WARNING: Risk of indigestion if eaten* is written on bricks.

OK, I made that last one up, but by my reckoning America is a bit OTT when it comes to personal safety.

I stepped out into spectacular afternoon sunshine. The autumn air was fresh and there was not a cloud in the sky. I checked my map and began walking. Now, I wasn't alone on the streets, but I did look a bit out of place. For a start I wasn't in a hurry and secondly I looked, um, clean. It wasn't long before I had company.

'Hey, buddy! You, sir. SIR!'

I stopped as a guy in a wheelchair, wearing old army fatigues under a clearly donated beige blouson leather jacket that was far too big for him, edged out of a graffitied bus shelter. 'Sir can you help? Anything at all, sir.'

He pulled himself towards me using his good foot. His left arm hung limp like the rest of that side of him. His other hand held a cardboard sign he'd written himself. It just said: *Veteran. God bless you.*

Not knowing quite how to engage, I offered: 'Oh hello, I'm just heading to the Bay Area.'

'Well, it'll take you around 20 minutes if you don't want to bump into more folk like me.' He grinned to show off a set of amazingly healthy, straight white teeth. Then he snatched the map from me and began to draw with a monogrammed steel Parker ballpoint.

'Beautiful day,' I said to fill the conversation void.

'Every day is . . . for somebody,' he murmured as he finished my route plan. 'There you go.'

'Thank you,' I said.

'That'll be ten dollars,' he said, glaring with one eye closed on his bad side. A very long pause was broken by a pirate cackle. 'Ha ha, just kiddin'. Anything you got will be just fine. Need a couple of bucks for a burger, that's all. I don't do meth or nothin', which is why I still got ma teeth. Free dentistry in the army, see. Lose them and you go downhill fast.'

'Well, there are certainly lots of hills here!' I said . . . to nothing in return. I dipped into my pocket. 'There you go,' I gave him the $10 he'd asked for. I didn't really know what to say next and so, like a lazy hairdresser, I ventured: 'You been here long?'

'Been here since the war in Eye-rack. The first war. Before the rush.'

'That's the second time I've heard that today,' I said. 'What was "the rush" anyway?'

'The second war, there was a lot more injured, a lot more refugees, a lot more shit all round. Less sympathy too . . . a lot less sympathy. Less help. First war was about oil, liberating Kuwait and stuff. Second war was just revenge. For the Towers. Folk didn't like the second war.'

'Right ho. . . . Thanks for the map.'

'Frank. The name's Frank. Frank with no rank. Not any more.'

'Well thank you, Frank. Appreciate it. The map.'

'You take care to follow it, friend.' And with that he was on his way slowly towards a McDonalds on the corner of another block.

As I watched him struggle, I was reminded of an old girlfriend called Sonja who was a physiotherapist. She came home from a visit to the United States in the mid '80s and cried as she recounted seeing numerous homeless stroke victims who could have been in far better shape with simple access to a physiotherapy programme. I think I had just met such a person.

I followed Frank's map for a couple of blocks before I gave up. I just didn't have the mojo any more to sit in a fancy bar sipping a beer and looking at the Golden Gate. *I'll go tomorrow*, I thought to myself and bought an early dinner from a tidy-ish looking Vietnamese takeaway and went back to the hotel.

The next morning I ordered a cab and went directly to the Rapha Clubhouse in what looked like a stripped-out building missing a floor or two on the inside. All minimalist painted brick and scaffold staircase, contrasting beautifully with the usual impeccably displayed Rapha products and, of course, the compulsory café and tray bake temptations. High up on the walls were large TV monitors for the expected crowd to keep an eye on the riders' progress. Filling much of the ground floor space were two banks of five training bikes, each linked to their own monitors set to a scene called Jarvis Island. It was like a window into a virtual ribbon of asphalt running through a psychedelic tropical rainforest.

Anyone who has not been living in a cave for nearly a decade will know a great deal about Zwift. It has been a phenomenal success in just about every sense. Virtual racing while training and getting a chance to measure yourself against similar riders or even stars of the road themselves, all set within a virtual racing scene of your choice, some even matching the very courses run in the Grand Tours and World Championships. There is even a virtual World Championship. Put simply, Zwift has transformed the training environment of millions of cyclists and introduced a level of competitive expression that has produced live competition and even new career paths for the best riders while entertaining and stretching the rest of us in a phenomenally engaging way.

Let's remember that at its heart cycling is about the numbers. If you want to get ahead, get the right parents. I'm talking genes, not dollars. And this is where Zwift's genius lies. It helps you find out if you have the legs and the lungs to go big in cycling. Jay Vine is the prime example. He won the Zwift Academy of 2020, a global e-racing competition that came with an amazing first prize: a Pro contract with Alpecin. Jay won and took the plunge. He sold everything in Oz and moved to Europe for his new racing life.

Alpecin loved everything about him, extended his contract and reaped the rewards. Jay went from virtual to reality with two stage wins in La Vuelta 2022. Not easy stages, either. In the mountains the man from Townsville in Queensland was beating some of the best Grand Tour riders on earth like Primož Roglič and eventual winner Remco Evenepoel. That right there was Jay saying thank you – in spades – to both Alpecin and, of course, Zwift.

Back in 2014, could anyone have predicted this? Even though the signals of this success were blazing bright green for go? The beta product opened on 30 September, 2014, the way to find any gaps in the program. Only 1000 places were available; 13,000 asked to be involved – an amazing response. These Lucky Thousand helped smooth out the program and eight months later it was time to invite the world to the lift-off event. I guess all were unsure how far it would fly. Well, it has since been a bit galactic.

Back in 2012, just as I was screaming Iljo Keisse home on Stage 7 of the Tour of Turkey, Eric Minn was meeting up with Jon Mayfield, a hugely talented 3D Programmer. Eric was keen to find out more about a revolutionary virtual racing game Jon had 'developed in his spare time'. You know much of the rest.

Since then, it has been an amazing feat for Eric and his colleagues. But it took more than faith and belief to get this off the ground. It was very, very brave. America is said to reward those who work hard and take risks. The team at Zwift did this exponentially. I was sharing a hoisin wrap with them the night before the launch. I'd just found out that these four guys had no other plans beyond Zwift. They had put all they had into this venture. They had mortgaged whatever they had financially and emotionally. The personal risk they were taking was clear. If this didn't work out, it would be the financial end for most of them. Put simply it would place unparalleled strain on both them and their loved ones. Yet each remained so full of energy and excitement. I had hope for them. But they had belief and, thank goodness, it proved to be very well founded.

'What will you guys do if things don't work out? What if the subscriptions fall away? What if —'

Jon interrupted me: 'We will just get on with the rest of our lives.'

'But what will that mean?

'Oh, I don't know, maybe I'll buy a Mobile RV and head for Hawaii . . . but it's not going to happen. *This* is going to happen.'

And it did. Brilliantly.

As we parted that night, we finished our beers and stepped out of the café over a man under a blanket. Waiting for us was something called an Uber. 'It's a new vehicle hailing transport system,' explained Jon. This unmarked car took me back to the hotel where I simply stepped out without the need for cash. All settled via an app . . . apparently. *I'll do the Golden Gate in the morning,* I thought to myself. I overslept.

I arrived in a fluster about an hour before the link. The team were all set up along with a mix of pro and top-end amateurs here to ride the launch. They were, for the first time, about to compare themselves to each other while racing in a virtual world. It was all taken very seriously with the spirit of competition feeling just as real as on the road itself. On the huge screen and the attached monitors, our peloton sped through a magical world where all riders were racing as named avatars; yet the bunch was made up of competitors thousands of miles apart. Wow!

The launch was amazing. Most of us had seen nothing like it before. Indeed, it's hard to quantify that bright sunny day in San Francisco because Zwift has now become so familiar.

After the launch the invited press went suitably wild. And so did we, actually. We duly dived into a post-event party. It's fair to say it was a heap of fun. I don't know where we went but it wasn't the Bay Area. Everywhere there was fully booked. We had not made a reservation in case an advanced party booking might jinx things; in case the link-up plans did not go smoothly. But that night our three global venues came together to prove that, with internet access, you can race a friend or rival anywhere on the planet.

So we crashed into a pizza parlour with a huge slab table and ordered a load of Anchors . . . it's a beer. Strong.

My flight was an early morning affair. I had to get home for some real-life racing. As my plane gained height out of San Francisco International, I caught sight of the Golden Gate Bridge. A modern-day wonder I have still to experience, yet that weekend in San Francisco I discovered three other amazing things along the way: Uber, Zwift and Anchor IPA whose first brew was in 2014; I think we drank most of the stock that fateful night. And like Uber and Zwift, the Anchor brewing company has also done rather well for themselves. How nice it is to be able to say that I was there for the first wave of each of them; you know, before the rush.

CARLTON COMMENTARY

'The only clean parts of Van Aert's face are the lines traced by tears.'
Third only, 2018 Strade Bianche

FINALLY

And so another cycling season comes to a close. It's a strange time. Once it would come to a dramatic end with Lombardia and you could all go for a jolly good piss-up, but these days the calendar rolls on.

Cycling nuts like you and me don't really have our Cup Final. There is, of course, the World Championships, but that doesn't mark the end. Once Europe is done with the road, it heads indoors with the Six Day scene while the remaining demigods make their way out East or Down Under to tidy up their palmarès.

Then, before you know it, the early form tester races start up in the Middle East and southern Europe. It's a merry-go-round that slows only enough for a few to jump off. The rest stay on board.

I haven't jumped yet, but I've been circling so long I do wonder when I might take a final ticket. For now, I'm still enjoying the ride.

There have been fun days and foul, but all have been memorable. I have had the pleasure of sharing my life with some fantastic people . . . and some real shits (which is another book for another day). I'm honestly glad to have met and played with them all; it's made for a fascinating ride.

And let's not forget your good self. If you are reading this, it likely means we share a love of a sport that has no equal in terms of drama and emotion. I like to think I invest heavily in both while calling races for you.

People often ask me how I think of some of the lines I come out with. Well, I have no idea. I plug in the headset and fully invest in the moment. It's the only way. What comes out of my mouth is not filtered, just me. And I wouldn't have it any other way. I tell you what I see . . . and how I see it. This can, of course, get me into trouble if it goes wrong.

So, like that lucky drunk in a minefield, I haven't blown up. Just yet.

Talk to you soon.

CK xx